FLORA TRISTAN was born in Paris in 1803, the daughter of a French mother and a Peruvian-Spanish father. Her first publication was a pamphlet, *Nécessité de faire un bon accueil aux femmes étrangères* (1835). This was followed in 1838 by her autobiography, *Pérégrinations d'une paria*, which made her name. In it she combines her personal search for independence with a remarkable portrait of Peruvian life and customs. In the same year she published her only novel, *Méphis*. In 1839 Flora Tristan visited England for the fourth time and wrote her popular *Promenades dans Londres*, first published in French in 1840, and translated by Jean Hawkes as *The London Journal* (Virago, 1982).

In 1843 Flora Tristan published her manifesto, *L'Union ouvrière*, calling for a world-wide Workers' International. Many of the ideas formulated in it were used by Marx in his 1848 *Manifesto*. The following year she travelled through France addressing workers' meetings, making a record of this in her *Tour de France* which remained unpublished until 1973. While on her journey, Flora Tristan contracted typhoid fever and died at Bordeaux at the age of forty-one and was mourned throughout France as 'the workers' saint'. Her last book, *L'Emancipation de la femme*, was completed by Alphonse Constant and published posthumously in 1845.

JEAN HAWKES is a graduate in French from St Anne's College, Oxford. She has been working on the writings of Flora Tristan for many years and her translation and editing of *The London Journal* for Virago has been highly acclaimed. She is married with four children and lives in Wales.

PEREGRINATIONS
OF A PARIAH
1833–1834

—❧—

FLORA TRISTAN

Translated, edited and introduced by
JEAN HAWKES

Virago

Published by VIRAGO PRESS Limited 1986
41 William IV Street, London WC2N 4DB

First published in French as
Mémoires et pérégrinations d'une paria 1838
First translated into English by Jean Hawkes, 1986
Translation copyright © Jean Hawkes 1986
Introduction copyright © Jean Hawkes 1986

British Library Cataloguing in Publication Data
Tristan, Flora
    Peregrinations of a pariah.—(Virago traveller)
    1. Peru—Description and travel
    I. Title   II. Hawkes, Jean
    918.5′045   F3423

    ISBN 0 − 86068 − 477 − 6

Typeset by Florencetype Ltd, Bristol
Printed in Great Britain by Anchor Brendon, Tiptree, Essex

The cover shows Arica, Peru, 1868.
Reproduced by kind permission of the Royal Geographical Society.
The drawing on page ii is of the author in Arequipa, 1833.
Map by John Flower.

In memory of Mary Hawkes (1927–1985)

Contents

Translator's Introduction

Over the past fifteen years there has been a revival of interest in the socialist and feminist Flora Tristan (1803–1844), author of the *Promenades dans Londres* (1840), an indictment of social conditions in England, and the *Union ouvrière* (1843), a blueprint for social revolution in France. Tristan was inspired by the teachings of Christ and the ideals of the French Revolution. She belonged to no school and left no doctrine, though she was familiar with the theories of the leading reformers of her day, Saint-Simon, Fourier and Owen, and took from each of them whatever accorded with her experience and judgement. Out of these gleanings she evolved an original synthesis in which the principal element was the total emancipation of women, the prerequisite, as she saw it, for the liberation of the working class and the achievement of a harmonious society. Tristan's socialism was her religion and she was its solitary prophet. To propagate its gospel she embarked on a gruelling tour of the industrial regions of France, in the course of which she contracted typhoid fever and died in Bordeaux on 14 November 1844 at the age of forty-one. She was christened the Workers' Saint and in 1848 a monument was unveiled to her memory, but her cult was short-lived, and had it not been for J.-L. Puech, who published an exhaustive study of her life and works in 1925 and spent years preparing her unfinished *Tour de France* for publication, she would probably have been forgotten.

Yet at one time Flora Tristan had been almost as notorious as her nearly exact contemporary George Sand, not for her political ideas but for the personal revelations contained in her *Mémoires et pérégrinations d'une paria*. This was the story of her visit to Peru in 1833–1834 to claim her share of the Tristan family fortune, a journey she undertook as a last desperate resort after leaving her husband André Chazal and trying for eight years to support herself and her children.

The book was published in 1838, at a time when women were becoming increasingly resentful of their inferior status. Few were sufficiently militant to join feminist clubs or subscribe to feminist journals, but a growing number were prepared to agitate for reform of the marriage laws. The *Gazette des femmes* presented a petition for the restoration of divorce to the Chamber of Deputies in 1836, Tristan herself presented one in 1837, and during the session of 1838–1839 there were no fewer than sixteen. However, it was on the literary front that women were most active, as the critic Sainte-Beuve observed in an article published in 1833. 'Nowadays women from all walks of life have taken to writing,' he said. 'Each has her own secret grievance, her own love story, which she uses to support her pleas for emancipation.' But while it was one thing for a woman to transmute her experiences into fiction, as George Sand had done in her novels *Indiana* and *Lélia*, it was quite another for her to write openly of her marital troubles, name the man responsible, and exhort other women to do the same.

Tristan had anticipated that her lack of reticence would arouse criticism. 'I speak often of myself,' she said in her Preface, 'not because I want to draw attention to *myself personally*, but to all women who are in the same position.' The *Peregrinations*, her first major work, was in fact her only essay in autobiography. The fifteen months it covers was a crucial period in her life, during which she discovered as much about herself as she did about the Peruvians to whom the book is dedicated. In this sense it is more than a travel journal: it is a personal odyssey, a record of the temptations she had to face in the course of her transformation from a self-centred young woman into a single-minded champion of the oppressed. Not that her personality underwent any radical change in the process. Her mother had brought her up to regard herself as a superior being by reason of her aristocratic birth, and the conviction was to remain with her all her life. This made her opinionated and impatient of criticism. But as she was also warm-hearted and impressionable she was able to appreciate the sufferings of others, and the indignation she expresses so vehemently on their behalf is one of her most attractive characteristics.

Tristan is disarmingly frank about the shortcomings of her younger self. 'In 1833 I was still very narrow-minded ... I did not see that all men are brothers and that the whole world is their home.' One hundred and fifty years later, modern readers, living in a world where critical observations about Africans or Asians are seen as evidence of racial prejudice, may find it difficult to reconcile Tristan's professed detestation of slavery and oppression with the revulsion she felt on her first encounter with the Black population of the Cape Verde Islands. Let me reassure them that Tristan's initial reaction to the white inhabitants of England's slums was just as spontaneous and uncontrollable. 'I felt my stomach heave, while a fierce pain gripped my head.' This involuntary reaction is invariably succeeded by a broader understanding. Tristan recognises that the most pernicious effect of slavery and oppression is their tendency to reduce humans to the level of animals. Hence the black children look like monkeys, while the white wallow in the mud like pigs. She has to remind herself that these are her fellow creatures, and from that moment, compassion for their plight takes over.

Flora Tristan is at her best when she allows the events so graphically recorded in her journal to speak for themselves. She is blessed with an enquiring mind, a quick understanding and an intuitive sympathy. Her eye for

detail makes her a good observer and many of her portraits are memorable, notably those of her uncle Pio, her
cousin Carmen, Pencha Gamarra and Colonel Althaus.
She is less successful at evoking a landscape. Despite her
knowledge and appreciation of art (on which she often
wrote articles for periodicals) her descriptions of nature
are laboured and she soon lapses into awe-struck contemplation. When the pace of events quickens and there is
scope for action — as, for instance, when civil war breaks
out in Arequipa — she is capable and decisive, but when
faced with the task of dismissing an unwanted suitor she
agonises for days. Her analysis of her motives and actions
always ends in triumphant self-justification because her
conviction that she has a mission to serve humanity
overrides any sense of her obligation towards individuals.

Yet Tristan also sees herself as a pariah, born to suffer,
and when she speaks of her unique and unparalleled
sufferings her tone rises to a pitch of exaltation inappro-
priate to the occasion. The passionate indignation which is
endearing and admirable when expressed on behalf of
others becomes tiresome and somewhat absurd when
concentrated on herself. It is tempting to dismiss this
failing as an excess of the much-maligned sensibility
which is the hallmark of Romantic literature, but I suspect
it may be due to the overwhelming sense of outrage and
humiliation which possessed Tristan at the very time
when she was preparing her journal for publication, and
which she could not help transferring to her younger self,
the Flora of 1833. For this reason it is relevant to trace the
sequence of events leading up to the publication of the
Peregrinations.

When Tristan returned to France in late 1834 or early
1835 (the date is uncertain) she had no immediate intention of publishing her journal. She had renounced all
hopes of love, wealth and happiness, and her only desire
was to be of some use to humanity. From now on
usefulness was to be her sole criterion, and it is a constant

theme in her writing. 'Why die?' the hero of her novel
Méphis asks the heroine Maréquita, 'when you could be,
if not happy, at least useful?' It was with this laudable
object in mind that Tristan made her first venture into
print, a pamphlet based on her wide experience of foreign
travel called *Nécessité de faire un bon accueil aux femmes
étrangères* (1835) which, while primarily concerned with
the welfare of women living abroad, calls upon all women
to broaden their horizons through travel and study,
thereby fitting themselves for their mission to bring peace
and love to the whole world.

Tristan was not slow to put her precepts into practice.
In 1835 she made her third visit to England and there is
evidence that she visited Belgium too that year. She had
been familiar with the basic ideas of Saint-Simon since
1827, when his school began to gain adherents in Paris
and the main provincial cities; now she turned her attention to the communitarian system elaborated by Charles
Fourier, though she was by temperament impatient of
theories and pinned her hopes of social change on action.
It was enough for her that both Saint-Simon and Fourier
advocated the total emancipation of women and the
peaceful reorganisation of society on co-operative lines.
She sent a copy of her little book to Fourier and offered
her services in the cause of reform. He was sufficiently
impressed to make her acquaintance and called on her
several times. During that autumn she also began to
attend the Thursday meetings organised by the *Gazette
des femmes*, where she met the feminists Eugénie
Niboyet, Anaïs Ségalas and Hortense Allart.

But these promising contacts had to take second place
when, in October 1835, Tristan's husband Chazal learned
that she and her daughter Aline were back in Paris. Up to
then she had managed to evade him by changing her
address every so often, but now that she was discovered
the harassment which had driven her to leave France in
1833 began all over again. This time Chazal succeeded in

abducting Aline on her way to school, but as she became hysterical and he was unable to calm her, he was forced to take her to a relative's in Versailles. When Flora caught up with him there were violent scenes. Eventually the case came to court, and at the Public Prosecutor's suggestion Aline was placed in a boarding-school where both parents undertook to visit her.

Now for a few months there was an uneasy truce which left Tristan free to resume her political activities. In March 1836 she wrote to her new friend Eugénie Niboyet that she was hoping to raise two hundred francs in subscriptions to start a periodical. Nothing seems to have come of this, but it may have been a similar desire to raise money that gave her the idea of publishing her Peruvian journal. (As late as 1843 she was thinking of dashing off a novel, *La Fille de Lima*, based on her experiences in Peru, as a means of financing the second edition of her *Union ouvrière*.) At all events she began to select passages from her journal for publication in periodicals, and she decided to dedicate the complete book to the Peruvians to repay them for the kindness and hospitality they had shown her. But as in fact she had been horrified by the backwardness and corruption of Peruvian society, she showed her gratitude by lecturing her hosts on their shortcomings, an illustration of her dictum that well-founded criticism is the truest form of friendship. To appreciate her concern for the Peruvians' welfare it is necessary to take a brief look at their history.

It was in 1807 that the Spanish colonies in South America, taking advantage of Spain's defeat by Napoleon, began to demand their freedom. Their struggle for independence produced one leader of world stature, Simon Bolivar from Venezuela; an outstanding soldier-statesman, José San Martín from Argentina, and a number of brilliant generals. Fighting between royalist and patriot forces continued on land and sea (with the unauthorised intervention, after 1815, of thousands of British soldiers and sailors on the patriot side) until one by one the colonies gained their independence and began to set up governments of their own. San Martín declared Peru independent in 1821 and was proclaimed Protector, but he was forced to abdicate in 1822. It was his conviction that only a constitutional monarchy could give Peru the stable government it so badly needed, but the ambitious generals thought otherwise, and they prevailed upon Congress to nominate Colonel Riva Aguero president. He was deposed in 1823 after only three months in office, and Bolivar arrived to take charge, but after three years he had to return to Venezuela and left Santa Cruz as acting president. In 1827 Congress elected José de la Mar president, but in 1829 he too was deposed and Agustín Gamarra seized power. He was the first president to complete his full term of office. Thus, by the time Flora Tristan arrived in September 1833, Peru had been independent for twelve years, during which there had been six different heads of state. Meanwhile the country's chief source of wealth, its gold and silver mines, fell into ruin, its upper classes lived in idleness and luxury, its prosperous citizens were stripped of their savings by the military, and its Indian and Negro populations were still slaves.

Tristan was appalled at conditions in Peru and the memory was still fresh when she wrote the dedication for her book. In it she proposed a number of reforms to set the infant republic on its feet. First came education: if the entire population, including the Indians and Negroes, could read and write, their political and religious leaders would no longer be able to exploit their ignorance. The next priority was employment: if all men had a trade, they would no longer need to depend on charity but would develop the self-reliance so essential for the citizens of a free country. When the Spaniards discovered Peru it was the most advanced civilisation in the whole of South America, thanks to the natural aptitude of its people and the abundance of its resources. It was her sincere wish that a progressive government would restore Peru to its former greatness.

Tristan signed this dedication 'your compatriot and friend' and finished it in August 1836. Meanwhile the arrangement to publish extracts from her journal in the influential *Revue des deux mondes* ran into difficulties when she quarrelled with the editor, François Buloz, over her style. She always refused to alter anything she had written, so she took her articles elsewhere, and they eventually appeared in the *Revue de Paris*. *Les Femmes de Lima* (part of Chapter 16) was published in September 1836, and *Les Couvents d'Aréquipa* (Chapter 11) in November. Both extracts illustrate Tristan's talent for observation and show her at her best.

But by the time they appeared in print Tristan was embroiled in a fresh domestic crisis. Chazal had taken advantage of her brief absence from Paris in July 1836 to place Aline in a school of his own choice, with instructions that her mother was not to be allowed to see her. The poor child was so desperately unhappy that in August she ran away to join Flora, who was by now back in Paris. Chazal accused the two sisters who owned the school of negligence, demanded 10,000 francs in damages, and started proceedings against his wife for the abduction of a minor, but he lost his case and was ordered to pay costs. In November he had Aline removed from her mother's apartment by force and took her to the shabby lodgings in Montmartre where he and the couple's surviving son Ernest were living. The loss of Aline distressed Flora so much that she felt she had to leave Paris, so she took a temporary post as lady's companion and was away for several months. Nothing further is known about this episode. In January 1837, during her absence, her *Lettres à un architecte anglais*, a detailed description of the buildings and monuments she had seen on her visit to London in 1835, were published in two issues of the *Revue de Paris*.

For despite the upheavals of her personal life Tristan still managed to contribute articles to periodicals and continue her political education. She was by now familiar with the ideas of Robert Owen, and on 4 August 1837 she had the opportunity to hear him address a meeting arranged by the Saint-Simonists. Owen had first achieved fame by successfully reorganising his New Lanark factory on humanitarian principles. Later, in 1834, he set up the Grand National Consolidated Trades Union for both men and women workers, and now, at the age of sixty-six, he was concentrating on expounding his moral, educational, rationalist and feminist views. It was the practice of the Saint-Simonists to place an empty chair on the speaker's platform to symbolise their quest for the female Messiah who was destined to regenerate humanity. When somebody in the audience objected that Owen's doctrine was incomplete because there was no woman at his side, Flora Tristan sprang to her feet and cried, 'Oh yes, there is!' She was to have a second meeting with Owen in London in 1839, when she was collecting material for her *Promenades dans Londres*. But this is to anticipate events.

To return to 1837: in April of that year the long-standing battle between Tristan and her husband reached a climax when she received a letter from Aline which convinced her that André had attempted to rape the eleven-year-old child. She immediately had him arrested on a charge of incest and he had to spend a month in prison before being released for lack of evidence. Meanwhile his appeal against the judgment given in his recent lawsuit was rejected and he was ordered to pay a further set of costs. At the hearing André's counsel, Jules Favre, concentrated his attack on Flora rather than on the two proprietors of Aline's school, an injustice which stung her into writing letters of protest to the editors of *Le Droit* and the *Gazette des Tribunaux*. But a heavier blow was in store for her: André published his version of her conduct since their marriage, in which he accused her of taking lovers, leading an immoral life, and being unfit to have charge of children.

This was the crowning insult for Tristan. She did not stop to consider how little impact Chazal's *Mémoire* was likely to have on the world at large. (In fact he could afford to have only thirty copies printed, and these he distributed among his friends.) The fact that the husband she loathed and despised had dared to blacken her name filled her with the desire to retaliate: she would reveal the identity of the man she held responsible for all her tribulations, and the means of doing so lay ready to hand in the journal she was preparing for publication. In a twenty-two-page preface more remarkable for grandiloquence than logic she justified her action on the grounds that it would benefit humanity, because the memoirs of an ordinary individual who had suffered were more useful than those of famous men who wrote only to gratify their self-esteem. But such an individual must have the faith of the martyr and not shrink from making enemies. The crimes of the oppressor must be exposed, but a veil should be drawn over the struggles of the oppressed. To publish a woman's love affairs was to expose her to oppression. She was confident that her example would inspire other women to publish their stories. An era of truth was beginning. She was fulfilling her mission and obeying the voice of her conscience.

This preface, like the foreword which follows it, is undated, but its references to the crimes of the oppressor and the iniquity of publishing the love affairs of women are indication enough that it was written after Chazal published his *Mémoire*. For all her rhetoric Tristan does not mention Chazal once by name in the main body of her narrative, though she refers to him as a contemptible creature and misses no opportunity of inveighing against the law which binds her to him for life. She does, however, name him twice in her foreword, which is pitched in a lower key than the preface and provides the reader with an explanation of the events leading up to her voyage to Peru. This is a summary of her story:

Her parents met and married in Spain, but her father never had the marriage registered, nor did he make a will, so when he died her mother had little money on which to bring up the two children of the marriage. After her brother's death Tristan and her mother returned to Paris, where her mother made her marry a man she could neither love nor esteem, M. André Chazal, an engraver. She left him when she was twenty (she was in fact twenty-two and expecting her third child: Translator) and resumed her maiden name, posing either as a widow or an unmarried woman, according to whether she had her children with her or not.

In 1829, when she and her little daughter were staying at a Paris hotel, she met a Captain Chabrié who asked her if she was related to the Tristans he had known in Peru. She denied the connection, but later she wrote to her father's family, and the reply she received was so encouraging that she would have gone to them immediately had she not feared that they would reject her when they learned that she had left her husband.

On several occasions the persecution of M. Chazal forced her to leave Paris. In 1832, when her surviving son Ernest was eight, her husband insisted on taking the boy, and offered to leave her in peace on that condition. She reluctantly agreed, but a few months later he demanded her daughter as well, so for the sixth time she fled, and for six months she wandered from one town to another with her daughter. When they reached Angoulême she fell seriously ill. There she had the good fortune to meet a lady who offered to take care of Aline, so in January 1833 she went to Bordeaux to wait for a passage to South America. She had an introduction to a cousin of her father's who received her kindly, and for two months she took her meals at his house and rented a room near by.

In February 1833 there were only three ships in port bound for Valparaiso. Two were unsuitable, which left only the *Mexicain*, whose captain turned out to be the very same Captain Chabrié she had met in 1829 when she was with her daughter – and now she was posing as an unmarried woman! After two days and nights of agonising she sent for the captain and made him promise not to reveal that he had known her as Madame Tristan and that she had a daughter. Then she went to choose her cabin and make arrangements about paying for her passage.

Now that everything was settled she was beset with doubts. First she considered seeking the protection of her father's cousin, for her daughter's sake as much as her own, but she decided against it when she saw that there was no warmth beneath his courtly manners. Next, she wondered whether to confide in her uncle's agent in Bordeaux, Felipe Bertera, but she could not bring herself to add to the troubles of a young man who had lost all his family and was quite alone in the world. So she kept silent, although her mind was in turmoil. She could not wait to cast off the society which had rejected her, but she could not bear to leave her daughter. This was her state of mind when she left Bordeaux on her thirtieth birthday. Her memoirs need no further introduction. It remains only to trace the course of events which followed their publication.

Tristan's book caused a minor sensation and was on the whole favourably received by the critics, though one reviewer, a lady writing in the *Revue de Paris* of 7 January 1838 and signing herself Mme M, found the personality of the author obtrusive and felt that, on the evidence given, Tristan had no reason to complain of being badly treated by society, since she had been received with kindness wherever she went. The modern reader may well share this view. As for the suppression of the right of divorce, Mme M was of the opinion that it weighed equally heavily on both sexes, and that to use the freedom of the press to expose the lives of private individuals was a dangerous precedent which should not be followed for fear of the consequences. Her apprehensions were soon to prove justified.

In March Tristan applied for a judicial separation from her husband, and her book provided André's counsel with plenty of ammunition to use against her when the case was heard. Nevertheless her application was granted, and the tribunal decreed that she should have custody of Aline while André should be responsible for Ernest (who had been staying with Flora's mother ever since the family crisis of the previous year). But Flora's mother refused to give him up, which proved the final blow for André. While Flora, unsuspecting, worked on her novel *Méphis*, André, obsessed with his wrongs, decided that the only course left to him was to kill his wife. He bought some pistols and began to practise marksmanship. On 10 September 1838 he lay in wait for Flora and shot her in the back. For some days it was uncertain whether she would live, but she recovered, and during her convalescence she put the final touches to her novel, which was published towards the end of the year.

Méphis, ou le prolétaire – to give the book its full title – is not a satisfactory novel: the plot is melodramatic and the characters lack depth. The hero and heroine represent two facets of a single personality, one intellectual, the other emotional, and their sole function is to express Tristan's views on the place of woman in society. The hero Méphis is a cultural Superman: scholar, poet, musician, artist, scientist and politician, he is capable of working fifteen hours a day. The heroine Maréquita, though not unintelligent, is governed by her emotions. She has neither interests nor accomplishments and suffers from melancholia. The problem Tristan poses is threefold: how to strike a balance between these two opposing aspects of human personality, one traditionally attributed to man, the other to woman; how to overcome the prejudice against women imposed on society by church and state; and how to raise the status of women so that all the advantages enjoyed by men are available to them as well. It is Méphis who provides the answer: only through education can women become conscious of their mission as humanity's inspiration and guide. In time Maréquita comes to accept his philosophy, and before her death she entrusts their baby daughter to her faithful friend Albert, to be brought up in accordance with her father's principles.

In addition to completing her novel Tristan accomplished a further task during her convalescence. She presented a petition to the Chamber of Deputies for the abolition of the death penalty. In those days the crime of attempted murder was still a capital offence, but when André Chazal went on trial in January 1839 his counsel pleaded extenuating circumstances, and he was sentenced to twenty years imprisonment. He served seventeen years and died in 1860, four years after his release, convinced to the end that he had been the victim of a conspiracy to protect his wife and thwart the course of justice. It should be remembered that under the law as it then stood, his claim to be granted custody of his children was no more than his right.

Tristan was by now something of a celebrity, but after a few months the pleasures of her new life began to pall and she went off to make her fourth visit to England, this time shunning the usual tourist attractions to investigate at first hand the prisons, asylums, factories and slums of the Monster City as well as the high-class brothels where no respectable lady ever set foot. This was the raw material for her *Promenades dans Londres* (1840) which, though largely ignored by fashionable society, was warmly welcomed by the reformist and working-class journals and established her as a serious writer.

By now Tristan was irrevocably committed to the cause of working-class emancipation and began to meet the workers' leaders. Their chief concern was the lack of unity in their ranks. The old *compagnonnages* or trade associations had degenerated into rival factions and one comprehensive organisation was needed to take their place. Tristan read what the workers' most articulate leaders, Gosset, Moreau and Perdiguier, had written on the subject and found their recommendations inadequate because they were merely palliatives and did nothing to eradicate the scourge of poverty. What was worse, they failed to mention the vital role of women in the movement for reform; Tristan was inspired to put forward her own plan. She could find no publisher willing to accept it, so she raised the money herself, tramping the streets of Paris in all weathers to call on possible subscribers. The first edition of four thousand copies was published in June 1843 under the title *Union ouvrière*.

This little book is indispensable for a proper understanding of Flora Tristan because it combines her vision of a harmonious social order with practical recommendations on how this is to be achieved. For Tristan was one of those rare beings whose life reflects their faith. She was not a Catholic, nor did she accept the divinity of Jesus, but she believed in a beneficent God and in the perfectibility of His creation; it followed that the best way for her to love and serve her God was to love and serve her fellow creatures, not through acts of charity, but by showing them how they could best help themselves. So in her book she called upon France's seven million workers — women as well as men — to proclaim their identity as one separate and distinctive social class by forming themselves into a single union in order to claim their rights under the Constitution, with the addition of the one essential right that all previous constitutions had omitted — the right to work. If each member of the Union were to contribute two francs per annum to a central fund, the workers would have sufficient money at their disposal to pay a Defender to represent their interests before the nation, and to build palaces for the education of their children and the care of their aged and infirm.

But Tristan knew that it was not enough for her to set down her plans on paper, for most workers could not read and the rest did not have time to read. Therefore she proposed to make a tour of the industrial regions to rouse the workers from their apathy and persuade them to join the Union. It was her sincere intention to do no more than set them on the right road, for she distrusted all elaborate systems worked out in advance, and loathed the regimentation of the workers advocated by Saint-Simon's disciple Enfantin. However, because she prided herself on being practical, she could not resist including in her book, under seventy-five separate heads, detailed suggestions for the structure and proceedings of the Union, the collection of funds, the election of the central committee, the appointment and salary of the Defender, the architecture of the palaces, the conditions governing admission to them, the type of education to be provided, and so on. She even prepared, in the workers' name, a series of petitions addressed to the king, the nobles, the clergy, the bourgeoisie, etc. asking them to support the Union and contribute generously to the palaces, because she saw human progress as a co-operative effort whereby the more privileged helped their less fortunate brothers and sisters to rise in the world.

Among these petitions was one addressed to all women, and Tristan devoted an entire chapter to explaining why she attached such importance to their emancipation. For centuries women had counted for nothing in society: the church taught that they were agents of corruption, while the law made them completely dependent on men. Workers should sympathise with the plight of women, for they too had had no place in society until the revolution of 1789, when they were astonished to discover that they were citizens with basic human rights. Now, in 1843, it was in their interests to demand equal rights for women, because the law which enslaved women also oppressed men. All the evils in the world proceeded from the neglect of women's natural rights. Only if they were given equality with men could they receive an education. Yet on the education of women depended the education of men, particularly of working men. All the sufferings of the working class came from poverty and ignorance. The only way out was to educate the women of the working class, because they were responsible for bringing up children. It was right for men to demand justice for themselves, but they should also prove that they were just by recognising women as their equals and making the equality of women one of the articles of their Charter.

The *Union ouvrière* came out in June 1843. In September Tristan spent several weeks in Bordeaux to promote the sale of her book and persuade workers to join the Union, as a trial run for the full-scale campaign she planned to launch the following year. That winter and the following spring she made preparations for her tour, and on 12 April 1844 she left Paris by boat for Auxerre, the first town on her itinerary.

Tristan's tour of France lasted from April to September and took her to seventeen manufacturing towns, including Dijon, Lyons, Toulouse, Marseilles and Toulon. She found conditions even worse than they were in England: most of the workers were so cowed that at first she had difficulty in communicating with them, but by encouraging them to talk about their wretched lives she overcame their apathy and awoke in some of them the first glimmer of self-respect. She learned that in many trades men worked from five in the morning until eight at night. The demand for labour fluctuated and there were long periods of unemployment when they had to pawn their belongings to buy bread.

Wherever she went Tristan assiduously collected facts

and figures with which to challenge the academic econ-
omists with their glib talk of 'average earnings' and the
bourgeois philanthropists who visited only a few carefully
selected model workshops and factories. Her daily round
was gruelling, especially so in the enervating heat of the
Midi. On a typical day she might see the printer about a
new edition of her book at eight, receive a deputation at
eleven, snatch a bite to eat at two, visit a hospital or
workshop in the afternoon, and hold a meeting at eight.
She has left an unforgettable impression of one such
meeting, held in a dimly lit fifth-floor room encumbered
with looms and packed to suffocation with shabby, half-
starved workers. She had a gift for gauging the mood and
intelligence of her audience, and despite initial opposition
from a few communists or republicans she invariably
succeeded in establishing a strong emotional rapport with
them. Then she would return to her hotel in such a state
of exaltation that she was unable to sleep, so she would sit
up into the small hours recording the events and impressions of the day in her journal.

But euphoria gave way to frustration whenever Tristan
reflected on the magnitude of her task. Ranged against her
were the entrenched forces of church and state: the one
disowned her because she was not a Catholic, the other
persecuted her because she was a socialist. In Lyons the
police confiscated her papers, in Agen they broke up her
meetings. As if this were not discouragement enough,
Tristan also had to contend with the workers' self-
appointed spokesmen, café politicians and journalists who
resented her presence and on one occasion even accused
her of being a government agent sent to sow discord
among the workers.

In spite of these obstacles Tristan's campaign achieved a
measure of success. In Marseilles, Avignon, Toulon and
Carcassonne branches of the Union were formed, and in
militant Lyons, with its bitter memories of the savage
repression of the silk weavers' rising of 1831, Tristan's

message of love and reconciliation made so strong an impact that workers not only flocked to join the Union, they also raised enough money to finance the third edition of the little book.

But as the tour progressed Tristan's health deteriorated. She had never been robust, and though she made light of the headaches, fevers, and bouts of dysentery which sometimes put her out of action for several days, only her strength of will and faith in her mission kept her going. She had planned to make Nantes the last stop of her tour, but when she reached Bordeaux on 26 September she collapsed with typhoid fever. Over the next few weeks her condition seemed to improve, but on 11 November she had a relapse and on 14 November she died.

Tristan's early death blighted hopes of a universal workers' union. The movement had many devoted and capable adherents, but none with her magnetic personality and capacity for self-sacrifice. Events were to confirm her contention that the majority of workers were more easily roused by the call to arms than the appeal to reason. In February 1848 massive popular demonstrations in Paris drove Louis Philippe into exile and the Second Republic was born; but in April fear of socialism drove an unrepresentative electorate to return a liberal government unable to cope with the crisis it had inherited. One of the new deputies was Louis Napoleon Bonaparte, the man Tristan had lampooned in her *Promenades dans Londres*. She was not taken in by his professions of liberalism. But he was an astute operator: in December 1848 he was elected President of the Assembly; in December 1851 he engineered a successful coup d'état, and in December 1852 he held a referendum in which the people voted overwhelmingly for the restoration of the Bonaparte dynasty and confirmed him as Emperor. For a time he managed to hold the various conflicting classes in equilibrium, but the gulf between them widened and there was no more talk of the peaceful transformation of society: Karl Marx saw to that.

Tristan's journal *Le Tour de France* remained unpublished until 1973. Its blend of messianic fervour, political shrewdness and sardonic humour is quite a revelation. Scribbled in haste, sometimes on odd scraps of paper, it retains, even on the printed page, an urgency and intensity which would have been lost had Tristan lived to revise it for publication as she intended. She left one other unfinished work, *L'Emancipation de la femme*, which was published posthumously in 1845. A few months before her death she had sent the manuscript to her friend Constant for revision, but he rewrote it, so although it reproduces her views on the evils of violent revolution, the abolition of the death penalty, the closure of all prisons and the rehabilitation of criminals, none of it is in Tristan's own words, except the appeal to all women which was reprinted from the *Union ouvrière*.

Twice in the present century Flora Tristan has been rescued from undeserved obscurity: once in France, after the First World War, when the demand for women's suffrage was renewed; and once in what is loosely termed the West, in the seventies, when the women's movement entered a new and militant phase. I hope that this translation of the *Peregrinations* will not only interest those readers who made Tristan's acquaintance through her *London Journal* (Virago, 1982) but will also win her many new friends.

Jean Hawkes, 1986

Translator's Note

The first edition of the *Mémoires et pérégrinations d'une paria* was published in two volumes by Arthus Bertrand in January 1838; the second was published by Ladvocat later in the same year. Volume I contains the Dedication, Preface, Foreword and chapters 1—8. Volume II contains the remaining chapters, numbered 1—10. The original work has 908 pages and runs to over 180,000 words, but considerations of space and economy have obliged me to reduce it by more than one-third, much to my regret. There is no complete modern edition to be had in France either: an abridged paperback version was published in 1979 by François Maspero in the series *La Découverte*. The book has fared better in Latin America, as complete Spanish translations appeared in Chile in 1941, and in Peru in 1959 and 1971.

In preparing the text for translation I worked from the first edition of the *Pérégrinations* in the Bibliothèque Nationale. I have followed Maspero in omitting the Dedication, Preface and Foreword altogether, but as they contain information which is necessary for the understanding of Tristan's story, I have summarised them in my Introduction. In the narrative proper, I have eliminated a number of minor characters, among them the sea captain Tristan met in Praia, various members of the French community in Arequipa, the other passengers on board the *Leonidas*, and the ladies Tristan met in Lima, including Calista Thwaite, who translated Byron into Spanish, and Caroline Riva Aguero, the Dutch wife of the first president of Peru. I have cut much of Tristan's moralising, telescoped descriptions of people and places, and excised a long conversation about politics between the officers of the *Mexicain*. These cuts vary in length from a few words (superfluous adjectives, pious exclamations, etc.) to twenty-five pages (letters Tristan received from David, Briet, Miota, de Castellac, and Crévosier, the manager of her uncle's sugar refinery, all of which she quotes in full). I was left with a text which, though shorter than Maspero's, contains several incidents he omits, but which struck me as either too amusing or too revealing to leave out: notably the bickering among the officers of the *Mexicain*, the excitement of the nuns at Santa Catalina as they investigate Tristan's underwear, and Tristan's brush with the French consul on her arrival in Lima. An abridgement seldom satisfies anyone who knows the original work, but I trust there is enough of Flora Tristan's attractive and contradictory personality in these pages to engage the interest and affection of readers, even if, like me, they find her exasperating at times.

In translating a text one is liable to be struck by minor inconsistencies that might escape the attention of the reader. For instance, two of the dates Tristan gives are obviously wrong: one, the date of her arrival at Callao, is easily corrected (from 1 May to 4 May) as she also gives the day of the week, which was a Sunday. The other date concerns Chabrié's visit to Arequipa, and remains an intractable problem. Tristan states that she learned that he was in Islay on 28 October, and that he arrived in Arequipa two days later. But his farewell letter to her, written after his six-day visit, is dated 29 October! Fortunately one of the letters David wrote her during Chabrié's stay in Arequipa is dated 24 October, so, bearing in mind that Chabrié's visit lasted from Saturday to Friday, there is some justification for the assumption that he arrived on 19 October, left on the 25th, and wrote his farewell letter to Flora on Tuesday 29th. So I have taken the liberty of changing the date on which Flora heard of his impending arrival to 17 October.

The reader interested in following Tristan's itinerary will not find the port of Islay in a modern atlas. The *Times Gazetteer of the World* (1922) gives its position as 17S and 72.7W; that is, just a little to the west of the modern port of Mollendo. But I have been unable to discover how and when Islay ceased to exist.

In conclusion I should like to thank my friends Edrica Huws and Diane Bataille for their generous hospitality; and the Assistant Librarian of the Taylor Institute, Oxford, for supplying me with material I needed for my Introduction.

I

The Mexicain

April 7th 1833, the anniversary of my birth, was the day of our departure. As the moment drew closer I felt so agitated that for three nights I was unable to enjoy a single hour of sleep. My body was broken, nevertheless I rose at daybreak so that I would have time to finish all my preparations, and this occupation calmed my mind. M Bertera came for me at seven o'clock and we went to the steamboat with the rest of my baggage. What a flock of unruly thoughts beset me on the brief journey to the port! The growing noise in the streets heralded a return to the bustle of daily life, and I leaned out of the cab in my eagerness to look again at the beautiful city where I had once spent so many tranquil days. The warm breeze touched my face; I felt an overwhelming sense of life, yet grief and despair filled my soul. Like a condemned man being taken to his death, I envied the lot of the country women coming into town to sell their milk, the men going to work. We passed the city park, and I bade farewell to its lovely trees, recalling with feelings of profound regret the times I had walked beneath their shade. When we reached the steamboat the sight of all the people saying goodbye to their friends or making their way towards the surrounding countryside only increased my distress. God only knows how I overcame the impulse to say to M Bertera: 'In heaven's name, save me! For pity's sake, take me away from here!' But the presence of so many people served as a grim reminder of the society that had banished me from its midst. At the memory my tongue froze and my body broke out in a cold sweat.

1

The signal was given to depart, the visitors went ashore and the boat began to draw away. I stayed below while the other passengers stood on deck waving their last farewells. Suddenly indignation gave me strength, and darting to one of the windows I cried in a voice choked with emotion: 'You fools! I pity you, I cannot hate you. Your disdain hurts me, but my conscience is clear. I am the victim of the very laws and prejudices which make your own lives so bitter, but which you lack the courage to resist. If this is how you treat those whose lofty souls and generous hearts lead them to champion your cause, I warn you that you will remain wretched for many years to come.'

This outburst restored my spirits and I began to feel calmer. The gentlemen of the *Mexicain* returned to the saloon. Only M Chabrié seemed moved: his eyes were full of tears. My sympathetic look drew him towards me and he said: 'It takes courage to leave one's country and one's friends, mademoiselle, but I hope we shall see them again. . . .'

By the time we reached Pauillac I appeared resigned to my fate. I spent the night in writing my last letters, and the following day at about eleven o'clock I went on board the *Mexicain*.

The *Mexicain* was a new brig of about 200 tons and looked from her lines as if she would do well under sail. Accommodation on board was comfortable enough but very limited: the living space was sixteen or seventeen feet by twelve and contained four very small cabins, with a larger one for the captain at the far end. The first mate's cabin was just outside the entrance. The deck, encumbered with hencoops, baskets, and stores of every description, allowed only a restricted space for movement. The vessel was the joint property of M Chabrié, the captain, M Briet, the first mate, and M David, the second. They owned most of the cargo as well. There was a crew of fifteen: eight seamen, a carpenter, a cook, a cabin-boy, a boatswain and the three officers. All were young, strong, and perfectly competent, with the exception of the cabin-boy, whose laziness and dirtiness were a source of constant irritation. The ship was amply stocked with provisions and the cook was excellent.

There were only four other passengers: an elderly gentleman called Don Jose who had wanted to see his native Spain again before he died and was now on his way back to Peru, accompanied by his nephew Cesario, a remarkably intelligent youth of fifteen. The third passenger, Firmin Miota, was a Peruvian born in Cuzco, the City of the Sun. He had been sent to Paris at the age of sixteen to complete his education, and was now twenty-four. He was accompanied by his cousin Fernando, a young Biscayan of seventeen. Of the four, only M Miota spoke French.

The captain, M Zacharie Chabrié, was a man of thirty-six, born in Lorient, and quite unlike the usual captain in the merchant fleet. He had an abundance of natural wit and an astonishing gift for repartee, but what was most remarkable about him was the goodness of his heart and the loftiness of his imagination. His temper, on the other hand, was quite the worst I have ever encountered: he was so intolerably touchy that every little thing upset him, and when he was in a bad humour he was incapable of moderation.

At first sight M Chabrié appeared very ordinary, but one had only to speak to him for a few moments to realise how cultivated he was. He was of medium height, and must have been a fine figure of a man before he began to put on weight. He was almost bald, and the top of his head was so white that it made an odd contrast with his face, which was dark red. The sea had ruined his eyesight, but his little blue eyes sparkled with a blend of malice, effrontery and tenderness difficult to define. Everything about him was contradictory, including his voice. When he spoke it was impossible to imagine a more discordant sound, but when he sang a Rossini aria, a Tyrolean folk song or a sentimental ballad, it was like being lifted up to heaven. To complete the picture, I should add that he was very particular about his dress. He was sensitive to the cold, and from the moment he felt the first twinges of rheumatism in his legs, he began to take the greatest care of his health, protecting himself against cold and damp with an assortment of garments piled one on top of the other in the most ludicrous fashion.

The first mate, M Louis Briet, also came from Lorient and was the same age as M Chabrié. He had been a member of the Imperial Guards in 1815, but the fall of the Emperor cheated him of his hopes of glory, so he became a sailor, took his master's ticket, and went to try his fortune in the Spanish colonies. By nature he remained more of a soldier than a sailor, as unlike sailors he was a stickler for order. As well as being neat and efficient in everything he did, he was a man of the strictest sobriety.

M Briet was a very handsome man, tall and well made, with good features and a distinguished countenance. It was not in his nature to be attentive, let alone gallant, towards ladies; but on board his manner towards everybody was always very polite and perfectly proper.

M Alfred David was thirty-four and typical of the Parisian who has seen the world. When he left the *Collège Bonaparte* at the age of fourteen, his parents sent him to sea aboard a merchantman bound for India to give him a taste of hardship. By the time they reached Calcutta the captain had had enough of this awkward customer and left him ashore, whereupon the lad boldly determined to earn his living, which he did. In turn sailor, language teacher, clerk, etc., he remained in India for five years. Back in France, he sought to settle down, but finding that he could not rely on the fine promises which are never lacking in Paris, he decided to try his luck once more in trade, and went off to Peru. In Lima he joined forces with

M Chabrié and the two of them returned to France in 1832: M David had been away for eight years.

M David was self-taught, and while he had no profound knowledge of anything, he was acquainted with a variety of subjects. As he was left poor and helpless at a tender age, he learned about the human heart in a good school and his early disappointments destroyed his illusions. He hated the human race: he looked on men as wild animals and was always on his guard lest they should attack him. The poor man had never loved anyone, not even a woman: the gentle emotions of the soul were stifled in him before they had a chance to develop. He was passionately fond of good cheer, enjoyed smoking cigars, and delighted in thinking about the pretty girls of any colour he would meet in the next port of call. That was the only kind of love he understood.

M David was extremely good-looking, tall and very slim, but strong and healthy nevertheless. His delicate regular features, pale complexion, black side-whiskers, jet-black hair and the smile forever playing upon his lips, combined to create an impression of cheerfulness very much at odds with his real feelings. M David was what people call an agreeable man. He was also a dandy who went round Cape Horn in silk stockings, trimmed his beard every day, scented his hair, recited poetry, spoke English, Italian and Spanish, and never lost his balance however much the ship was rolling.

Such were my companions on the *Mexicain*.

From the moment we set foot on board, each of us was busy settling into his own little space as best he could. M David helped me arrange my things, and with his experience of sea voyages he was able to show me how to make myself as comfortable as possible.

I was seasick an hour after I came aboard my floating home. I shall spare my reader the tedium of yet another description of this affliction, except to say that it is quite unlike any of our common illnesses: it is a permanent agony, a suspension of life. Persons of an emotional nature feel its cruel effects more intensely than others do. As for me, I suffered from it so consistently that not one of the one hundred and thirty-three days of the voyage passed without an attack of nausea.

Our vessel was moored at the mouth of the river. The weather did not seem to favour our braving the perils of the Bay of Biscay, nevertheless at about three o'clock the captain gave orders to raise the anchor, and the ponderous machine, light as a feather on the waves, began to move across the immense expanse of water bounded by the sky. Hardly were we in the Bay than the shrill whistling of the winds and the tumult of the waves announced the impending storm which broke soon afterwards in all its fury. This was a new experience for me: I felt it though I did not see it. I would have found it fascinating to watch if I had had the strength, but all my faculties were absorbed by my sickness; I knew I was still alive only by the shivers that shook my body and seemed to presage my death. We had a dreadful night. The captain was lucky to be able to get back into the river. One wave had carried off our sheep, another our baskets of vegetables, and our poor little ship, so neat and trim the day before, was already crippled. The captain, though dropping with fatigue, went ashore to buy fresh sheep and replace the vegetables the sea had stolen from us. During his absence the carpenter repaired the ravages caused by the storm and the crew restored the order so necessary on board ship.

This first attempt did not make us any wiser, and we knowingly exposed ourselves a second time to dangers which very nearly claimed our lives, thanks to a false notion of honour, which all too often makes sailors brave unnecessary hazards and endanger the lives of men and the safety of vessels entrusted to their charge. The next day, April 10th, as the sea continued rough, our officers, who were very prudent, judged quite rightly that they ought to keep the pilot aboard until the weather improved sufficiently to send him back safely; but there were two other vessels moored close by, the *Charles-Adolphe* and the *Flétès*, which had left Bordeaux at the same time and were bound for the same destination. The latter, out of bravado no doubt, sent back her pilot and made for the open sea; the other, not wishing to be left behind, did the same. Our gentlemen of the *Mexicain* began by blaming the foolhardiness of the other two ships, but although they were not the sort to let themselves be influenced by the example of others, the fear of being thought *cowards* made them abandon their earlier decision. Towards four o'clock in the afternoon they sent back their pilot and we found ourselves amid the mountainous waves. We were nothing but a speck on the ocean, and if two waves had struck us at the same time, we would have been buried beneath them.

It was three days before we could struggle out of the Bay. We were constantly battered by the storm and our situation was critical. During those three long days of agony our brave captain never left the deck; he told me afterwards that several times he had seen our brig in imminent danger of being dashed against the rocks or swallowed up by the waves. Thanks to God we came out if it alive. You would think that such dangers ought to make sailors more careful, but no, they commit similar reckless acts every day.

Between two and three o'clock on the afternoon of the 13th, our captain, looking absolutely exhausted and as wet as if he had fallen into the sea, came below for the first time in three days. Seeing all the cabins closed and hearing no sound of life, he shouted in his hoarse voice:

'Hallo there! Passengers! Is everybody dead down here?'

Nobody answered his kind enquiry. Then M Chabrié half-opened my door and said with a solicitude I shall never forget:

'Mademoiselle Flora, you have been very ill, so David tells me: poor young lady, I am really sorry for you as I used to suffer from seasickness myself, but take heart, we are out of the Bay at last and have come into the open sea — can't you feel it from the gentle rocking motion, so unlike the horrible convulsions we felt before? The weather is magnificent; if you felt strong enough to get up and come on deck, it would put new life into you. The air is so fresh and pure up there it's a pleasure to feel it.'

I thanked him with a look, as I felt too weak even to attempt to speak.

'Poor young lady!' he repeated with an expression of kindness and compassion, 'this weather will allow you to sleep. I am going to sleep too: I need it.'

In fact we all slept a full twenty-four hours. I was awakened by M David opening all the cabin doors because he wanted to know, or so he said, if all the passengers were definitely dead. We were not dead, but dear God, what a state we were in! M Chabrié, who was above trading on his position of authority and spoke to his crew and passengers alike as a friend, now invited us to get up, so that we could change our linen, take the air on deck, and — most important of all — drink a little hot broth. For my part, I consented, on condition that I was excused from eating anything. The gentlemen were good enough to make me up a bed on deck, but it took me all my courage to get up and dress, and without their help it would have been impossible for me to climb on deck.

For the first fortnight of the voyage I felt quite numb, apart from brief intervals when I was conscious of my existence. From sunrise until about six in the evening I was so ill that I was unable to put two ideas together.

I was indifferent to everything: my only desire was that death would come quickly and put an end to my sufferings — but an inner voice told me that I was not going to die.

As we approached the Canary Islands our officers noticed that the ship was taking in water, so they decided to put in to the nearest port and get it caulked. We had been at sea for only twenty-five days, but the time had seemed so long and life aboard had become so much a part of me, that when I was told that we should soon sight land, the happiness I felt overcame my infirmities and I was immediately restored to health. You have to have been at sea to understand the powerful emotion contained in the word *land*. To hear it after long months spent between heaven and ocean means everything to the sailor: his country, the pleasures of society, cool shades and flower-strewn fields, love and liberty.

We all gathered on deck, eager to catch sight of this land which each of us was already investing with every imaginable delight. Our hearts beat faster as we rounded the tip of the tongue of land forming the bay of Praia. What were we about to see? It was at this anchorage that the first disappointment of the voyage awaited me. I was not very good at geography, and as I had never read a description of Praia I invented one in my head. I imagined that an island called Cape Verde was bound to greet the voyager with a green landscape, otherwise how account for its name? But there is something so monotonous about this uniformly black and arid land that it inspires the deepest melancholy. The whole bay is surrounded by high rocks upon which the waves break with a roar. In the middle a higher mass of rock projects in the shape of a horseshoe, and it is on the plateau which crowns it that the town of Praia is built.

From a distance it is not unimpressive. In the centre is

mounted a battery of twenty-two high-calibre cannon, with a guard of quite presentable soldiers. To the left is a pretty church, newly built; to the right, the American consul's house, surmounted by a white belvedere which serves as a lookout from which to observe ships at sea. Here and there you see a clump of banana trees, a few sycamores and other broad-leaved trees.

II

Praia

No sooner had we cast anchor than there were signs of great activity ashore, and a few moments later a small boat came towards us, rowed by four half-naked negroes. Sitting proudly in the stern clutching the tiller was a little man with enormous side-whiskers whose copper-coloured skin and fuzzy hair showed that he was not of Caucasian origin. His costume was quite grotesque: his nankeen trousers went back to about 1800 and had plainly seen better days before coming down to him. He wore a white piqué waistcoat, an apple-green frockcoat and a voluminous red silk scarf with black spots, tied like a cravat with its ends floating gracefully in the breeze. To complete the picture he had a big straw hat and gloves which had once been white, while in his free hand he held a splendid yellow silk scarf which he used as a fan. He was protected from the sun by an enormous pink and blue striped umbrella, the sort which used to be made thirty years ago. When he came alongside us this ridiculous individual began to declaim a list of his titles: he was harbourmaster of Praia and secretary to the Governor, besides being a wholesale and retail merchant, etc. Clearly the law against pluralism has not yet reached the coasts of Africa. This character was Portuguese: he told us that the island belonged to his illustrious master Don Miguel, and as he pronounced the name he removed his hat. He attempted to draw us out on the subject of politics, accepted our brandy and biscuits, paid me elaborate compliments in Portuguese, and after spending a long time on board devoted more to spying than carrying out

11

his proper business, he climbed back into his boat, where he assumed the lofty attitude of a Turkish pasha sailing out of Alexandria at the head of his fleet.

While the little Portuguese was talking to us we were visited by two other individuals no less remarkable for their appearance and manner: one was captain of an American brig, and the other commanded a little schooner from Sierra Leone. Our captain and his officers thought it advisable to go ashore and see the Governor, so that they could have the ship's papers examined and find some workers to help our carpenter with the repairs. As I have resolved to tell the whole truth, I must confess how proud I felt as I compared our boat with the three others manned by negroes or poor American sailors. How trim our boat was, and how fit our sailors looked! M Briet had the tiller: with his noble bearing he was a worthy representative of the French navy, while our captain, with his polished boots, white duck trousers, dark blue tailcoat, black taffeta cravat and fine straw hat, was just as worthy a representative of the merchant fleet. As for the amiable M David, he was the man of fashion *par excellence*, with his grey kid boots, close-fitting grey duck trousers and short green frogged jacket. He wore no cravat but had tied a checked cotton scarf negligently about his neck and sported a little purple velvet toque over his left ear. He stood amidships waving me farewell and laughing heartily, presumably at the preposterous appearance of the notables of the port. I must admit that in 1833 I was still very narrow-minded: I thought only of my country and hardly considered the rest of the world at all. I judged the opinions and customs of other countries by the standards of my own: the name of France and everything related to it had an almost magical effect on me. At that time I thought of the English, the Germans and the Italians as so many *foreigners*: I did not see that all men are brothers and that the whole world is their home. But I am telling you what I felt then, when I saw how superior we were to the representatives of other nations in Praia at the time.

The gentlemen were gone a long while, and during their absence we speculated on the pleasures Praia might offer us. M Miota wanted to escape life on board and take refuge in a hotel, while Cesario and Fernando planned to accompany our lieutenant and the cook on their daily trip into town for provisions. I too was making plans for our stay: I wanted to live in a Portuguese house so that I could study the manners and customs of the people and take note of everything I found worth recording. Meanwhile old Don Jose was quietly enjoying the inexpressible happiness of being able to take a dozen steps at a time without the risk of falling down. He stopped only to make yet another of his little cigars, and from time to time he smiled as he listened to us. I was curious to know what lay behind that smile, and asked him what *he* was planning to do in town.

'Mademoiselle,' he replied with that Spanish calm he possessed in the highest degree, 'I shall take good care not to set foot in it. I do not think it worth the trouble of leaving the ship only to be even more uncomfortable ashore. That is what will happen to you, but the young need to find things out for themselves. Well, go and see, and then tell me if I was not right.'

We all protested at this, but the old Spaniard would not be moved. He merely repeated, 'Go along then, and when you come back, tell me if I was not right.'

When we saw the boat returning our curiosity revived: hardly were the gentlemen back on board than we overwhelmed them with questions, but the moment was not propitious as MM Chabrié and Briet were busy explaining to the workmen what had to be done, while M David, with his passion for everything English, was entirely occupied in speaking the beautiful language of Lord Byron with his new friend the young and elegant American consul, whom he had invited to dine on board.

The next day after breakfast the three young Spaniards, M David, the captain and I went ashore.

As there is no jetty at Praia a sailor had to tow our boat ashore, while the rest of the crew used their oars to prevent the waves from dashing it against the rocks. It is very difficult to land without getting wet, especially in the morning when the sea is always rough. However, thanks to all the precautions our gentlemen took, I did not get wet: a sailor picked me up in his strong arms and set me down on a patch of dry land. A narrow track over the rocky foreshore leads to Praia; this is not without its hazards as the black sand which covers the rocks is liable to crumble beneath your feet, and the slightest false step could send you tumbling into the sea below. After this you come to a stretch of soft smooth sand caressed by the rippling silver waves. It is a relief to walk upon this firm surface constantly washed by the sea, but after barely two or three hundred steps you have to leave it for an exceedingly difficult rocky path, a kind of ladder cut into the rock on which the town is situated. It takes at least a quarter of an hour to climb up. I was so weak that I had to stop and rest three times. I could hardly walk: my good friend M Chabrié almost had to carry me. M Miota shaded me with his umbrella (for my own would have offered me little protection) while M David, agile as a deer, went on ahead and showed us the best way to go. The tropical sun blazed down immediately overhead: there was not the vestige of a breeze to dry our faces bathed in sweat, and a raging thirst parched our throats. At last we reached level ground and M David hastened to warn the consul of our approach so that he could have refreshments prepared for us. We went through the town, which we found almost deserted: it was noon, and from then until three o'clock the heat is at its strongest, so the townsfolk do not venture out, but shut themselves indoors and sleep away the afternoon. The reflection of the sun's rays was so intense that it blinded us. M Chabrié was in despair at having brought me into such a furnace and this put him in an evil humour. The three young men were already regretting their little cabins, while as for me, I was thoroughly vexed to be feeling so ill, as I feared this might stop me from exploring the town. Such were our thoughts when we arrived at the residence of the American consul, whom we found sitting with M David at a little table drinking spirits and smoking excellent Havana cigars.

The American consul had brought to that dismal spot all the comforts his nation holds so dear. This young man of about thirty had been living there for the past four years. His house was large, well appointed and maintained in meticulous order. He had us served with a very pleasant meal consisting of ham, butter, cheese, cakes and many other things, all imported from New York. There was also fresh fish and a plentiful variety of fruit grown on the islands.

The room in which this meal was served was furnished entirely in the English style: the floor was covered with a pretty carpet, the windows were fitted with blinds depicting views of different ports, and the walls were hung with fine engravings of hunting scenes, departing coaches, children playing with dogs, and those delicate portraits of women for which the English are so famous.

The food too was served in English, or rather American style. We ate off big plates with a blue pattern, we drank ale out of tall stemmed glasses and port out of smaller ones. Our large steel knives and forks were so highly polished they looked like new. Finally, we had no table napkins, so everybody made do with the portion of tablecloth in front of him. The consul, overjoyed to have met in M David an anglophile who knew the language of his beloved country so well, spoke to him all the time. He also spoke English to the two negro servants, so that I, a silent observer, began to imagine that I was in a country house on the outskirts of New York.

After the meal, while M David stayed to talk English and drink tea, we went to visit a lady who claimed to be almost French, as she had been married to a Frenchman from Bordeaux called M Watrin. This Madame Watrin was the wealthiest lady in the whole of Praia. She was in her fifties, tall and very fat, with a skin the colour of strong coffee, slightly frizzy hair, and fairly regular features. She had a pleasant expression and a refined manner. She spoke a little French and could read and write the language tolerably well, as her husband had taught her all she knew. She said she missed her dear husband very much: he had been dead for four years.

Madame Watrin received us in a large room with a roughly tiled floor and a gloomy aspect. This was what she called her drawing-room. There was something odd about the way it was furnished: we noticed this the moment we entered. It was easy to see that it had been lived in by a Frenchman: the walls were lined with bad engravings of Bonaparte at four or five different stages in his career, together with every general of the Empire and every battle, all arranged in symmetrical order. At the end of the room was a glass-fronted bookcase on which stood a bust of the Emperor draped in black. This bookcase contained a few of the works of Voltaire and Rousseau, the fables of La Fontaine, copies of Télémaque, Robinson Crusoe, etc. arranged in no apparent order on the shelves. On another piece of furniture stood two globes and a glass jar containing two foetuses preserved in alcohol. Here and there one noticed things which had obviously come from France: a little mahogany work table, a lamp, two black armchairs stuffed with horsehair, several bird-cages, the fine cloth upon the table in the centre of the room, and a number of other little things. When we entered, Madame Watrin came up to me, took my hand, and made me sit in one of the armchairs. She had put on all her grandest clothes and assembled several of her friends who were curious to meet a young lady from abroad. Perhaps our Parisian ladies would like to know how the ladies of Praia dress for special occasions. Madame Watrin's costume was in glaring contrast with the rest of her person. She wore a short gown of cherry-coloured silk with short sleeves and a very low neck. A voluminous sky-blue crêpe-de-Chine scarf embroidered with white roses covered her shoulders and head, while her plump arms were adorned with bracelets of every hue and her fingers were weighed down with rings. A coral necklace of seven or eight strands encircled her neck and enormous ear-rings hung from her ears. She wore stockings of white silk and shoes of blue satin. The other ladies were no match for her in finery: they were wearing simple cotton gowns of blue, red or white, but the style of their dresses and scarves was similar to hers in every respect.

Madame Watrin asked me many questions about Bordeaux as her husband had told her so much about it; then, with an affability rare among the people of these islands, she undertook to satisfy my curiosity and tell me everything I wished to know. She took me round her house and garden, and invited me to stay with her while our ship was in port. I was grateful for this courtesy, but I must confess that I was not tempted to accept it, for however much you long for the sight of land when you are at sea, it soon loses its charm when you find yourself among people so far removed from the sort of society to which you are accustomed. When M Chabrié heard Madame Watrin make her offer, he turned red and looked at me with an expression of painful anxiety. I declined, however, and we took our leave, promising to return in a few days' time.

We made a tour of the town: it was by then six o'clock in the evening. The sun was going down and a light breeze made the heat easier to bear. The entire population seemed to be out on their doorsteps for a breath of air, and it was then that we first became aware of the characteristic negro smell: there is nothing quite like it, it follows you everywhere you go. If you approach a group of children to watch them play, you have to beat a hasty retreat, the odour they give off is so repellent. As for me, I am particularly sensitive and the slightest smell affects my head or my stomach, so we had to quicken our pace to escape from the *effluvium Africanum*.

When we reached the foot of the rocks, I sat down to rest. M Chabrié sat beside me while the three young men wandered along the shore looking for shells. M Chabrié took my hand and pressed it affectionately to his heart, saying in a tone I had never heard from him before:

'Oh, Mademoiselle Flora, how thankful I am that you did not accept that lady's offer: how unhappy that would have made me! To be separated from you when I am responsible for you, when you are so ill! Oh, I would never have consented to it — and then, who would look after you if I were not there?'

The passion with which M Chabrié uttered these words affected me in a way I find difficult to describe: a mixture of gratitude, affection and terror. Since leaving Bordeaux I had never once considered how extraordinary my position must appear in M Chabrié's eyes. My being so ill had prevented me from thinking about it: I attributed our captain's kindness towards me and the attentions he showed me to his natural goodness. I had never dreamed that he might feel anything for me beyond the sympathetic concern that my position inspired in everybody on board.

For those beings endowed with a loving heart and a sensitive nature, a single glance is enough for them to penetrate another's secret thoughts. M Chabrié's look let me read his mind as he read mine. I pressed his hand and he said sadly:

'Mademoiselle Flora, I cannot hope to make you fond of me. All I ask is to help you bear your sorrows.'

I gave him a grateful smile, and pointing to the sea I said, 'My heart is like the ocean: adversity has ploughed such deep furrows in it that no human power can fill them.'

'Does that mean you think adversity is stronger than love?'

The question made me tremble, for at that time I could not hear the word *love* without the tears springing to my eyes. M Chabrié hid his face in his hands and I looked at him as if I had never seen him before, He was weeping; I went on watching him and blissfully abandoned myself to the most melancholy thoughts.

Somebody called us: the boat was waiting and we slowly made our way towards it. I leaned on M Chabrié's arm for support; we were absorbed in our thoughts and neither of us felt inclined to break the silence. On board we found M David with his consul and two musicians he had brought to give me a taste of native music. We all gathered on deck; I reclined on a double layer of carpet, the gentlemen settled themselves around me, and everybody lent as much attention as his thoughts permitted to the monotonous music of the two Africans. The concert would probably have continued well into the night had not one of the musicians been suddenly overcome with seasickness, although the ship was perfectly still. This circumstance obliged the consul to return to the town and delivered me from the boredom of listening to his English speech and his African musicians. We stayed on deck talking until very late: these tropical nights are so beautiful!

Next morning M David and M Miota left the ship to visit a Frenchman who had a small plantation about forty miles from Praia. They were intending to buy provisions from him, as well as to see what the island was like.

In the two days that followed, I felt that M Chabrié was no longer at ease in my company, and this increased the anxiety and sadness which our conversation on the seashore had caused me.

At that time I still had all the illusions of the young

woman who has seen little of the world, even though I had already suffered cruelly; but as I had been brought up in the depths of the country and since then had led a very quiet life, I had gone through ten years of disappointment and misfortune without becoming any the wiser.

In 1833, love was a religion in my eyes: from the age of fourteen my ardent soul had worshipped it. I considered love as *the breath of God*, the life-giving force from which all goodness and beauty proceed. I put my faith in love alone, and judged any human being who could live without a pure, devoted and eternal love as scarcely higher than the other animals God created. I loved my country, I wanted to help my fellow men, I admired the marvels of nature; but none of these were sufficient to fill my soul. Only a passionate and exclusive love for a man afflicted with the sort of misfortune that exalts and ennobles its victims could have satisfied me.

I had loved twice: the first time, I was still a child. The young man to whom I gave my affection was worthy of it in every way, but his soul lacked strength, and he died rather than disobey the proud father who spurned me. The second time, the man on whom I lavished my whole affection was one of those cold, calculating beings who regard a great passion as madness. He was *afraid* of my love: he feared that I loved him *too much*. This second betrayal broke my heart, and I vowed never to be the cause of similar suffering in others. I was not sure whether M Chabrié loved me, but I felt it would be kinder not to encourage a feeling I could not share. The absence of MM David and Miota gave me a little more freedom: the other three passengers did not understand a word of French, so I could talk to M Chabrié without the risk of being overheard.

In the evening I went up on deck, and when I had arranged a couch for myself on one of the hencoops, I began to talk to M Chabrié.

'What a beautiful night it is!' I exclaimed. 'I have never

seen all these bright stars before: can you tell me their names?'

'I do not know enough about astronomy to tell you very much, but I am particularly fond of the Southern Cross, those four stars there, one smaller than the rest.'

'And what about those two very bright ones beside it?'

'They are Gemini, the twins. How lucky you are, Mademoiselle Flora, to be so interested in everything! I do admire your childlike curiosity. How happy you must be to have illusions! Life is very dull when you have none left.'

'I hope you have not reached that stage, M Chabrié. Anyone with a heart as good as yours stays young for a long time!'

'Mademoiselle, to stay young you have to love and be loved, but the man with no love in his heart is old at twenty.'

'So you think we cannot live without love?'

'I am convinced of it, unless you call it living just to eat, drink, and sleep as animals do. But I imagine you understand love too well, mademoiselle, to dignify such an existence with the name of living. Still, that's how most men live. When you think of that, don't you feel the same as I do — ashamed to belong to the human race?'

'No, the human race suffers and should not be despised. I pity it for the misfortune it has brought upon itself, and I love it because it is unhappy.'

'And you never feel the need to revenge yourself upon it?'

'Never.'

'But perhaps nobody has ever given you cause to complain: you have probably only come across people who loved you, and you have never felt the grief and horror of betrayal.'

'That is true, but I know something even worse than betrayal, and that is insensitivity. Yes, the cold creature incapable of enthusiasm who responds to the sentiments of the heart with reason and claims he can measure the lofty flights of the soul: yes, the automaton who is not inspired by the breath of God, who cannot feel the sublime beauty of devotion and disdains the love he has inspired is worse than a betrayer. Yes, the man who is afraid of being loved too much and is indifferent to the suffering of the woman who loves him is worse than a betrayer. For *she* is always motivated by love, M Chabrié, while *he* is motivated by egoism and loves only himself.'

In uttering these words, which had escaped me almost in spite of myself, I had forgotten the reserve which up to then I had so scrupulously observed. M Chabrié was struck by my expression and said with a look of concern:

'Merciful Heavens! Could you have loved a man with so vile a nature? Tell me, is this the grief that weighs so heavily upon you?'

I could not speak: I could only bow my head in token of assent. I looked up at the sky as if to implore its aid, then, stretching out my hand towards M Chabrié, I managed to utter these words: 'How I suffer! Oh, God, how I suffer!' Then, letting my head fall back upon my pillow, I closed my eyes, weary of external things, and, plunged in a welter of confused memories, I tasted the indefinable charm of excessive grief. I remained in this position for several hours, overcome by the feverish activity of my brain.

Meanwhile M Chabrié had covered me with my cloak and arranged a scarf around my head to protect me from the dampness of the night. I was aware of him beside me: from time to time he sighed heavily, and occasionally he rose, took a few turns about the deck and returned to his seat.

When I emerged from my reverie the pale moonlight was investing everything around us with a melancholy sadness. The town was silent and the sea calm. M Chabrié was still sitting on the end of the hencoop beside me, leaning his head upon his hand in a pose entirely appropriate to the scene.

I remained a long time in silent contemplation. Little by little I became aware of the gentle influence the moon exerts upon the whole of nature, calm flowed back into my soul and I marvelled anew at the majestic beauty of the heavens. I did not dare speak to M Chabrié for fear of disturbing him, but I made a slight movement. He turned immediately, and seeing that I was awake, he got up precipitately and asked if there was anything I wanted.

'I should like to know what time it is,' I replied.

'Past midnight.'

'So late! Then why haven't you gone to bed? You were planning to have a few good nights' sleep now that you no longer have to go on watch.'

'I am like you, Mademoiselle Flora, I like the beautiful tropical nights; besides, now I am your *friend*, your old friend who is too fond of you to let you sleep on a hencoop without someone to watch over you.'

I took his hand and clasped it tightly in my own. 'Thank you, oh, thank you!' I exclaimed. 'How grateful I am for your friendship and how I need it! You too have had your sorrows; well, I shall help console you for them, and they will seem nothing to you compared with mine.'

'Then you accept me as your friend?'

'How can you ask such a thing!'

And I kissed him on the forehead in a gesture of gratitude which made my tears flow.

It was nearly two in the morning when I went to bed, and I slept until ten. I was awakened by the melodious voice of M Chabrié singing an old ballad about friendship. I got up and the cabin-boy served me breakfast: everybody else had finished. M Chabrié came to keep me company, peeled my oranges and bananas for me, and talked to me with so much trust and frankness that I grew fonder of him every minute.

Around three o'clock MM David and Miota reappeared, bringing with them the Frenchman they had been visiting. M Miota was exhausted and went straight to bed; as for

M David, he was not so much tired as bad-tempered because he had not been able to shave for three days and he was not his usual immaculate self. We had to evacuate the saloon for him so that he could make a completely fresh toilet. This was no hardship for us, as the deck had become a very agreeable saloon in itself, thanks to the awning which sheltered us from the sun.

What little M David had told us about this Frenchman, a landlord on the island, made me want to talk to him. He was a squat little man with angular features, a swarthy complexion, and thick black hair brushed forward over his forehead. He was dressed like one of our peasants in Sunday best. I greeted him cordially, as one would on meeting a compatriot when far from home. M Tappe (that was his name) clearly appreciated my interest, and although he was not by nature very talkative, I could see that he would not need much encouragement to tell me his life history.

M Tappe had been on the Cape Verde Islands for fourteen years. I asked him how he had come to choose such an arid spot.

'I didn't choose it, mademoiselle: God, whose ways are truly incomprehensible, decreed that I was to live in this dry and desolate land. I had been destined for the priesthood since childhood: I was brought up in the seminary at La Passe, near Bayonne, where my burning religious zeal soon attracted the notice of my superiors. When the usurper fell and the monarchy was restored, our holy religion recovered all its former power, and in 1819 it was decided that all the seminaries in France should send their most enthusiastic evangelists to convert the idolatrous savages. I was one of those chosen, and we departed to go wherever our apostolate called us. We put into Praia because our ship, like yours, was in need of repair. I went ashore, where I became friendly with an old Portuguese who told me what the country had to offer. I saw that with very little money it was possible to make a quick fortune, so I decided to change course and stay on these shores. But alas! God, whose will I respect, has not permitted my hopes to be realised, and for fourteen years I have been leading the most wretched and aimless existence imaginable.'

I was curious to know what kind of business had made M Tappe decide to abandon the apostolate for the chance of a fortune, so I asked him what was the quick method of making money which had led him astray.

'My God, mademoiselle, there's only one kind of trade on this coast, and that's the slave trade. When I first settled on this island, ah, those were the days! There was money to be had then for very little trouble. For two years it was a good business; even after the abolition of the slave trade you could still sell as many negroes as you liked. But now those accursed English insist on such strict enforcement of the treaties that it has become too dangerous and expensive to transport the negroes, and the most profitable trade of all time has been completely ruined. Besides, nowadays everybody wants his cut from the business, so you make no more out of it than if you were selling bales of wool or cotton.'

All this and more M Tappe told me with an air of simplicity and good nature that left me dumbfounded. The very sight of him inspired me with such instinctive repugnance that as I could not rid myself of his company in any other way I went down to the saloon. There I found M David, in splendid dishabille, sitting at the table with his consul, who it was clear could no longer live without him. When M David saw me, he threw away his cigar and said:

'Well, mademoiselle, what do you think of the amiable compatriot I have brought you? I hope you will agree that there are one or two Frenchmen on the Cape Verde Islands with a little culture. Here's a man who speaks Latin better than Cicero and cannot mention his green lemons or stunted cabbages without quoting Horace,

Juvenal or Virgil at you, to say nothing of the Scriptures: the fellow knows Hebrew as well. I am sure you must be delighted, mademoiselle, to see our beautiful France so well represented. . . .'

'Not another word, monsieur; that man is no Frenchman, he's a cannibal in sheep's clothing.'

'Well said, mademoiselle! That's quite charming — I really must translate it for the consul.'

And from that moment M Tappe was nicknamed *the cannibal sheep*.

'All the same, M David,' I went on, 'I really cannot guess what made you bring that man on board. Can there be many more like him?'

'Unfortunately there are, mademoiselle, and as we are speaking frankly, I will make bold to assert that most of the human race resembles the worthy M Tappe in every respect.'

'If I thought that were true, monsieur, I should throw myself into the sea without more ado; but here is M Chabrié, and I can see from his face that he has no use for your facile misanthropy.'

'What has that David been telling you, Mademoiselle Flora?' asked M Chabrié as he entered. 'That all men are wicked, I'll be bound. It's always the same old tune with him, he doesn't know any others.'

'Ah, but this time I can prove it, that's why I've brought the holy and righteous M Tappe all the way from Saint-Martin to dine with us, if you'll be good enough to allow it.'

Then M David turned to me and said, 'Now, mademoiselle, I'm not joking any more, I urge you to study this man. I will put him next to you at dinner, so try to overcome your distaste a little, you are lucky to meet somebody like him on your travels.'

All through the first course the former seminarist ate and drank with a gusto that gave him no time to utter a single word: his faculties were concentrated on his plate and his glass. I never partook of this course, so I had ample leisure to observe the man. How his little eyes shone at the sight of the enormous leg of mutton and all the other meat set before us! His nostrils dilated, he licked his pale thin lips, the sweat ran down his face. I thought he looked like a wild animal. When he had gorged himself thoroughly, his features gradually resumed their normal expression, or rather lack of it, and he took up the thread of our conversation where we had left it.

'Your captain has just given us an excellent dinner, mademoiselle. Eating is the very stuff of life, but as for me, stuck on this wretched island, I am deprived of that kind of living.'

'Do you mean you have nothing to eat here?'

'Only mutton, poultry, vegetables, fresh fish and fruit.'

'But it seems to me that with all these things it should be possible to live perfectly well.'

'Yes, if one had a cook and the means to prepare food, but there is nothing here.'

'Why do you not train one of your women to do the cooking?'

'Ah, mademoiselle, it is plain that you do not know the black race. They are so wicked that I could never trust any of them with the responsibility, for fear of being poisoned.'

'You must treat them very badly for them to hate their master so much!'

'I treat them as you have to treat negroes if you want them to obey you – with the lash. I assure you, mademoiselle, these creatures are more trouble to control than animals.'

'How many have you at the moment?'

'I have eighteen men, twenty-eight women, and thirty-seven children. For the past two years the children have been selling very well, but it is very difficult to get rid of the men.'

'And what do they all do?'

'They cultivate my farm and look after my house: everything is very well kept, as these gentlemen can tell you.'

'M David said you were married: is your home life happy?'

'I was forced to marry one of my negresses to make sure of staying alive: they had already tried to poison me three times. Then I thought that if I married one of them, she would take an interest in me, especially if I led her to believe that everything I had belonged to her as well. So I make her do the cooking, and she has to taste everything before I will eat it. This makes me feel much safer. I have had three children by this woman: she loves them dearly.'

'So you no longer think of returning to France, if you have ties here?'

'Why do you say that? Is it because of this woman? Oh, that doesn't bother me. As soon as I have made a nice little fortune, I shall bring her here one day when the sea is very rough and I shall say to her, "I'm going back to my country, will you come with me?" As these women are all terrified of the sea, I am sure she will refuse; then I shall say to her, "Well, my dear, you see that I am doing my duty, I offer to take you with me, you refuse to obey your husband. I am too good to force you against your will, so I wish you every happiness" – and then, off I go!'

'But what will become of the poor woman?'

'Oh, she won't complain, never fear: she'll sell her children for a good price, then she'll find another husband to cook for: she's a fine-looking girl and still only twenty-six.'

'But that woman is your wife in the eyes of God, M Tappe; she is the mother of your children, so how can you leave them to the mercy of whoever will buy them in the marketplace? It's a wicked thing to do!'

'Mademoiselle, in our society such things are done every day.'

By now I was crimson with indignation; M Tappe

looked at me in amazement. Then he muttered another of his Latin tags and said with a disagreeable smile:

'You are still very young, mademoiselle, and I imagine you have seen little of the world. I advise you to see more of it, as it is good to know what sort of people you have to live with, otherwise you are taken in by everybody.'

After dinner M Tappe returned to the town. When I was alone with M David he said to me: 'Well, what do you think of the pupil of those gentlemen from the famous seminary of La Passe?'

'I tell you once more, M David, I would rather not have met him.'

'Mademoiselle, I beg you to forgive me if in my desire to serve you I have caused you a few unpleasant moments; however, you are too sensible not to realise that sooner or later you will have to learn a little more about the world in which you have to live. Society is not a very pretty sight at close quarters, I agree, but it is important to recognise it for what it is.'

A week had gone by, and I had still not returned to the town. My aversion to the smell of the negroes held me back: nevertheless, courtesy obliged me to overcome my reluctance, and I resolved to pay my farewell visits to Madame Watrin and the American consul.

At the consul's I was able to witness one of those scenes of cruelty so common wherever slavery, that monstrous outrage against humanity, persists.

This young consul, the representative of a republic; this elegant American, so courtly towards me, so agreeable towards M David, was from that moment no more than a barbarous master in my eyes. We found him below-stairs, savagely beating a big negro lying at his feet. The man's face was covered with blood. I ran forward to defend him against his oppressor, since slavery had paralysed his strength.

The consul charged M David to explain to us why he was beating his slave: the man was a thief, a liar, etc. As if it was not the slave who had suffered the greatest loss of all! I cannot describe what a painful impression this dreadful scene had upon me. I pictured the wretched Tappe among his slaves; my God, I thought, could M David be right? Could all men be wicked? These reflections completely overturned my notions of morality. The evils we encounter foster doubt, and I began to fear that goodness was not as widespread as I had hitherto imagined. On my way to see Madame Watrin I closely examined every negro I saw: the men looked surly and the women stupid. As for the children, they were horribly ugly, quite naked, thin and sickly; you would have taken them for little monkeys. As we passed the town hall we saw soldiers beating negroes by order of the slave-owners, and this cruel practice only increased the depression which the scene at the consulate had caused me. When we arrived at Madame Watrin's I complained bitterly to her about the cruelty I had witnessed in the town, and this lady, who seemed so kind, just smiled and said gently: 'I can understand that such customs seem strange to you, because you were brought up in a different society, but if you were to live here for a week, you would no longer even think about them.' I found such a callous attitude revolting and could not wait to get away from this society and all it stood for.

At last, after spending ten days at Praia to repair our vessel, we put to sea again.

III

Life on board

For the first week, I was just as ill as I had been when we left the river at Bordeaux. After that my illness followed a regular pattern: I was sick every morning, I began to feel a little better about midday, from two until four I felt very queasy, and from four o'clock until the following morning I was perfectly well. This daily pattern continued until we reached Valparaiso, but when the sea became rough I was ill day and night without interruption.

Fourteen days after we left Praia we were on the Equator, and there our troubles began. Our vessel had been carefully repaired and no longer leaked, but this had a serious drawback, for we soon became aware of an overpowering stench arising from the hold. We attributed this to the foul water trapped inside, which could no longer be washed away by the sea. The odour was so corrosive that all our silverware turned black. The whole ship was contaminated: we had to abandon our cabins for fear of being suffocated if we remained below.

For the next twelve days we suffered abominably. We were forced to stay on deck day and night: every quarter of an hour or so we had squalls, then the fierce equatorial sun blazed down directly overhead. The heat was intolerable: we could not put up our awning to protect ourselves because the wind was constantly changing direction. Everybody tried in vain to find a shady corner. We were a pitiful sight, drenched to the skin and exhausted from lack of sleep. We all suffered from a raging thirst, but there was no fresh fruit to assuage it. The ship's water supply was stored on deck in barrels which became so hot that the water inside was quite warm.

In spite of the kindness and consideration shown me by the gentlemen of the *Mexicain* on this occasion and indeed throughout the voyage, I thought I should collapse from exhaustion as we were crossing the line. M Chabrié had the bottom knocked out of an empty barrel to serve me as a shelter, and thanks to this rolling home I was the only passenger to be protected from the sun and the rain. M David lent me some boots and M Briet gave up his voluminous fish-skin cape to me. This garment, made in China, was waterproof, exceptionally light and of exquisite workmanship. M Chabrié contributed a big oilskin hat, and this too was waterproof. Thus attired, I sat in my barrel like a latter-day Diogenes and reflected sadly on the human predicament. M David must have had some special secret which enabled him to bear the extremes of heat and cold with equanimity, for he was always active, cheerful and immaculately dressed. The other gentlemen wore just a shirt and trousers: M David alone appeared in cravat, stockings and white cotton jacket. He and our cook were, each in his own sphere, the life and soul of the ship. Nothing could damp their spirits. M David always had some fresh treat in store for us: he had water slung over the side in bottles to cool it, he prepared lemonade from the bitter lemons the unctuous Tappe had sold us for good ones, he gave one of us soup, another bananas, a third tea, a fourth punch — in a word, he was everybody's nurse.

We remained in the equatorial latitudes for about seventeen days. Gradually the infection disappeared and the saloon was thoroughly cleaned and fumigated with vetiver and vanilla. Everybody gave what perfumes he had to sweeten this chamber, the capital of our little world.

As the crew of the *Mexicain* were all men of progressive views, there was no ceremony when we crossed the line.

The ship, which was on her maiden voyage, had been launched without being christened, so she had no god-parents; she had put to sea on a Friday, which was unlucky; and now the captain was refusing to allow the customary celebrations on board. These three significant facts made Leborgne, who considered himself the only *true sailor* on board, declare that his sisters would very likely see the cherry trees blossom twice more before we saw land again. Nobody dared to disobey the captain, but a conspiracy was hatched in the fo'c's'le with our cook at the head. In the guise of Neptune's secretary, he wrote the captain a letter on behalf of his master. Leborgne offered to deliver it, and, dressed in a piece of sailcloth soaked in seawater, he looked as if he might well have come from the god of the sea.

I am sorry that I no longer have that letter: in style, sentiment and spelling it was characteristic of its author. The artful cook declared that Neptune was angry at seeing his empire invaded by *philosophers*, and threatened to swallow them up unless they agreed to pay him the tribute they owed him. Our captain had no difficulty in interpreting this ingenious fable, and to appease Neptune's wrath, he sent his worthy emissaries a gift of wine, brandy, white bread, a ham and a purse to which everybody who was crossing the line for the first time contributed a gold coin. We felt the god must have been grateful, to judge from the general rejoicing of his servants, among whom the discordant voices of Leborgne and the cook nearly drowned all the rest.

Between the Equator and Cape Horn we had some beautiful days, and I marvelled at the magnificence of the sunrise: what an impressive spectacle it is in these latitudes! But I found the sunset even more splendid. The human eye cannot contemplate anything more sublime than sunset in the tropics. Words are colourless to describe the magical glow its dying rays cast on sea and clouds. Such ravishing spectacles elevate the soul to the Creator, but it is not given to us to reproduce the emotions they excite.

After a beautiful sunset I liked to remain for part of the night on deck. I would sit in the stern and there, while talking to M Chabrié, I would watch with keen pleasure the sparkling patterns of phosphorescent light caused by the play of the waves. What a brilliant comet our vessel drew in its wake! What a rich hoard of diamonds the dancing waves disclosed! I also loved to see the big porpoises come alongside, leaving long trails behind them like rockets lighting up the whole vast stretch of sea! Then it was time for the moon to rise: its light gradually invaded the empire of the night, the flashing diamonds returned to the depths, and the waves, pierced by moonbeams, now shone with a reflected light and glittered like the stars in the firmament.

How many delightful evenings I spent in this way, plunged in sweetest reverie! M Chabrié told me of the sorrows he had encountered in his life, especially the last betrayal which had so cruelly broken his heart. He suffered, so did I, and this established a close and unsuspected bond between us. Each day M Chabrié loved me more, and each day I felt inexpressibly happy in the knowledge that he loved me.

Then came Cape Horn with all its horrors. They have been described so often that I shall not dwell on them here. My readers need only know that the temperature varies from 12° to 25° Fahrenheit, depending on the season and the latitude at which you round the Cape. Our latitude was 58° and the time was July—August, which gave us temperatures between 20° and 24°, together with a good deal of snow, hail and ice.

It was there that we underwent a second series of hardships. Around Cape Horn the sea is always appallingly rough, and the winds we encountered were nearly always contrary. The cold sapped the strength of our crew, even the strongest among them. Our sailors were all in the full vigour of youth, nevertheless several were afflicted with carbuncles, while others were seriously hurt slipping on the icy deck. One fell from the topmast onto the capstan and dislocated his shoulder. Those whose health remained unaffected were overcome by fatigue because they had to perform the duties of those who were sick. To crown their misfortunes, these unfortunate sailors had barely a quarter of the clothes they needed. Their adventurous life makes them irresponsible, so when they embark on a long voyage they often have nothing sufficiently light to wear on the Equator and only one spare woollen shirt to take them round Cape Horn.

Now I saw one of the most horrifying things that can happen to men: I saw sailors whose shirts and trousers were *stuck fast to their bodies*, unable to move without the ice scraping the flesh from their frozen limbs. As so often happens on small ships in heavy seas, their sleeping quarters were under water and they had nowhere else to rest. How dreadful it is to see men suffer so! Extreme physical hardship has such a demoralising effect on them that it is impossible to get any work out of them. The gentlemen of the *Mexicain* told me that sometimes captains going round Cape Horn have had to enforce obedience with a loaded pistol in each hand when their sailors refused to go aloft. Extreme cold can make a man insensitive to entreaties and blows alike: nothing will make him move. Yet if they were properly dressed and had a suitable diet, they could withstand any amount of cold. What happened on board our ship proves my point: five of our men were well equipped, and four had barely a rag between them. The former suffered no ill effects, whereas the latter had so many ailments that they were quite unfit for service. They had a perpetual fever, and their bodies were covered with boils. They could not eat anything and grew so weak that we feared for their lives.

This crisis displayed yet again the indomitable courage

of our brave captain. He was always on deck encouraging the men with his example: he gave a cape and a pair of gloves to the man at the helm, a hat to one man, a pair of trousers to another, boots, stockings, shirts, everything he could spare. Then he would visit the sick in the fo'c's'le, nurse them, comfort them, give them new life. On his return he would tell me about the conversations he had with them. Sailors are not like other men: unless you have lived among them it is impossible to imagine the bizarre ideas they get into their heads.

The *true sailor*, as Leborgne used to say, has neither family nor country. His language does not belong to any nation: it is compounded of words from every tongue. He has nothing but the clothes on his back, he lives from day to day and gives no thought to the future. When in port he squanders in a few days on prostitutes all the money he so painfully earned in months at sea. He deserts whenever he can and signs on again next day with the first ship that needs him, be it English, Swedish or American. He is content to see the world without seeking to understand it. He is just an instrument for navigation, as indifferent to his destination as the anchor itself. If the sea spares him and he survives into old age, he settles wherever his final voyage leaves him. There he begs his bread and eats it in the sun, gazing lovingly at the sea, the companion of his youth. In the end, lamenting his failing strength, he dies in hospital.

Such is the life of the *true sailor*. Leborgne was my model, but as everything degenerates in our society, men like him are becoming rarer every day. Nowadays sailors marry, take a well-stocked chest with them, and desert less because they do not want to lose their belongings and the money they have earned. They take pride in learning their profession and are ambitious to do well. When their efforts come to nothing they end up toiling in small boats and barges in seaports.

Apart from its disastrous effects on the sailor's health,

the cold of Cape Horn undermines the morale even of those who take most precautions against it. The officers, with their dry cabins and everything human ingenuity can devise to protect them from cold and damp, do not fall ill like the sailors, but the bitter climate makes them morose. In fact the only individual who never acted out of character was our cook, whose cheerfulness and courage were admirable. He always managed to do the cooking, even when the frightful weather overturned his stoves; he tended the sick, helped our cabin-boy wait on us, lent a hand on deck when necessary, and often even took the night watch. He had not a day's illness the whole of the voyage, although to see him so thin, pale and undersized, you would not have thought him very robust. He was from Bordeaux, but as he had done his training in Paris, he had acquired all the habits of a Parisian. He was a great talker, a great reader of novels. He had served as cook aboard a frigate of the Royal Navy and had sailed round the Cape of Good Hope.

As we were sailing towards the southernmost point of South America in July and August, we had only four hours daylight, and when there was no moon we were in total darkness for twenty hours. These long nights increase the hazards of navigation and are responsible for much damage to vessels: the violent lurching of the ship and the frightful hissing of the waves make it impossible for anybody to concentrate. I could not read or take exercise: I could not even sleep. What would have become of me if I had been left to myself, without the pure and gentle affection of M Chabrié to warm my heart?

Before he went on watch, M Chabrié would come to my bedside and say, in the softest voice he could manage: 'Mademoiselle Flora, I beg you to say a few kind words out of friendship, to help me bear four hours of cold, snow and ice.'

'My poor friend, how happy I would be if my friendship could lighten your burden! You know it is yours for the asking, but when you say I can ease your suffering, aren't you treating me as if I were God?'

'Well, Mademoiselle Flora, you *are* God, at least, you are for me. You have so great a power over me that one word, one look, one smile from you is enough to give me fresh heart. I shall think of you for the next four hours, and then I shan't feel the cold.'

'How honoured any woman would feel to hear such words! They fill my heart with joy; thank you, Chabrié, I shall treasure the memory all my life. Go, then, dear friend, and since the thought of me can make you happy, let me assure you that the friendship I feel for you is far greater than the love you have had from other women.'

Meanwhile I would press his hand as I put on his gloves for him, and sometimes as I wrapped an extra scarf around his neck to protect him from the cold, I would even kiss him on the forehead. I liked to give him these little attentions and caresses, as if he had been my brother or my son.

Here I see what a difficult task I have set myself, not that anything I have to say gives me cause for repentance, but I am afraid that the portrayal of a true love on the one hand and a true friendship on the other may be accused of implausibility in our materialistic century. M Chabrié was too sensitive not to be moved by my suffering. He had intended to treat me just as a friend, but love entered his heart against his will. I must say that the mystery which surrounded me and the warm friendship I showed him combined to arouse in him a feeling to which he might not have been susceptible had the circumstances been different.

In following the plan I had made for myself, I had been obliged to lie to M Chabrié. When I told him briefly about my life, I had kept my marriage from him. However, I still had to account for the birth of my daughter. Oh, when people begin to lie in order to get out of a difficult situation, how little do they realise what an endless road they will have to travel! Their only hope of ever escaping from its twists and turns is to return resolutely to the truth. But I told M Chabrié that I had had a child, though I was not married, and that this was why I displayed so strong an aversion to the subject of marriage.

This confidence only made M Chabrié love me the more, and he conceived the idea of restoring me to the society which had banished me by offering me the protection of his name. I was deeply grateful to him for so generous a proposal, but at the same time I recoiled in fear as I thought of the consequences which might follow from the lie I had been forced to tell. So when he offered to marry me, I hid my face in my hands lest he should read in my face what was going on in my heart. I stayed for a long time unable to utter a word. Then I looked at M Chabrié and I saw that he truly loved me. The discovery made my heart leap in ecstasy. But this burst of gratitude was followed by despair at the thought of my position. An infernal mocking voice kept repeating: '*You are married!* Married to a contemptible creature, it is true; but you are chained to him for the rest of your days, and you cannot break that chain here any more than you could in Paris!' I thought my head would burst. I was sitting on my bed with M Chabrié at my side: I drew his head onto my knees, I was about to tell him the whole truth, but my tears were choking me, they fell like rain upon his face. M Chabrié could not understand me: he saw that I was overwhelmed with grief, yet at the same time he felt I loved him with the most sincere affection. I begged him to leave me: I was struggling to suppress my sobs for fear that my neighbours would hear. I asked him not to stop loving me, but to give me two days to recover from the agitation our conversation had caused me.

From the offer M Chabrié had made me, I could no longer doubt that he loved me passionately and sincerely, just as I had longed to be loved all my life. But alas! this love, so pure and devoted, in which I could still hope to find happiness, filled my heart with bitterness and despair by bringing home to me in all its horror the ignoble marriage I had been forced to contract.

For two days I remained in the most agonising uncertainty. At times I almost yielded to my inclination to tell M Chabrié the whole truth, but then I saw him rejecting me as all the others had done, I saw myself alone, abandoned, and I shrank from the additional burden of suffering so indiscreet a revelation might bring about.

In my perplexity it occurred to me that if I could induce M David to talk about M Chabrié, I might learn more about his character, so one night when we were talking in my cabin and M Chabrié was on watch, I brought up the subject of love and friendship by way of introduction.

'M David, do you really believe it is not in men's nature to feel a pure love entirely free from personal interest?'

'Mademoiselle, I am convinced of it, and the same is true of women. We all go in search of beauty, wealth and talent for the sake of the pleasure we hope to get out of them, and we love only in proportion to the pleasure we obtain.'

'You always say such depressing things! Love *is* a selfish sentiment, I admit, but is friendship the same? Surely you can have a totally disinterested friendship?'

'I really cannot help admiring you, mademoiselle! To reach the age of twenty-six and still have this childlike belief in friendship! Let me tell you, then, that the word *friendship* which you come across in books stands for an ideal which has never existed. Women are too often rivals for them to have any genuine affection for one another, and their relations with men, when not based on love, are purely selfish. As for men, they come together or drift apart as self-interest dictates, and what they feel for women is always love and never friendship. Friendship, as poets and philosophers describe it, is just a trap for the unwary.'

'Does that mean, monsieur, that the great friendship you profess for M Chabrié is nothing but an illusion?'

'That is a very delicate question, mademoiselle. There is nobody in the world I love more than Chabrié, but this sentiment rests entirely on the advantage I find in our association, and I am sure his feeling for me is the same.'

I looked at M David with an expression which showed him how much his words had hurt me: he took my hand and said affectionately: 'What do you expect, my dear? One must take the world as it is. But what does an intelligent woman like you need with the affection of men? Believe me, mademoiselle, there are enough treasures in nature to occupy all one's faculties, so why bother with the miserable little dramas of men?'

I had not realised how long we had been talking, and I had still not managed to get down to discussing M Chabrié when midnight struck and that gentleman came off watch. Finding M David in my cabin he was visibly annoyed and curtly refused my gracious invitation to stay and talk. It was one of his failings that when he was angry he was abrupt with his best friends, and made them, as well as himself, miserable for days.

That night, I could not sleep for one moment. What M David had said about friendship chilled my heart. If he were right, I told myself, Chabrié could never be just a friend, and if I told him I was married, he would stop loving me, because he wanted to make me his wife, not his mistress, and the moment he was forced to renounce any hope of marrying me, he would avoid my company, I knew how honourable he was. The thought terrified me. I was afraid of being abandoned: my very life might depend on the protection of others, and I clutched at the love of M Chabrié as the shipwrecked mariner clings to the floating plank. Besides, I was hoping to make him understand that my friendship could be as sweet to him as

the love of other women had been. This was not arrogance
on my part: I acted in good faith, but I was completely
mistaken.

When I was alone with M Chabrié, he asked me what
was to be his fate.

'I have decided that you will be my friend, my very
good friend, all my life,' I told him, 'and I shall always
have a tender affection for you.'

'No more than that?' he demanded in deep distress.
'Ah! how unhappy I am!' And he buried his face in his
hands.

I sat and watched him for a long time: the veins on his
forehead stood out, he shuddered convulsively, and his
whole person showed how profoundly he was suffering.
Suddenly he started out of his reverie, his expression
scornful, his smile sardonic, his voice harsh.

'So, mademoiselle,' he said, 'you do not love me? Of
course I understand that the love of an old sea-dog like
me must seem ridiculous to somebody accustomed to the
elegant manners of the young dandies in Paris, who are so
good at making pretty speeches but have no feelings —
but no, I'm wrong, I should have said they are capable of
feeling *fear*, for didn't you tell me one night in Praia that
one of them was *afraid of your love?*'

'Chabrié, you are bringing back memories that break
my heart.'

'Forgive me, mademoiselle, I thought in my simplicity
that anybody who could remain unmoved at the sight of
the appalling misery she was causing could hardly be
affected by a memory.'

'Chabrié, you are hurting me: what you say is unjust
and you cannot love me as much as you say.'

'Not love you as much as I say! But don't you realise,
Flora, I love you so much that I cannot help myself.'

'If that is so, give me proof!'

'What sort of proof? Tell me, and I will give you all the
proof you want!'

'Well then, love me as a friend.'

'There is no need to ask me that; you know I am your friend, and your daughter's friend, until my dying breath.'

'Then hasn't this affection the power to make you as happy as I so fervently want you to be?'

'No.'

'Ah! Chabrié, what a difference there is between us! The friendship I feel for you makes me happy; if you felt the same for me, my happiness would be complete, but it pains me deeply to see that this will never be enough for you.'

'Listen, Flora! If I loved you less, I might be tempted to lie to you, just as others have lied to me. Tell me, do you think a man of my age can stay close to you for hours at a time without falling in love? You must know that it is impossible. You see these things in books, but they lie, and you, my dear friend, are still innocent enough to believe what they say.'

'Why shouldn't I believe them, if I know I am capable of behaving as well as they say?'

'Perhaps you are, dear, because you are an exceptional being. But as for me, I've always lived life to the full, and I still have a heart left for loving, so how can you expect me not to be affected by all the charms you possess. All my life I have wanted to enjoy what I would describe as a *complete* love, that is, a beautiful soul inside a beautiful body. The last woman I loved was not beautiful; I was fascinated by the qualities I imagined to be hers. But she deceived me; her ingratitude hurt me very much, but thanks to you, my sweet Flora, I have stopped thinking about it.'

'My friend, perhaps that woman deceived you because she wanted your friendship and you wanted her love.'

'My dear Flora, you are so naive you astonish me! Let me tell you, my child, there is no such thing as friendship anywhere in the world, only self-interest in the wicked and love in the good — and you know where to place your old friend Chabrié!'

My heart contracted, and I thought to myself: M David, you were right.

Next day M Chabrié resumed his daily visits to my cabin, where the conversation continued on the same note. The love he showed me remained as pure as it was true, but I saw that I must give up any hope of inspiring him with no more than friendship. I do not know whether my fellow voyagers noticed how attentive and loving he was towards me; his behaviour was so irreproachable that in spite of his long and frequent visits, these gentlemen showed me more respect and friendship every day, so great is the influence a pure love exerts on all who witness it.

During the rough days of the Cape, I often had to act as peacemaker for my companions, whose bad temper and incivility towards each other poisoned every word they uttered. Life on board ship is antipathetic to our nature: it is not just the perpetual torture of the ship's motion, the lack of fresh food and exercise, and the effect these constant trials have upon the temper, it is also the cruel ordeal of living in a little saloon only ten to twelve feet across in close proximity to seven or eight people morning, noon and night. To understand such torture you have to experience it yourself.

M David would rise at the crack of dawn so as to have the whole table to himself when he shaved and did his hair. This was not accomplished without noise: his imprecations against the poor cabin-boy were enough to make an atheist tremble. The lad was as dirty as he was lazy, it is true, but as he was only sixteen and always ailing, I felt he was entitled to a little indulgence. I had placed him under my personal protection: M David had never dared to lay a finger on him after the time when he nearly killed the boy and I got M Chabrié to forbid anybody to touch him again.

When he had finished his toilet M David would go along to the store-room and vent his spleen on the quartermaster Emmanuel, whose negligence left everything in disorder; next it was the turn of the captain's bitch Cora. Then M David got down to general causes and fulminated against the trade, the sea, the wind, and the whole of creation, particularly the Peruvians. What with his shouting, the cabin-boy whimpering, Emmanuel protesting and the dog barking, there was so much commotion that nobody was able to sleep. The officers who had just come off watch complained bitterly: M Briet declared that never had he heard so much noise on board ship, M Chabrié upbraided M David, and the ensuing argument only increased the uproar. Then it was nine o'clock and breakfast was served. The contending parties were forced to sit down together and the dispute continued.

From the beginning of the voyage I had absented myself from this meal, and this became my rule. As I ate very little and was nearly always unwell in the morning, I preferred not to rise until breakfast was over and everybody on deck, as I found this gave me more freedom to attend to my toilet. There was nothing but a curtain shutting off my cabin, so I could see and hear everything that went on without being seen myself.

BRIET: I must say, M David, you would make an excellent alarm-clock! I am surprised your swearing does not stop Chabrié's precious Cora from fouling the deck, nor does it make our cabin-boy any more attentive, though he spends the whole morning heating soft water for your white hands, nor does it seem to have any effect on the good Emmanuel. From what I have heard this morning, he pays no more heed to your orders than he does to mine. Well, at all events, *you* are responsible for a fair number of the tribulations we have to put up with on the *Mexicain*.

CHABRIÉ: Briet, I am annoyed to hear that my dog has been a nuisance. I ordered Lebarre to tie her up; why hasn't he obeyed me?

BRIET: My dear friend, I don't dislike your dog, but on a little ship where there is hardly room to turn round, it is not very agreeable to have a big brute of a dog getting under your feet when you are trying to keep the ship on course at night. One of these days she will make one of us break his neck.

CHABRIÉ: But before we left I asked you if you minded having her, and you said no.

BRIET: My dear friend, you must realise that if each of us could choose an animal to have on board — a monkey, say, or a squirrel, or a parrot — life would be sheer hell. But enough, let's say no more about it.

DAVID: I'm glad Briet has spoken up: you see, Chabrié, I'm not the only one who complains about your dog.

CHABRIÉ: David, you are as stupid as you are selfish! My dog may annoy Briet, but you never set foot on deck except to smoke a cigar, and you are snug and warm in bed by eight o'clock — when you're not chatting with Mademoiselle Flora — so how can Cora be a nuisance to you? I can read your mind, my dear David: you want to change the subject. Well, let's get back to what Briet was talking about: I ask all these gentlemen to say whether your perpetual swearing and the row you make every morning doesn't upset them more than my Cora does?

BRIET: Oh, as for that, Chabrié is right. I am sure M Miota and Don Jose are of the same opinion.

MIOTA: I confess it is not very pleasant to be woken at six in the morning by M David and hear him calling the Peruvians thieves, rogues, scoundrels and bandits.

DAVID: But my dear M Miota, you don't know your fellow countrymen: you left Peru when you were sixteen. I don't deny that there as elsewhere you find thoroughly respectable families like yours and Mademoiselle Tristan's, but, I repeat, most of the inhabitants are thieves.

BRIET: Has it ever struck you, M David, that if we took

you seriously we would have to accept that we too are no better than thieves and scoundrels, which would not be very encouraging for the partnership we have formed?

CHABRIÉ: For God's sake, Briet, take no notice of what David says; don't you see that his greatest pleasure in life — after sprucing himself up and smoking masses of cigars — is railing against mankind? And as our friend David, for all his wit, is in my opinion pretty stupid, he is always at odds with his principles. . . . Yes, my dear fellow, when one loathes mankind, one goes and lives in the woods with the animals — not like you, who cannot remain an instant without company!

Almost every day started in this fashion. Hardly had I risen than M Miota came to me with his grievances and tried to make me share his indignation. I always did my best to calm him and made him promise not to say a word to M David. This made the proud and headstrong Cesario furious, and he would try to provoke his uncle and Fernando to anger as well. I had to exert all my influence on the boy to prevent him from making scenes.

I talked less often with M Briet, but when I did, he confided to me that never again would he enter into partnership, and never in his life would he set foot on a ship whose captain forgot the first duty of his command, which was to make himself respected.

At about three o'clock M David would come to my cabin and ask me what I would like for dinner. Not one day of the voyage did he omit this courtesy, but he always contrived to make me choose the dishes *he* liked, without worrying whether this would suit the others. I profited from one such visit to scold him for his conduct of the morning.

'Dear lady, forgive me this once. I promise you that from now on I will not swear so much. Upon my word,

I thought you were asleep; you know I never swear in front of you.'

'Yes, but what about the way you curse the Peruvians? Do you think M Miota and I are happy to hear you treat our nation like that?'

'But, mademoiselle, you are French.'

'I was born in France, but I belong to my father's country. Where we are born is just a matter of chance. Look at me and tell me which is my nation.'

'You coquette! You ask me that so that I shall compliment you on your beautiful eyes and your lovely Andalusian hair.'

'Monsieur David, you should know better than anybody that I am not affected by compliments: you are trying to escape my just criticism. I tell you for the twentieth time, M Miota is deeply hurt by the way you speak about the Peruvians in front of him.'

'You cannot believe that I ever intended any insult to M Miota, mademoiselle, much less to yourself. When you both know the Peruvians, you will say, David was right. . . . Dear lady, you know how much I honour you: I have heard nothing but praise for your family, and everybody says your uncle Pio is a most respectable man, but I assure you that taken as a whole the Peruvians are the worst bunch of scoundrels imaginable.'

'If that is so, monsieur, why did you spend ten years there, and why are you going back now?'

'Because there is money to be had there.'

'But it is ungrateful to speak ill of people who have helped you to make a fortune.'

'Well, it's no thanks to them! I sold them my merchandise at the market rate, and if they bought it, it was because they needed it. I see no reason why I should feel grateful to them.'

As self-interest was the only motive M David recognised, he was hardly likely ever to feel gratitude. However, it seems to me that we ought to be grateful to the country which protects our persons, our property and our labours. If M David had been consistent he could never have accused the Peruvians of dishonesty, and if he had been charitable, he would have pitied their ignorance.

Then it was time for dinner: everyone made a little effort to look presentable, and the conversation too was very different from that at breakfast. Our mood was grave or gay according to the direction of the wind, but when we were making good progress and the ship was not rolling too much, the talk became lively and amusing. At dessert the topic was usually politics, travel, or places for which our gentlemen had a special affection. M Chabrié was a republican, M David a Carlist and M Briet a Bonapartist, and in their discussions the two seasoned mariners were always more than a match for poor David. When he saw his position was desperate he would skilfully change the subject by leading Briet on to talk of his travels, or Chabrié of his native Lorient. Briet was the only one who had been to China, so there was nobody to contradict him. Everybody listened and grew calmer. The conversation on Lorient was more stormy. M Chabrié had the disadvantage of having been born there, and his life of travel had done nothing to diminish his exclusive love for his birthplace: in his eyes it was perfect and he was always quoting it as an example. There were interminable arguments between him and M David about the rival merits of Lorient and Paris. M Briet was not interested: he disliked urban life and it was his dream to retire to the country. As for me, I seldom took part in these conversations: my situation imposed restraint, and I was always conscious of the painful task I had undertaken in posing as an unmarried woman. I had to forget the whole of my past life, my eight years of marriage, the existence of my children – in short, the role of *dame* which is so different from that of *demoiselle*. As I am extremely frank by nature and not a little naive, I am often drawn into an animated conversation by the sheer heat of my imagination, and speak my mind without realising what I am saying. For that reason I could not trust myself and did not dare to say a word for fear of mentioning my daughter or inveighing against the French marriage laws, so I held my tongue and replied in as few words as possible when anybody asked me a question.

Such was the life we led aboard the *Mexicain*. What saved it from boredom was the diversity of our characters and social position, as well as the efforts we made to relieve the tedium. We celebrated Sunday by eating pastries and preserved fruit at dinner and drinking champagne or claret. After the meal M Chabrié would sing us ballads or selections from the opera. The gentlemen were always most attentive and would often read to me: if he were feeling well enough, M Miota would come to my cabin and read aloud from the authors he favoured, such as Voltaire and Byron; M David read *The Voyage of Young Anacharsis*, Chateaubriand or La Fontaine; M Chabrié and I read Lamartine, Victor Hugo, Walter Scott, and above all Bernardin de Saint-Pierre.

When we left Bordeaux we had expected to reach Valparaiso in eighty or ninety days, yet here was M Briet writing in the ship's log: Day 120: on a bad course. Then we became discouraged. It was feared that we might run out of water, and a little padlock was fitted to the barrel in current use. This caused endless trouble: the sailors stole water whenever they had the chance, while the cook drank what he was given for cooking and served us soup so thick it was impossible to eat it. Don Jose lost his philosophy as his stock of *cigaritos* diminished, M Miota's boredom and impatience increased when he had nothing left to read. Leborgne, the true sailor, never stopped repeating that as long as a single pig was left on board we would have contrary winds.

As the two men responsible for sailing the ship, MM Chabrié and Briet were the most fatigued by the length of the voyage, but the moral anguish it caused them was an even greater strain than the fatigue. The three partners knew it was unreasonable to hope that the two ships which had left Bordeaux with us bound for the same port could have encountered the same difficulties. They grew worried about the prospects of selling their cargo if their two rivals had already filled every warehouse in the country with goods similar to those the *Mexicain* was carrying. As they were honourable men and foresaw that the voyage would turn out badly, they were tortured by the fear of being unable to fulfil their obligations. M David cursed the wind and gave himself up to despair, while M Briet said to me sadly, 'I am not an ambitious man, so I cannot understand what made me risk going to sea again. But when I last returned to France, I had no friend, nobody close to me to ask me why I was going back, so as like most sailors I had no plans and could think of nothing better to do, I embarked again out of sheer habit.'

Of the three partners, only M Chabrié bore the threat of disaster with fortitude. If the worst happened, he would pay his creditors with everything he possessed, and if this were not enough, he counted on his boundless energy, his professional skill and his knowledge of commercial affairs to extricate himself.

I was in despair to think that my friend, who had up to then been so unlucky in his affections and his enterprises, could even now be ruined by the outcome of this voyage. I was forever asking which way the wind was blowing, and the reply, together with the expression of M Briet or M David, caused me the deepest distress.

These circumstances confirmed the delicacy of M Chabrié's sentiments towards me. I have already told how I accepted his love as much to save him from despair as to assure myself of his powerful protection. From that moment he never stopped making brilliant and optimistic plans for us, so convinced he was of finding happiness in our union. At first I listened to these plans with no hope of sharing them, then gradually his love awoke such admiration in me that I came to accept the idea of marrying him and going to live with him in California. I can hear people comfortably settled in respectable married bliss protesting against the consequences of bigamy and demanding that anyone guilty of such shameful conduct should be treated with contempt. But wherein lies the crime, if not in the absurd law which makes marriage indissoluble? Are we all so alike in our affections and inclinations that affairs of the heart should be treated in the same way as affairs of business?

My feeling for M Chabrié was not the passionate love I had experienced before, but it was one of admiration and gratitude. Once I became his wife I would have grown to love him more, and even if I did not discover the supreme happiness I had dreamed of when I was young, at least I would find the peace I longed for, the true and lasting affection one values so highly after the disappointments of a stormy life. I do not know whether M David had already guessed M Chabrié's secret intentions, or whether he was trying to influence them, but he would often say to him, 'What a splendid person Mademoiselle Flora is! And how lucky we would be if we could persuade her to go and live in America! I don't know where she gets her prejudice against marriage, but she is very fond of you and I think that in the end she will probably decide to marry you. I am a sworn enemy of marriage too, but I would stay with you and help rock the cradle, as I adore children until they reach the age of seven or eight.'

As for me, I had grown accustomed to M David: he was considerate and not without education, so I would not have found his presence in my household disagreeable. He had not the slightest desire to return to Europe: on the contrary, he had a marked preference for the climate of America, and if he had been able to live there with congenial companions, he would have been perfectly happy to settle down for good. This is how things stood as we drew near the end of the voyage.

I think it must have been the evening of the 128th day when M Chabrié said to me: 'Comfort me, my dear Flora, for I am very upset to see David in such despair. Briet is ill, and I feel guilty at having involved him in this business.'

'My poor friend, what can we do? It is not in our power to change the wind, The *Charles-Adolphe* and the *Flétès* probably reached Valparaiso long ago. The voyage is a loss — but you still have me, my dear!'

'Oh, you excellent creature! It is only because of David and Briet that I regret the voyage; for me it is a time of happiness, the dawn of felicity!'

'My dear, up to now, when we have spoken of our marriage, neither of us has thought about the financial advantages we might find in it. Let me just mention this for the first time: you know that I am going to see my family in the hope of obtaining at least a part of my father's estate. If I were to get it all, I should have a million, but as my status as a legitimate child may be contested, I am not counting on so much. Let us only hope that, as a natural child, I shall receive a fifth of that amount, plus the gift my grandmother will probably make me: well, then, dear friend, everything I possess is at your disposal. With this sum you will be able to pay your debts and still have enough to give David a fresh start.'

'It is like you to be so generous, my dear Flora, but now I am going to open my heart to you: as for this fortune you hope for and which you are so worthy to enjoy, it terrifies me, I tremble at the thought that it may fall to your lot.'

'But why, dear friend?'

'Dearest, let me tell you once again, you know nothing of the wickedness of men, their malice and the absurd prejudices which govern society.'

'But, Chabrié, I do not understand. . . .'

'Listen, Flora, at the moment you have nothing; if I marry you now, people will say I have done a foolish and headstrong thing, but anyone with a noble and generous soul will approve and say: "He has done right to marry the woman he loves." If on the contrary I marry you when you have become rich, people will jump to the conclusion that my only motive was self-interest. Flora, the thought tortures me: the nearer we get to Valparaiso, the more I feel it burning into my brain!'

'Ah, Chabrié, that is too horrible! I am as frightened as you at what might come of our marriage; in my ignorance I had not even thought of it.'

I buried my head in my hands, terrified at the consequences of my lie.

'Do not be so distressed, dear friend,' continued M Chabrié. 'No doubt our position is very difficult, for I know that once I am your husband the first blackguard who permits himself an insinuating word or smile at your expense will pay for it with his life, or I with mine. But let us not think any more about such possibilities: perhaps you will never get a single piastre of that great fortune. Dear God, I wish with all my heart it may be so!'

I was dumbfounded. A pariah in my own country, I had believed that in putting the vast ocean between myself and France I should be able to recover a vestige of freedom. Impossible! I was as much a pariah in the New World as I had been in the Old. From that moment I renounced all the plans for peace and happiness that had grown out of M Chabrié's love for me. If the fear of being abandoned and the need of a protector had made me accept that love, once ashore I could no longer compromise the happiness, the prospects, and perhaps even the life of the honourable man to whom I owed the most sincere gratitude for the five months of devotion he had given me.

At last, on the 133rd day of the voyage, we sighted the *Pierre-Blanche*, and six hours later we anchored in the roads of Valparaiso.

IV

Valparaiso

The considerable number of vessels moored in the bay of Valparaiso gave me an immediate idea of its importance as a trading centre. The day we arrived, twelve foreign ships entered port, a fact which did little to raise my friends' hopes. As they were very well known in these parts, hardly had we cast anchor than they were hailed by a number of acquaintances.

When it became known that the *Mexicain* was in port, the French hastened to the quay and waited for us to disembark. The two ships which had left Bordeaux with us had arrived more than a month earlier and were by now making their way along the coast. The two captains had announced my imminent arrival, and as they were unwilling to admit the reason why I had not sailed with either of them, they had had the impudence to claim that I had chosen M Chabrié because of the good-looking young men on board. So the good folk of Valparaiso were expecting to see *a very pretty young lady*, as to complete their revenge the two malicious captains had made certain insinuations about me. People were also expecting to see the handsome young men of the *Mexicain* fighting duels over me, which they would have found vastly entertaining.

They were all gathered on the sea wall when we stepped ashore. The scene astonished me: I thought we must be in some French town, as all the men I encountered spoke French and were dressed in the latest fashion. I noticed that I was the centre of attraction, but at the time I could not understand why. M David conducted me to a hotel run by a Frenchwoman called Madame Aubrit. He did not think it proper for M Miota to stay there as well, so he took him to another hotel, run by another Frenchwoman. Madame Aubrit's house was on the seafront: my window overlooked the sea, and my room was very well furnished in a style half French and half English.

I found that after one hundred and thirty-three days at sea I could no longer walk straight, and the soles of my feet were so tender that a sharp pain shot through them every time I stood up.

M Miota came to see me in the evening and I begged him to enquire in the town for news of Arequipa and my uncle, and particularly whether my grandmother was still alive.

That night I was unable to sleep. I had a presentiment that some new misfortune was about to fall upon my head. At every crisis in my life I have had similar premonitions. I believe that when we are destined for great suffering, Providence prepares the way for us with secret warnings which we would heed more carefully if we were not invariably led astray by our reason. After a thousand conjectures I assumed the worst: my grandmother dead, my uncle rejecting me, and myself alone, six thousand miles from home, with no friend, no fortune, no hope. The prospect was so appalling that its very horror restored my courage, and I awaited events with resignation.

M Miota returned the next day about noon. The moment he appeared, I read in his face that he had bad news for me. 'My grandmother is dead!' I said. He had wished to break it to me gently, but the blow had already fallen. She had died the very day I left Bordeaux. I confess that for a moment I felt my strength falter. Her death robbed me of my only refuge, my sole protection, my last hope. M Miota took his leave, knowing that at such times one needs to be alone. As he left, he said he would ask M Chabrié to call. The kind young man did not know that for me Chabrié too was *dead*!

Some forms of suffering are so far removed from normal experience that no words can describe them. Such were the pangs I felt at this death which destroyed all my hopes. I did not shed a single tear, but remained motionless for more than two hours, staring fixedly at the sea. They brought me food and I ate: during this crisis of inextinguishable grief, my soul was completely detached from my body. There were two selves inside me, one physical, responding to questions and conscious of the exterior world, the other spiritual, with its own life of visions, memories and premonitions.

In the evening M Chabrié came and sat beside me, pressed my hands affectionately between his own, and wept. He is one of those fortunate individuals whose grief flows away with their tears.

'My God!' he said after a long silence, 'what can I say to comfort you, my dear friend? I am quite overcome. Ever since this morning I have been unable to think straight. I did not dare to come to you, my poor Flora; your suffering lies here in this old heart of mine like an anchor dragged down by its own weight. What is to become of us? In the name of my love, tell me what I can do?'

In my distraction I continued to gaze at the sea: I would have liked Chabrié to fling me into its depths.

'Do you want me to take you back?'

'Take me back? Where would you take me?'

'My dear Flora, what is the matter with you? Your hands are so cold, and your forehead is burning hot! Calm yourself, dearest, your suffering is killing me!'

He too gazed at the sea and large tears fell from his eyes. Suddenly he broke the silence and said:

'Well, Flora, the more I think about it, the more I am convinced that what has happened is fortunate for us both. Suppose you had met your grandmother in Arequipa: then everything would have turned out as you wanted, and you would have been rich. Oh, my dearest, doesn't the thought make you tremble? You rich and I poor! Do you not understand, in that case I would have to give you up — that would kill me, Flora! But now, because of this death, you are mine! Oh, I cannot believe in so much joy, for all my life I have been so unlucky. Happiness always seemed just within my reach, but whenever I tried to grasp it, it disappeared. My good Flora, have pity on my joy, my grief, and all the cruel uncertainties which assail me. . . . I have been through so much since I heard of your grandmother's death that I feel I am losing my reason.'

Never before had I seen Chabrié so agitated: he strode up and down the room, stopped at the window, returned to my side, wrapped my shawl about me, chafed my frozen hands, told me how happy he was, spoke of our marriage and the steps he would take to hasten it, consulted me about his affairs, and asked me to decide whatever I wished. Chabrié was happy, and at the sight of his happiness I felt a thousand serpents gnawing at my heart.

He left me, and I threw myself upon my bed, my body shattered with fatigue. Now my body slept and my soul remained wide awake. Those who have experienced such nights can truly say they have lived centuries in other worlds. The soul breaks free from its outer covering and soars aloft in the realms of thought. In its thirst for knowledge it flies like a comet past thousands of spheres, absorbing in its course waves of light which it reflects on its dear ones below. Freed from the body and its demands, the soul responds to the power which emanates from God, and in its freedom it is conscious of its identity and of its destiny.

The day after we arrived at Valparaiso, the fine three-master *Elisabeth* set sail for France. As I watched the preparations for her departure, I had a strong desire to go with her, so much was I dreading the reception I might get from my uncle, but the fear of hurting Chabrié held me back. His friendship had become more necessary to me than ever: his devotion gained a stronger hold over me every day. Besides, my health was weakened by months of suffering, my morale shattered by my recent loss. It was all too much for me, and I longed for rest and affection. At times I was ready to throw myself into Chabrié's arms, confess everything, and beg him for his aid and protection. But the fear of causing him pain prevented me: his conduct towards me throughout the voyage, those five months of love and self-sacrifice, inspired me with so much gratitude that I did not have the heart to hurt him. I do not know whether I would have been strong enough to obey my conscience, or indeed what would have been the outcome, had not a stroke of good fortune enabled me to come to a decision.

M David visited me every evening, for the gentlemen had made my chamber their meeting place. Their affairs did not look very promising: they had found the market glutted with merchandise, they had no money coming in, and they were dreadfully worried about paying their bills. Then one evening M David arrived with an air of complete satisfaction. 'My dear lady,' he said, 'I have good news for you. We no longer have to worry about our debts: we have just heard from M Roux of Bordeaux that he will stand surety for us and undertake to pay our bills as they fall due. He says he looks upon Chabrié as a member of his family, almost as a son. . . . You see,' he added, 'before we left Bordeaux there was talk of Chabrié marrying Mademoiselle Roux, but the idea did not please our friend because he thought the lady too young. Well, whatever happens, it has proved very lucky for us; our operation is saved, though without the help of M Roux it might have failed as we are having to wait so long for any money to come in. Now it will be easier for us to wait.'

What M David told me opened up new vistas for Chabrié's future. This marriage with Mlle Roux would be ideal for him: he loved M Roux's family as his own, the two men were intimate friends, born and raised in the same town, serving for years on the same ship. Chabrié was eighteen years older than Mlle Roux, but if the girl loved him, what did the difference in age matter? I do not know if my faculty of second sight was active on this occasion, but I saw very clearly that in marrying his friend's daughter, Chabrié could find the happiness and tranquillity he needed so much, and from that moment I determined to use every effort to convince him of the fact. Meanwhile I rejoiced with M David in the generous offer which extricated them from their difficulties, and when Chabrié came we spoke of it at length.

The following day I announced to M Chabrié that I could not wait until he was ready to leave for Islay, as the delay was harming my interests, so I had decided to go direct to Arequipa, alone. Chabrié was so astonished at my sudden decision that he could not believe it and made me repeat it three times. I calmed his distress by pointing out that *our common interests* demanded it. He begged me to wait at least two days longer to give me time for reflection. I persuaded M David that it was urgent for me to leave immediately, and he helped me to reconcile Chabrié to our approaching separation. From the moment I took my decision I felt strong and free from all anxiety. I experienced that inner satisfaction so beneficial when we know we have done right. I found I was quite calm: I had just won a victory over the *self*. The voice of virtue had prevailed.

As I was now entirely free from any inner preoccupation I could devote myself to the role of observer, and I explored the town in every direction. I stayed in Valparaiso for only fourteen days, so I can do no more than sketch its external appearance.

M Chabrié told me that he had seen Valparaiso in 1825. At that time the town consisted of between thirty and forty wooden huts. Now every hill overlooking the sea is covered with houses and there is a population of thirty thousand. The town has three distinct parts: first, the harbour and customs district, one single street running for about two and a half miles along the seafront. It is not yet paved and in the rainy season it is a morass. The customs house faces the quay: it is a large building perfectly adequate for its purpose but lacking any interesting feature. In this quarter are the big trading companies from various nations, the warehouses, the stores and the fine shops which sell luxury goods: all is bustle and activity. Leaving the commercial centre one comes to the *Almendral*, the only promenade the residents possess. It is here that you find the *retiros* – imposing mansions set in beautiful gardens. The third district is called *Quebradas* after the gorges separating the mountains which encircle the town. This is where the Indians live.

I thought the Chileans seemed cold by nature, with stiff and arrogant manners. There is a kind of rigidity about the women: they speak little and dress in the height of luxury, but the general effect is lacking in taste. From the little I had to do with them, I was not impressed with their affability, and in this respect they seemed inferior to the women of Peru. They are said to be excellent at managing their households, which would seem to be confirmed by the fact that all the Europeans who come to Chile marry there, whereas considerably fewer marry in Peru.

V

The Leonidas

I had booked my passage on the American three-master, the *Leonidas*. The captain sent me word that the ship was to sail at noon on Sunday, September 1st, 1833.

I rose very early that day as I had no servant to help me with my trunks and other preparations for the voyage. I had several letters to write, and these occupations gave me a brief respite from the worries which lay heavy on my heart. In the middle of all this I had a number of visitors, and thanks to the general confusion I was able to receive them with every appearance of calm. These people came to bid me farewell, some out of affection, but most out of curiosity. Poor Chabrié could not keep still for a moment: he went to and fro between my chamber and the balcony, fearful lest these importunate visitors should notice how upset he was. His eyes were full of tears, his voice trembled so much he dared not utter a word. I was quite overcome by his distress.

I saw that the *Leonidas* was about to weigh anchor, so I took leave of my visitors. I had known them only briefly, but some had come with me from France, while others were my compatriots and spoke my language, so it wrung my heart to see them go. I remained a few moments alone with Chabrié.

'Oh, Flora!' he said, 'swear that you love me, swear you will be mine and I shall soon see you again, for if you do not, I shall not have the strength to see you depart.'

'My dear friend, do I need to swear to you that I love you? Haven't I proved it by my behaviour towards you?

62

As for our plans to marry, only God knows what the future holds in store for us.'

'But what do *you* want, Flora? Tell me that from this moment I may look on you as my wife: oh, tell me!'

I would have preferred not to have to renew a promise I knew I could not keep, but his distress frightened me, I was afraid he would lose control of himself, so, moved by his tortured expression and fearful lest David or someone else might enter and find him in tears, I promised that I would be his wife and stay with him in America, to share his lot for better or for worse. The poor man, delirious with joy, was too agitated to notice the profound sorrow which overwhelmed me. He was unaware that he was embracing a lifeless body incapable of responding to his caresses. He left me, as he did not feel strong enough to accompany me to the ship, and I went with M David. I bade farewell to Madame Aubrit and greeted the crowd of French residents I encountered on my way with a calmness that surprised me and was due entirely to the numb state of my mind.

It was when we were in the boat and I was silently struggling to contain the anguish which was consuming me that M David said: 'Mademoiselle Flora, we are just passing the *Mexicain*: don't you want to say goodbye to the poor old ship? You may never see her again.' His words had an indescribable effect on me: I was seized with such an uncontrollable fit of trembling that even my teeth began to chatter. M David could not help noticing, and I told him I was cold. For a moment I feared I was going to faint.

We went on board the *Leonidas*, where we found a large crowd of Englishmen and Americans. M David first commended me warmly to the captain, then escorted me to my cabin, together with the steward, whom he enjoined to take the greatest care of me. Both of them helped me to arrange my belongings and put my cabin to rights. Then M David, taking me aside, warned me about the ways of foreigners, so that I would be on my guard against them and behave with the extreme reserve a woman must adopt in their company if she wishes to be respected. There were several Englishmen and Americans sitting at a table in the saloon drinking grog. All eyes turned towards me and although they were speaking English I knew I was the subject of conversation. Their insolent stares and derisive laughter disgusted me, and I felt how *alone* I was among these men of dissolute habits who cared nothing for the consideration due to a woman or for the first social law, which is decency. Already I felt all the horrors of isolation. M David saw my distress and tried to restore my courage and revive my self-confidence, but they were weighing anchor and he had to bid me farewell. I accompanied him on deck, and after I had watched him embark in his boat I sat down in the stern of the vessel, where I remained until the captain and the doctor (to whom I had not yet spoken) came to conduct me below.

I was ill for the first two days, but after that I recovered my strength, and with it, my morale. I was soon on as good terms with the captain as it was possible to be, considering that we spoke different languages, he English and I French. The doctor was called M Victor de Castellac, and we had long conversations on every conceivable subject. I talked about Paris, Algiers, and a thousand other things with an enthusiasm that astonished me. The doctor never tired of hearing about Paris as he hardly knew it, having spent the whole of his life since leaving college in the Spanish colonies. After staying six years in Mexico, where he amassed a small fortune, he came to Paris in 1829 and entrusted all his money to a bank which failed during the revolution of 1830, so he lost everything. At first he was inconsolable, but in time he became resigned to his loss and decided to return to South America. He was now on his way to Cuzco.

The doctor was a great gossip and his curiosity was

boundless. An excellent man at bottom, he was however self-centred and suspicious, because he knew the world, and, like M David, he had suffered at its hands.

We had a very smooth passage, and on the eighth day, at nine o'clock in the evening, we anchored in the Bay of Islay, off the coast of Peru.

VI

Islay

On the day we arrived, I could hardly see the coast of Peru. Just as we were drawing near, a very fine rain began to fall, and hid the coast from sight. The sea was quite calm, and had it not been for an English vessel which sent its launch to tow us into port, I do not know how we would have managed. We were all disappointed that we could form no opinion of what the country looked like.

The entire coast of Peru is extremely arid: Islay and its environs present a scene of utter desolation. In spite of this, the port is surprisingly prosperous. Don Justo, the postmaster-general, assured me that when it was first established, it consisted of nothing but three huts and a large customs shed, but now, after six years, Islay had a population of between one thousand and two thousand people. Most of the houses are of bamboo and have earth floors, but there are also some very pretty wooden houses with elegant windows and wooden floors. The residence of the English consul, which was nearing completion when I returned to Islay the following year, is quite charming. The customs-house is a very large wooden building: the church is not unattractive, and its size reflects the importance of the settlement. The port of Islay is better situated than Arica and has taken over all its trade. If it continues to prosper as it has done over the past six years, it could have as many as four or five thousand inhabitants in ten years' time, but the sterility of the region will inhibit its growth for some time to come, as it is entirely without water and there is no tree or vegetation of any kind. The day of the artesian well has

66

not yet dawned in this backward country. Islay has only a tiny stream to water it, and when this dries up in summer, as frequently happens, the inhabitants are forced to abandon their homes. The soil consists of a black and stony sand which would undoubtedly be very fertile if only it could be irrigated.

At about six o'clock in the morning the harbour-master came on board to make his inspection, a universal practice whenever ships enter port. The customs officials asked us for our passports, and when they examined mine, they gave a cry of astonishment and asked me if I was related to Don Pio de Tristan. I replied that I was, and there followed a long conversation conducted in low tones: they seemed to be deliberating whether they should offer me their services or await orders from their superiors. The outcome was that they began to treat me with the deference reserved for persons of eminence in the republic. The harbour-master informed me respectfully that he had formerly been in my uncle's service and owed his present position to the generosity of Don Pio when he was Prefect of Arequipa. Putting himself entirely at my service, he gave me to understand that my uncle was not in Arequipa, but had for the past month been staying with his family at Camana, where he had a large sugar refinery on the coast, some sixty miles from Islay and the same distance from Arequipa. I took advantage of the harbour-master's offer to ask him if he would precede me into Islay and deliver my letters of introduction to Don Justo de Medina, Don Basilio de la Fuente and my uncle's agent. At eleven o'clock, after we had breakfasted and dressed, we left the *Leonidas* with all our baggage.

There is still no jetty at Islay, so it is just as difficult to disembark there as it is at Praia. On my entry into this, the first important settlement of Peru, I was received with all the honours due to the rank and office of my uncle Don Pio. The collector of customs, Don Basilio, invited me to stay at his house; so did the postmaster-general,

Don Justo. I gave my preference to the latter, as I felt I had more in common with him.

We went through the whole of the settlement: just one straggling main street where the surface has never been levelled and you still stumble across rocks from the sea or sink up to your knees in sand. There, even more than in Valparaiso, I was the centre of attraction. Don Justo installed me in the best room in his house, while his wife and daughter hastened to offer me everything they thought would please me. Poor Dr Castellac clung to me like a limpet, and to reward him for taking such good care of me during the voyage, I appointed him my *personal physician* so that he too could enjoy the generous hospitality offered to the niece of Don Pio de Tristan. He was given a room in Don Justo's house as well, and from that moment he never left my side.

For the better understanding of the reader I should perhaps explain at this point how matters stood between my uncle and me, and what was my uncle's position in relation to his own people.

As I said in my preface, my mother's marriage had not been regularised in France, and as a result of this omission, I was regarded as illegitimate. Up to the age of fifteen I was completely unaware of this absurd social distinction and its monstrous consequences. I worshipped my father's memory and still hoped for my uncle's protection, as my mother often spoke of him and encouraged me to love him, although she knew him only through his correspondence with my father. I had read this correspondence many times over: it was an extraordinary monument of fraternal love.

I was fifteen when, because of a marriage I wished to contract, my mother revealed to me how the circumstances of my birth affected my position. My pride was so deeply wounded that in the first flush of indignation I renounced my uncle Pio and all my family, but in 1829, as the result of a long conversation with M Chabrié about

Peru, I wrote my uncle the following letter, in which, to translate the picturesque expression used by the President of the Court in Arequipa, I cut my head into four pieces:

To M Pio de Tristan

Monsieur,

May the daughter of your beloved brother Mariano take the liberty of writing to you? I imagine that you are unaware of my existence and that not one of the score or more of letters my mother wrote you ever reached its destination. Had fate not dealt the crowning blow to my misfortunes, I would never have approached you. I have found a reliable means of conveying this letter to you, and I hope it will succeed in touching your heart. I enclose my birth certificate: should you still have any doubts about me, the illustrious Bolivar, who was a close friend of my parents, will be able to dispel them. He can testify that I was brought up in my father's household, as he was a frequent visitor to our house. You could also see his friend, who is known to you by the name of Robinson, as well as M Bompland, whom you must have known prior to his imprisonment in Paraguay. I could mention other names, but these two should suffice. Now I will proceed to a brief account of the facts.

To escape the horrors of the revolution, my mother went to Spain with a female relative. They settled in Bilbao, where my father formed a friendship with them, and where the bond between him and my mother soon grew into a love so strong that it was impossible for them to live apart. The two ladies returned to France in 1802, and my father was not slow to follow them. As a military man, your brother needed to obtain the king's consent to his marriage, but as he chose not to seek it (and I have too much respect for my father's memory to try to guess what could have been his motive) he proposed to my mother that they should be joined in wedlock by means of a religious ceremony, which has no validity in France.

My mother, feeling that she could not live without him, consented to this proposal. The nuptial blessing was given by a responsible priest, M Roncelin, who had known my mother since she was a child, and the couple settled in Paris.

On my father's death, M Adam of Bilbao, later to become a deputy in the Cortes, who had known my mother either in Spain or in France as the lawful wife of Don Mariano de Tristan, sent her a document signed by more than ten people attesting that they had all known her by that title.

You know that at that time my father's sole fortune consisted of the six thousand francs his uncle the Archbishop of Granada had left him as head of the Tristan family. You sent him money on several occasions, but most of this was lost: 20,000 francs was seized by the English and 10,000 went down with the *Minerva*. Nevertheless, thanks to my mother's thrift, my father was able to keep up his position. Thirteen months before his death he purchased a house at Vaugirard, near Paris. When he died, the ambassador, Prince Masserano, took possession of all his papers, which would have come to you, including the document confirming the purchase of the aforesaid property, through the Spanish ambassador.

My father had paid for the property in part, and if it had been left to my mother, this would have helped her to raise my brother and me, but ten months after my father's death it was confiscated by the state on the grounds that it belonged to a Spaniard, for by that time France and Spain were at war. It was subsequently sold, and the state profited by a sum exceeding the 10,000 francs still outstanding on the original purchase price; yet my mother was never reimbursed for the 554 francs she had paid to have the ownership of the property transferred to my father's heirs.

You will appreciate, monsieur, how much suffering this has meant for my poor mother, left penniless and burdened with two children. (My brother lived for ten years.) In spite of her straitened circumstances she did not wish the memory of the man who had been the object of her tenderest affections to be sullied in any way. Because of the war my father received nothing for twenty months, and as a consequence he was in desperate need of money. In response to my mother's entreaties, my grandmother lent him 2,800 francs, without asking him for any written acknowledgement of his debt, so when he died she had no legal claim to the money. My mother paid her the interest due in full, as she needed it in order to live, and when my grandmother died she paid one-third of the sum borrowed to her sister, and the remaining third to her brother.

But I do not want this glimpse of the misfortunes I have so inadequately described to expose you to all the painful details. You still cherish the memory of the brother who loved you like his son, and it would cause you untold suffering if you were to contrast my fate with the happier destiny which might have been expected for his daughter. When he was struck down by the thunder-bolt of a sudden and untimely death, he was only able to utter these words: 'My daughter, you still have Pio. . . .' Unhappy child!

However, whatever the effect my letter may have upon you, monsieur, do not think that my father's spirit could ever be offended by any grievance of mine: his memory will always be dear and sacred to me.

I look to you for justice and generosity. I entrust myself to you in the hope of a better future. I ask your protection and pray that you will love me as the daughter of your brother Mariano has the right to claim.

I am your very humble and obedient servant,

FLORA DE TRISTAN

The reader will find proof of my sincerity in the above letter, which illustrates my complete ignorance of the world, my belief in honesty, and that blind trust in good faith which assumes that others are as good and as just as oneself. My uncle, who had professed so great a love for his brother, was soon to open my eyes. Here is the reply he sent me, which I have chosen to present in a literal translation from the original Spanish:

> Mademoiselle Flora de Tristan
> Arequipa, 6 October 1830.

Mademoiselle and my estimable niece,

I received your dear letter with as much surprise as pleasure. I knew from General Bolivar's visit here in 1823 that at the time of his death my beloved brother Mariano de Tristan had a daughter: M Simon Rodriguez, whom you know by the name of Robinson, had already told me as much; but as neither of them gave me any further news of you or where you were living, I was unable to let you know about various matters of interest to us both. I was officially informed of your father's death by the Spanish government, acting on information received from Prince Masserano. As a result I invested General Goyeneche, now Count Guaqui, with my power of attorney so that he could investigate the question of my brother's estate, but he was unable to take any action at that time because of the French invasion of Spain, which obliged him to go to the continent of America on a mission of great urgency. Another consequence of the aforesaid invasion was that we remained for many years without any means of communication, and then the American war occupied us so completely that we were unable to think of other matters, and in any case it would have been difficult to settle them because of the distance which separated us. However, on 9 April 1824, I authorised M Changeur, a merchant in Bordeaux, to try to discover, through his agents in Paris, where you were living and what property the deceased had left. I gave him the address of the house where my brother was living at the time of his death. Before and after the despatch of my power of attorney, I particularly recommended him on several occasions to take every possible step to discover whether you and your mother were still alive. All I had to show for it was an account of the sums of money so unprofitably expended in searching for you, and I can produce proof of these enquiries. How could I imagine that you were still alive when twenty years had passed since the death of my brother Tristan without any news of you or your mother? Yes, dear niece, it is a tragedy that not one of the letters your mother wrote ever reached me, whereas your very first letter arrived without delay. I am very well known here, and for the past eight years communications between our shores and yours have been frequent enough for at least one of her letters to have arrived. This proves plainly enough that you were somewhat careless in this respect.

I have examined the birth certificate you sent me and I am fully convinced that you are my brother's acknowledged daughter, although the document is not authenticated and signed by three lawyers, as it should have been, to certify that the signature of the priest who issued it was genuine. As for your mother and her status as the legitimate spouse of my deceased brother, you yourself admit and confess that the manner in which the nuptial blessing was bestowed is null and void and has no validity in this country or anywhere in Christendom. Indeed, it is extraordinary that a cleric who claims to be respectable, like M Roncelin, should have allowed himself to proceed to such an act, seeing that the contracting parties had not observed the proper formalities. It is also quite irrelevant that when you were baptised he declared that you were legitimate, as is the document which you tell me was sent from Bilbao by M Adam, in which ten persons from that city state that they knew and regarded your mother as the legitimate spouse of Mariano: all that this proves is that she was granted this status purely and simply as a matter of propriety. Moreover, in the correspondence I maintained with my brother until shortly before his death, there is strong, albeit negative, proof of what I affirm: my brother never once mentioned this union, an extraordinary fact when we had no secrets from one another. Added to that, if the union between my brother and your mother had been legitimate, neither Prince Masserano nor any other authority would have been able to set his seal upon the property of a deceased person who left legitimate descendants, recognised and known as such in that country. Let us accept, then, that you are only the natural daughter of my brother, that does not make you any less worthy of my consideration and my tender affection. I willingly give you the title of my dear niece, I will even add daughter, for nothing about any person who was the object of my brother's love can fail to interest me; neither time nor death can ever efface the tender affection I bore him and which I shall preserve all my life.

Our esteemed mother is still alive and has attained the age of eighty-nine. She still has her reason and all her physical and moral faculties. She is the delight of the whole family, and she has been generous enough to divide all her property among them now, so that she may have the pleasure of seeing it enjoyed before her death. We were busy with this distribution when your letter reached me: I read it to her, and when she learned of your existence and your unhappy fate, she complied with the wishes of the family and arranged to leave you an appreciable legacy of 3,000 piastres, which I beg you to regard as proof of my special interest in you, of our mother's undying love for her son Mariano, and of the eternal remembrance of all the members of the family.

Meanwhile, as you have some slight claim on my deceased brother's estate, which I have administered by virtue of the power of attorney he gave me on 20

November 1801 in the presence of the royal notary of Our Lady of Begona in Biscay, Senor J. Antonio Oleaga, I am sending you a copy of the account as it stands at present. This will convince you that nothing of my dead brother's is left, as the Ibanez affair absorbed all that remained at the time of his death. This business would have been settled immediately had I known anything about it, or if the creditors had not been so negligent as to let eleven years elapse before taking steps to secure payment, although they must have heard of my brother's death. Thus the interest on the debt, though only 4 per cent, doubled the amount to be repaid. Everything about my brother's death was marked by fate: the time and manner of his passing were the cause of your misfortunes and my eternal grief. But let us forget all that and try to remedy it as far as possible.

My agent in Bordeaux is M Bertera, through whom I am sending you a draft for 2,500 francs. To obtain the money you will have to send him a copy of your birth certificate witnessed by a lawyer. Try to manage on this sum while I find a way of sending you your legacy of 3,000 piastres, which will be made payable at your risk, though I will take all the necessary steps to guarantee its safety. I advise you to invest the money in government stocks, or, if political developments make them too risky, in other stocks, so that you have a guaranteed income paid to you every six months. What I have done for you may not amount to very much, but it is incontestable proof of my affection for you, and if I live long enough for us to meet, time will tell how much I love the daughter of my brother Mariano.

Write to me often as you can and address your letters to M Bertera in Bordeaux: I shall write to you myself through the same channel. Let me know where you live, tell me how you are, what are your plans, what are your needs. My sincerity should inspire you to trust me. I am writing to you in Spanish because I have forgotten all my French.

I am married to one of my nieces, Joaquina Florez: we have a son called Florentino and three daughters aged eight, five and three. May it please God that one day they may embrace you in person and that you too may lavish your caresses upon them here in this country. In anticipation of this pleasure let me assure you of all my affection.

(signed) PIO DE TRISTAN.

When I received this reply, in spite of the good opinion I had of men, I realised that I could expect nothing from my uncle, but I still had my grandmother, and all my hopes turned to her. It seems that my uncle had deceived me when he wrote that he had read my letter to my grandmother and all the family, for before I appeared on the scene, hardly any of them knew of my existence, and I am now convinced that my grandmother did not know of it either, because I learned later that not long before she died, my uncle persuaded her to make a will in which his wife benefited by 20,000 piastres, and I was included with a bequest of 3,000. This will is very long, and my grandmother, who trusted her son Don Pio blindly, signed it without knowing all its provisions. I was not designated as the daughter of Don Mariano, but only by my name, Florita, lest anybody should discover why such a bequest should have been made. When the property was divided, my existence was revealed to the interested parties, as my legacy was set aside in advance, and my uncle had a good deal of trouble to persuade them to give it to me: they demanded: 'But why give 15,000 francs to a complete stranger?'

'Because she is presumed to be my brother's daughter.'

I had not informed my uncle of my departure for Peru, and as I had not had time to forewarn him, he was still unaware that I had arrived. Such was my position with regard to him: now I shall give a brief account of his position with regard to his country.

Don Pio de Tristan returned from Europe in 1803 with the rank of colonel. He took part in the terrible wars of independence, when the Peruvians fought so fiercely to win their freedom. My uncle was one of the ablest soldiers Spain ever sent to those parts. When the armies of King Ferdinand were forced to evacuate Buenos Aires and the territory of the republic of Argentina, he was second-in-command, under our cousin M Manuel de Goyeneche, brother of M Mariano de Goyeneche, of whom I have already spoken. My uncle was then a field marshal. They retreated in the direction of Upper Peru (Bolivia) crossing the immense distance between Buenos Aires and Lima, where they were frequently forced to engage in combat, cross rivers, and make their way through terrain where no roads had ever run. These magnificent warriors, glittering with gold and accustomed to the comfortable life of the Spanish-American cities, endured great hardships in these wild regions. On their epic march they subsisted on wild animals they hunted, provisions they obtained at bayonet point, and anything whatever they were able to purchase. My uncle has often told me how, when there was no money left in the army's coffers, he made his cavalry officers, who all wore spurs of *solid gold*, draw lots to decide which of them should sacrifice one of his spurs to pay for food. One soldier alone had more than enough gold about him to equip two hundred on the republican side. This arrogant display of wealth gave the Spanish armies in South America an exaggerated idea of their superiority to the colonial populations, whose submission they were meant to ensure; but a display of wealth quickly loses its effectiveness. With the money it cost to equip one Spaniard, the king could have maintained twenty Germans. The local populations were not conspicuous for their warlike qualities, and as they were spread over a vast area, they could easily have been kept in a state of submission had Spain sent more troops, which she could have done without any increase in expenditure. People who knew South America considered that the day of its independence was still a long way off, and that Spain was more than strong enough to repress the revolts sparked off by Bonaparte's invasion of the Peninsula. But events do not turn out according to expectations. The insurrection led by Riego paralysed the efforts of the Spanish monarchy by turning the forces intended to subdue the colonies against the king, and South America achieved independence. M de Goyeneche and my uncle had five thousand men under their command when they left the shores of the River Plate, but when after two years of forced marches, battles and continual hardships they reached Peru, barely a third remained to answer the roll. In Peru the war between royalists and republicans lasted fifteen years: my uncle fought in every battle, including the last, the famous battle of Ayacucho (1824) which assured the triumph of the republican cause. He was appointed viceroy in the interim, and had the courage to accept high office at a time when it was more of a danger than an advantage. After its defeat in battle the royalist party was in total disarray: the viceroy and his officials had no choice but to leave the country, and my uncle announced that he proposed to return to Spain with his family and his fortune. But the republican leaders, appreciating his valour and his military skill, and realising how much their new government needed to attract such men, proposed that he should retain command of the army, merely exchanging his former title of viceroy for that of General of the Republic. My uncle declined this offer, preferring to be appointed Governor of Cuzco, which he proceeded to administer for the next six years. By taking this prudent course, dictated entirely by self-interest, he hoped to avoid offending either side, but matters turned out otherwise. My uncle's administrative ability could not conceal his lack of political conscience and commitment. He aroused the gravest suspicions of the republicans and permanently alienated the royalists, who regarded him as a *traitor*. In vain did he exert every effort to win the support of both parties: loving the old yet serving the new, he was bound to fail. For a long time my uncle fought against the harassments he suffered from all sides with an obstinacy I am almost tempted to admire, but in the end feeling against him grew so intense that he judged it prudent to leave a place where his life was no longer safe. He tendered his resignation and retired to Arequipa, where he could have had as good a life as anybody with an income of 200,000 francs may expect to enjoy anywhere on earth. But he had acquired the habit of command, and the mere enjoyment of wealth no longer had any charm for him. He had to be surrounded by a brilliant retinue and a flock of servitors: in short, he did not feel he was alive unless he was engaged in some great enterprise. In his desire to satisfy this need, he made a prolonged tour of all his sugar refineries and had a magnificent country mansion built, but none of these activities could distract him from his ambition. He plotted behind the scenes, and his machin- ations were so successful that he came within five votes of being elected President of Peru. To compensate for this disappointment his supporters had him appointed Prefect of Arequipa. My uncle carried out the new duties en- trusted to him with as much intelligence as zeal: he made many improvements to the town and did his utmost to increase public prosperity. Nevertheless, as his claims to the respect of his fellow citizens increased, the hatred against him intensified. The republicans retained their suspicions, the royalists renewed their accusations. The newspapers, which are more virulent in Peru than else- where, attacked my uncle so remorselessly that at the end of two years he was again forced to resign, and again his life was threatened. When I arrived in Peru, he had been back in Arequipa for only ten months, and was thinking of accepting nomination as President. His decision to hasten his return owed at least as much to his ambition as to his desire to see his family again. The Peruvians are all political opportunists: when this is taken into account, together with the considerable influence my uncle had with the government, it is easy to understand their behaviour towards me. So now let us return to Islay and the house of Don Justo de Medina.

From my chamber I had a good view of everybody who came to see Don Justo or visited the ladies in the room adjoining his study. I was surprised to see how much coming and going there was in this house: I also noticed that everybody seemed anxious or ill at ease. Though I spoke little Spanish I understood it very well, and from the few sentences I picked up I gathered that I was the cause of all these visits. The doctor, who had been to the customhouse for our baggage, came to me on his return with an air of mystery and satisfaction, the reason for which I could not guess.

'Ah, mademoiselle,' he said in a low voice, 'if only you knew what a terrible country we are in! These Peruvians are just as untrustworthy as the Mexicans. Oh, my beloved France, why can't a poor little doctor make a nice little fortune in Paris?'

'What, doctor, cursing the country already? What harm have these people done you?'

'None as yet; but let me give you a little sample so that you will know what to expect. I pretend I don't know Spanish so that they will speak freely in front of me; well, let me inform you that these rascals have been discussing whether they should welcome you with open arms or whether it would be more prudent to keep their distance for fear of displeasing Don Pio de Tristan. Fortunately for you there is a sworn enemy of your uncle here, a priest who is also a member of the government. He is looked upon as the leader of the republican party and his name is Francisco Luna Pizarro. He is on his way to Lima and is staying with Don Basilio, the collector of customs, who was not sure how he ought to behave towards you and asked his advice. The priest replied without hesitation that you should be received with every courtesy and that he wished to visit you in person; you will see him arrive any minute.'

In fact, a few moments later the famous priest Luna Pizarro came to visit me, together with Don Basilio de la Fuente and other notables of the town. After this official visit there came in quick succession all the ladies of Arequipa, who were in Islay for the sea-bathing, followed by people of lesser rank. Don Justo gave us an excellent dinner, and as an entertainment worthy of the occasion he assembled the local musicians and dancers to regale me with a ball in Peruvian style. The dancing continued until after midnight.

I waited impatiently for all the guests to depart, as I was dropping with fatigue. At last I was able to retire, but, alas, hardly was I in bed than I felt I must be in a veritable nest of fleas. Ever since I arrived they had been bothering me, but never as much as this. I was unable to sleep the whole night long, and I was bitten so much that I had a fever. I rose as soon as it was light and went into the courtyard to take the air. There I found the doctor washing his face, neck and hands and cursing the fleas. For sole response I showed him my hands, which were covered with swellings. The good Justo was much distressed to hear that the fleas had prevented us from sleeping. Madame Justo said with some embarrassment: 'Mademoiselle, I did not dare to tell you what to do so that they trouble you less, but this evening I will show you.'

In the morning my uncle's agent came to tell me that he had despatched a courier to Camana to inform my family of my arrival. He felt sure my uncle would send some-body for me as soon as he knew that I was in Islay. I reflected for a few moments, and from what I knew of my uncle I felt it would be unwise to go immediately to his country house and place myself in his hands. I thought it would be much better to go direct to Arequipa, spy out the land, collect information and wait for my uncle to broach the question of my interests. So I told the agent that I would leave the following day for Arequipa as I felt too fatigued to go to Camana. I charged the doctor with the preparations for our journey so that we could set out at daybreak.

The rest of the day was spent in receiving farewell visits and exploring the surrounding countryside. In the evening I called on the collector of customs, who had invited me to take tea. To add to the splendour of his hospitality, he, like Don Justo, had assembled the town's musicians and dancers, and the ball continued until one in the morning. I was obliged to drink several cups of coffee to keep myself awake: it was very good but it made me very restless. When I retired to my chamber, Madame Justo came and showed me how to keep the fleas at bay. She placed four or five chairs in a row with the last one next to the bed, and made me undress on the first. I proceeded to the second wearing only my shift, while Madame Justo took all my clothes out of the room, advising me to wipe myself with a towel to remove the fleas still clinging to my body. Then I went from chair to chair as far as the bed, where I put on a white nightgown liberally sprinkled with eau de cologne. This procedure gave me two hours peace, but after that I could feel the fleas returning to the attack, thousands of them converging upon my bed. You have to have lived in countries where these insects abound in order to imagine the agony caused by their bites: the irritation sets the nerves on edge, inflames the blood and gives you a fever. Peru is infested with fleas: in the streets of Islay you see them hopping about in the sand. It is impossible to protect oneself from them completely, but if the country were a little cleaner in its habits, the fleas would trouble one far less.

VII

The Desert

At four o'clock in the morning the muleteer came for our baggage, and while he was loading it, I got up. I felt quite exhausted, so, as usual, I restored my strength by drinking quantities of coffee.

When I was ready to mount my mule, I found it was a very poor specimen, and the harness in particular did not look as if it would stand up to such a long journey. I observed as much to the doctor, but he assured me that he had scoured the entire neighbourhood and been unable to find anything better. I believed him: at that time it would never have occurred to me that a man for whom one has done service should so quickly forget all about it. However, Don Justo lent me a piece of carpet to place on top of the cushion stuffed with straw which serves as a cheap saddle in those parts, and I made myself as comfortable as I could. Everybody told me that I was most unwise to set out on such a poor mount; but with the self-confidence of youth I ignored the entreaties of the good Don Justo and his wife and daughter, who declared that they had nearly died of exhaustion the last time they went to Arequipa, and set out: it was five o'clock on the morning of 11 September 1833.

At the beginning of the journey I found that I was tolerably comfortable on my mule. The coffee I had drunk gave me an illusion of strength, so I felt full of energy and well satisfied with the course I had taken. Hardly had we left the plateau of Islay and begun to penetrate the mountain regions than we were joined by two horsemen, cousins of the collector of customs: one was called Don Balthazar de la Fuente and the other Don Jose, and they asked me if I would like their company on the journey. I was delighted at such a fortunate encounter and thanked them for their courtesy, for I was not entirely happy about the doctor's courage. M de Castellac, accustomed to travel in Mexico, where the roads are infested with bandits, had feared that Peru would be the same, so he had armed himself to the teeth. He had a brace of pistols in his belt, then a sword-belt from which hung a big cavalry sabre, then a shoulder-belt to which was attached a hunting knife, and finally, two huge pistols in his saddle-bow. All this was in comical contrast with his diminutive stature and shabby costume. He still wore the same leather breeches, top-boots and long spurs that had served him on his Mexican travels, while his short green hunting-jacket was so tight and threadbare that I was afraid he would burst out of it. On his head he wore a black silk skull-cap surmounted by an enormous straw hat. In addition to all this, he had a collection of bottles and baskets in front of him and a pile of blankets, rugs, mufflers and cloaks behind: in short, all the paraphernalia of the seasoned desert traveller who is afraid of leaving anything behind. As for me, I had no idea what such journeys were like, so I had set out just as I would if I were going from Paris to Orleans. I was wearing grey duck half-boots, a brown cloth wrapper, a silk apron, in the pocket of which I kept my knife and my handkerchief, and a little blue grosgrain hat. I had however brought along my cloak and two shawls.

We descended the mountain by a perilous path which took us to Guerrera, about three miles from Islay. There we saw streams of running water, trees and a little vegetation, as well as five or six huts inhabited by muleteers. Don Balthazar and Don Jose began to talk about the astonishment my unexpected arrival had produced, as my uncle had never mentioned me, then they went on to speak of my grandmother, and, quite oblivious of the pain they were causing me, deplored the loss I had suffered in this estimable woman, as generous as she was just. This upset me so much that I could not restrain my tears. They attempted to change the subject, but they had reawakened my grief and now I felt an imperative need to weep, so I let them go on ahead with the doctor while I lingered behind and gave free rein to my tears. At first I thought this would make me feel better, but soon afterwards the heat became intense, my head began to ache exceedingly, and the thick white dust raised by the animals' hooves only increased my suffering. I had to exert all my will-power to stay on my mule. Don Balthazar kept up my morale by assuring me that once out of the mountain gorges we would come to a plateau where the air was pure and fresh. I had a raging thirst which I tried to assuage by drinking a mixture of wine and water, which is usually effective, but now it made my headache worse, as the local wine is very strong. At last we emerged from the stifling gorges where there is never a breath of wind and the sun makes the sand as hot as a furnace. We climbed the last mountain, and when we reached the summit, the vast chain of the Cordilleras and the three giant volcanoes of Arequipa spread before us. At the sight of this magnificent spectacle I forgot my sufferings and lived only to admire. I let my gaze wander over the bright billowing sand to the point where it met the azure heavens, then upon the lofty mountains which stretched like an endless ladder to the skies, their thousand snow-capped peaks reflecting the sun's rays and marking the western limit of the desert with all the colours of the rainbow. Then I turned my gaze towards the three volcanoes of Arequipa, joined at their base and branching out like a triple candlestick, symbol of a trinity beyond our human understanding.

Meanwhile Don Jose and the doctor, instead of spending their time in ecstatic contemplation of endless ice and burning sand, had prepared a couch for me upon some carpets and set up a little tent to protect me from the sun. I made myself comfortable and we began to eat. There was an abundance of everything: the good Madame Justo had given the doctor a basket full of roast meat, vegetables, cakes and fruit. The two Spaniards were just as well supplied: they had sausage, cheese, chocolate, sugar and fruit, as well as milk, wine and rum to drink. We made a leisurely meal, then it was time to leave. We had eighty-five miles to go and not a drop of water to be found; we had covered only fifteen miles and it was already ten o'clock.

Don Jose gave me his mare because she went better than my mule, and we set off once more. My soul was still full of the magnificent panorama which kept my senses too under its powerful spell for a time, so we had been making arduous progress for close on half an hour before the frightful desert began to affect me. Then physical suffering snatched me from my mental ecstasy: my eyes suddenly opened and I thought I was in the middle of a sea as limpid and blue as the sky it reflected, but as I felt the furnace heat arising from it, the stifling atmosphere, the stinging dust upon my face, I thought this illusory ocean was really liquid fire, and lifting my eyes towards the Cordilleras I suffered all the torments of the fallen angel banished from heaven.

'Don Balthazar,' I asked him fearfully, 'can this sand be liquid?'

'It is the effect of the mirage that makes it appear so, mademoiselle: these *pampas* are covered with tiny hillocks of sand piled up by the wind. You can see that they do in fact resemble waves, and from a distance the mirage gives them the appearance of movement; indeed, they are no more stable than the waves of the sea, for the wind is always dispersing them.'

'Then it must be very dangerous to travel through the *pampas* when there is a strong wind?'

'Oh, yes: a few years ago some muleteers on their way

from Islay to Arequipa were buried by a whirlwind together with their mules; but such events are very rare.'

We were silent: I thought how frail man is in the presence of the dangers to which he is exposed in these vast wastes, and I was seized with a sombre terror. I fervently invoked God's aid and surrendered myself to His providence.

Towards midday the heat intensified and made my headache so much worse that I could no longer stay on my horse. The sun and the heat reflected from the sand burned my face, a raging thirst parched my throat; finally a general lassitude overcame my will and I collapsed. I was so ill that twice I fainted right away. My three companions were in despair: the doctor wanted to bleed me, but fortunately for me Don Balthazar prevented him, or I am sure I would have died. They laid me down upon my horse, and I am tempted to believe that an invisible hand sustained me, for now by the grace of God I did not fall off once. At last the sun disappeared behind the towering volcanoes and gradually the fresh evening air revived me. To raise my spirits Don Balthazar told me that I would soon see the light of the inn which lies half-way along the route, although he knew very well that we were still more than fifteen miles away and was counting on the first star to appear above the Cordilleras to lend credence to his deception, but the night was completely dark.

In the pampas, just as the days are burning hot because of the sun and the heat reflected by the sand, so the nights are icy cold because of the breeze which has crossed the mountain snows. The cold did me much good, and I spurred on my horse with a vigour that astonished my companions: two hours before I had been at the point of death, and now I felt full of life. I had not been taken in by Don Balthazar's trick, and I was the first to see the real light. We were still a long way off, but the sight of that little lantern kept up my courage. We reached the *tambo* (inn) at midnight. Don Balthazar had gone on ahead with his servant to have soup and a bed prepared for me, so when I arrived I went straight to bed and drank my soup, but I was unable to sleep. Three things prevented me: the fleas, which were even more plentiful than in Islay, the incessant noise in the inn, and the fear that my strength would fail me and that I would be unable to complete the journey.

The inn had been there for only a year: before that travellers had been forced to sleep on the ground in the middle of the desert. The house consisted of three rooms divided by bamboo partitions: the first was used by muleteers and their animals, the second by travellers, and the third by the proprietors of the place. It also served as kitchen and store. Travellers of both sexes usually slept in the middle room, but Don Jose and Don Balthazar, who always treated me with the utmost delicacy, left it entirely to me, in spite of my protests, and went to sleep with the doctor in the kitchen. Although they spoke in low tones, I overheard enough to frighten me: Don Balthazar was saying to the doctor: 'I must confess I do not think it wise to take that poor lady with us this morning: she is so weak that I fear she may die on the way, especially as the worst part of the journey is yet to come. I am of the opinion that we ought to leave her here and send a litter for her tomorrow.'

At this the innkeeper observed that he was not sure that there would be any water as his stocks were exhausted, and if none arrived I might die of thirst. These words made me shudder with horror: the thought that I might be abandoned in the desert and that the rough folk to whose care I was entrusted might leave me to die — perhaps all for want of a glass of water — revived my strength; whatever happened, I preferred to die of exhaustion rather than thirst. The fear of such a frightful death wrought me up to such a pitch that by three in the morning I was ready to depart. I had done my hair, split open my boots to make my swollen feet more comfortable, dressed myself as suitably as possible, and got all my things together. Then I called the doctor and asked him to get me a cup of chocolate. The gentlemen were amazed to see me so well: I told them I had slept and was feeling quite better. I urged them to hasten the preparations for our departure, and we left the inn at four in the morning. It was bitterly cold: I had both hands wrapped round with scarves, and Don Balthazar lent me a big poncho lined with flannel. Thanks to these precautions, I went on without suffering unduly from the temperature.

On leaving the inn the landscape changes completely: the pampas comes to an end and you enter a mountainous region equally devoid of any kind of vegetation — a scene of utter desolation. Not a bird in the air, not even the tiniest animal on the ground, nothing but black and stony sand strewn with the bones of animals which have perished of hunger and thirst in this dreadful desert: mules, donkeys, horses, oxen. As for the native *llamas*, they are not exposed to this sort of crossing, which is too much for them: they need plenty of water and a cool climate. I was deeply moved at the sight of all these skeletons. Animals belong to the same planet as we do: are they not our companions? Are they not God's creatures, like us?

At about eight in the morning we reached the *Quebradas*, mountains renowned throughout the country for the difficulties they present to travellers. As we climbed the peaks which stretched before us on our way, I lay down upon my mule and trusted to the mercy of Providence, but as we descended it was impossible to do this, as the path was fraught with dangers, and although my mule was very sure-footed, I was still forced to take the greatest care. We had to make our animals jump across crevasses, climb huge rocks and sometimes follow narrow tracks where the sand crumbled beneath their feet and we risked falling into the fearsome precipice which ran alongside the mountain. Don Balthazar always went ahead to show us the way. His cousin, the gentlest and most considerate man I have ever met, stayed close beside me so that he could help me if need arose. The doctor, the very soul of caution, brought up the rear, as he was afraid that if one of us fell, he would be taken with us. Every time his mule stumbled he would commend himself to God, curse the track, the sun, the dust, and bemoan his terrible fate.

I managed to get down the first two mountains quite well, but when we reached the summit of the third, I felt so weak and ill, the jolting of my mule had given me such an agonising pain in my side, that it was impossible for me to hold the reins. We made a brief halt on the summit where the air is pure and fresh. Don Balthazar decided that as I could not sit on my mule without risk of falling into the precipice, I should try to make the descent on foot, so he and his cousin supported me under the arms, almost carrying me, while M de Castellac led the animals. As this method proved successful we adopted it for all the other peaks — and there were still seven or eight to come.

On the way we encountered two wretched animals, a mule and a young ass, which had been overcome by hunger and thirst and were struggling in their death throes. I cannot describe the effect this scene had upon me. The sight of these two creatures expiring in such dreadful agony and the sound of their feeble hollow groaning made me sob as bitterly as if I were at the deathbed of two fellow humans. Even the doctor was moved, in spite of his cynicism, for in these abominable places the same fate threatens us all.

As we were toiling up the very last peak, I was forced to undergo one more trial which death, the divinity of the desert, had kept in store for me: a tomb, built right beside the path so that it was impossible to ignore, met my eye. Don Balthazar wanted me to pass quickly by, but an uncontrollable curiosity led me to read the inscription.

It was for a young man of twenty-eight who had died there while on his way to Arequipa. He was already ill when he set out from Islay, where he had been taking the waters, and the fatigue of the journey was too much for him. He died, and the greatest grief there is, the grief of a mother mourning her son, is commemorated there in the desert to add the crowning touch to its horror. For a terrible moment I feared that I too was going to die in the same spot. I thought of my poor daughter and begged her to forgive me for seeking death six thousand miles from my native land. I prayed God to take her under his protection, I forgave all who had done me harm, and I resigned myself to quitting this life. I clung to the tomb, prostrate, unable to move. Once again Don Balthazar was my saviour: he carried me to my mule, fastened me onto its back with his poncho, held me up with his strong arm and transported me, as if by magic, right to the top of the final peak. They laid me down upon the ground and all speaking at once, cried: 'Open your eyes, dear lady, and look at the green countryside! Look at Arequipa, see how beautiful it is! Has France anything as lovely?'

I tried in vain to open my eyes: I was utterly exhausted. We still had a little water left, and they bathed my face, then they rubbed my hands and forehead with rum and gave me oranges to suck, but it was the fresh breeze, more than anything else, that restored me to life. Little by little my strength returned and I was able to open my eyes. Then I looked at the smiling valley and felt so sweet an emotion that I wept, but these were tears of joy. For a long time I lay there: the view made hope spring up again in my heart and I felt my will revive, but my body was still exhausted. I wanted to rise and try to descend the last mountain, but it was impossible for me to stand. This time Don Balthazar decided to take me up behind him; the path was better now, and it was only half an hour's journey to Congata, which we reached at last at two in the afternoon.

Congata is not a village, for it consists of only three or four houses and a fine farm whch also serves as staging-post, inn and general meeting-place for travellers crossing the desert. The owner is called Don Juan Najarra. Don Balthazar told him immediately who I was and how much I needed care and attention. My uncle's name was a powerful recommendation: Senor Najarra, his wife and their numerous servants bustled around me with such energy that in less than ten minutes I was served some very good soup, my boots were removed and my feet, face and hands were washed in warm water and milk. Then I was carried into the little chapel attached to the farm, where a bed had been placed on the floor for me. Madame Najarra, helped by a black maidservant, took off my clothes, dressed me in a fresh white batiste nightgown, carried me to the bed, settled me there with the greatest care, placed a cup of milk beside the bed, then withdrew, closing the door of the chapel as she went.

From the information I had been given in Islay, I judged that my uncle would not return to Arequipa before two months were up, and that I would have to look to other relatives for hospitality, so on the eve of my departure I had written to our cousins, the Bishop of Arequipa and his brother M de Goyeneche. The doctor knew of this and relayed the information to Don Balthazar so that when he arrived in Arequipa he could let the Goyeneche family know of my arrival at Congata and the alarming state of my health. No sooner had Don Balthazar heard all this than he clapped spurs to his horse and shook off in a burst of speed the boredom our slow progress had caused him. For on account of me, he and his cousin had made the greatest sacrifice any Peruvian could make, in resigning themselves to travel so slowly. Had they been alone they would have made the crossing in eighteen hours at the most, whereas we had taken forty.

I rose about six in the evening: my body was bruised

and my feet swollen, but I wanted to take a turn in Senor Najarra's little wood. After two days in the desert, what joy it was to be back in cultivated fields, to hear the murmur of the broad stream which ran beside our path, to see such large and beautiful trees! I was discussing agriculture with Senor Najarra when a negro came to announce the arrival of a visitor, Don Juan de Goyeneche, the first member of the family I had met in person. He made a favourable impression: his manner was extremely gentle and courteous. On behalf of his brother, his sister and himself, he invited me to look upon their house as my own, adding however that my cousin, Don Pio's niece, had told him that she would not hear of my staying anywhere but in my uncle's house, and that on the following day she would send and invite me to come and take possession.

M de Goyeneche was accompanied by a Frenchman, M Durand, who had come on the pretext of acting as interpreter but was in fact a busybody acting out of curiosity. After their departure I retired to my chapel and went to bed in a state of inexpressible happiness.

When I awoke next day I felt completely recovered. Senora Najarra was kind enough to have a bath prepared and sent in for me. I stayed in it for half an hour, then went back to lie between my beautiful embroidered sheets of finest cambric and was served an excellent breakfast.

Towards midday M de Castellac came to bid me make haste to rise, as four horsemen had arrived from Arequipa and wished to be presented to me. As I left the chapel I saw approaching a young man of eighteen or nineteen who bore so strong a resemblance to me that he might have been taken for my brother: this was my cousin Emmanuel de Rivero. He speaks French like a native: he was sent to France at the age of seven and returned only a year ago. We took to each other immediately. His first words to me were: 'My dear cousin, how is it I never knew of your existence until now? I spent four years in Paris all alone without a single friend; you were living in the same city, yet God never allowed me to meet you. What a cruel thought! I am inconsolable!'

Emmanuel brought me a letter from my cousin Dona Carmen Pierola de Florez inviting me on behalf of my uncle Pio to stay at his house, as this was the only place where it befitted me to live. The whole letter was couched in this style, and I saw that I had to do with a woman of character, yet prudent and very politic withal. To carry me to Arequipa my cousin sent me a beautiful horse with a superb English saddle, as well as two riding habits, shoes, gloves and many other articles she thought I might have need of, since I did not have my trunks with me. The three gentlemen who had come with Emmanuel were Senor Arismendi, Senor Rendon and M Durand, all good friends of my cousin Carmen. I talked with them for a while, then left them with the doctor so that I could take a walk with Emmanuel. Through him I learned that my arrival was the talk of the town: everybody was convinced that I had come to claim my father's inheritance. Emmanuel told me something of my uncle's character and position. He too had every reason to complain of harsh treatment, as my uncle had refused to pay him an allowance for the mere three years it would have taken him to complete his studies in France. Emmanuel's father had squandered a huge fortune and reduced his family to poverty. My grandmother had come to the rescue of the children by leaving them an annuity which gave them just enough to live on. My cousin related all his family troubles with affectionate frankness, just as if we had known each other for ten years. For my part, I loved him as I would my brother.

We were anxious to depart, as my cousin had made it clear that she was expecting us for dinner, but our excellent hosts were so insistent that I should have a last meal with them that I accepted gladly, touched by the warmth and concern they had shown on my behalf.

After dinner, towards six in the evening, I left the farm at Congata. Wearing a smart green broadcloth riding habit and a man's hat with a black veil, I rode at the head of the little cavalcade, with the inseparable doctor bringing up the rear. The road from Congata to Arequipa is good compared with the other roads in the country, but it still presents some difficulties to the traveller. Fording the river can be dangerous at certain times of the year. When we crossed there was not much water in it, but the stones in the river bed sometimes cause a horse to slip, and a fall could have fatal consequences. My horse was so fresh that I had a great deal of trouble to control it, but Emmanuel was my squire, and thanks to his attentions I emerged safe and dry. As we left the river behind us I observed well-cultivated fields and hamlets which looked poor and sparsely inhabited.

At Tiavaya we found a large cavalcade coming to meet us, led by my saviour Don Balthazar and his cousin. The other gentlemen were friends of my cousin Carmen and seven or eight Frenchmen resident in Arequipa.

The distance between Congata and Arequipa is about thirteen miles and it was dark when at last we entered the town. I was glad of this because it hid me from being observed: all the same, the noise of our large cavalcade attracted the curious to their doorsteps, but it was too dark for anybody to be recognised. When we came to the street of Santo Domingo I saw a house blazing with light. Emmanuel told me: 'There is your uncle's house!'

A group of slaves stood at the gate; as we approached they hurried inside to announce us. My entry was just like one of those scenes of pomp and ceremony that you see in the theatre. The entire courtyard was lit with resin torches fixed to the walls. The great drawing room occupied the whole of the far side and had a large door in the middle, with a porch forming a vestibule in front of it, approached by a flight of four or five steps. The vestibule was lit with lamps and the drawing room positively blazed with the light from a splendid chandelier and a multitude of candelabra holding candles of every colour. My cousin, who was wearing full evening dress in my honour, came to the top of the steps and received me with all the ceremony prescribed by convention. I dismounted immediately in front of her. I was greatly moved: I took her hand and thanked her with all my heart for everything she had done for me. She conducted me to a large sofa and sat by my side. Hardly was I seated than a deputation of five or six Dominican monks advanced towards me. The Grand Prior of the order made me a long speech extolling the virtues of my grandmother and the magnificent gifts she had made to the monastery. During his harangue I had time to study the people who thronged the room: it was a rather mixed company. I had the impression that the men belonged to a higher rank of society than the women. Each of them presented his compliments in pompous terms together with offers of service so exaggerated that they could not possibly be genuine. I was led to conclude that I should not count on them in an emergency for even the smallest service, and that everything they said was just servile homage addressed to Don Pio in the person of his niece.

My cousin told me that supper had been prepared for me and that we could sit down as soon as I gave the word. But I was tired and did not care to be a magnet for the curious any longer, so I begged my cousin to excuse me from appearing at supper and to permit me to retire to the apartment she had made ready for me. I saw that my request, which my cousin could not refuse, displeased the honourable company exceedingly. I was escorted to a suite of two large and positively shabby rooms in another part of the house. A number of people accompanied me right inside my bedroom, including the monks, who laughingly offered to help me undress. I bade Emmanuel tell my cousin that I wished to be left alone. Everybody retired, and at last, when it was nearly midnight, I succeeded in having my room to myself, with just the little negress I had been given to wait on me.

VIII

Arequipa

— ❧ —

So here I was in the house where my father was born!
This was the house to which I had so often been transported in my childhood dreams, when the presentiment
that I should see it one day had first taken root in my
heart and thereafter had never left it. This presentiment
sprang from the idolatrous love I had borne my father, a
love which still keeps his image alive in my thoughts.

When the little negress was asleep, I could not resist the
impulse to explore the two vaulted chambers in which I
had been lodged. I wondered if my father had ever lived
there, and the idea lent all the charm of the paternal roof
to a place which had chilled my heart with its cold and
gloomy air from the moment I had crossed the threshold.
The furniture in the first room consisted of a massive oak
chest which looked as if it dated from the reign of
Ferdinand and Isabella and must have reached Peru hard
upon the heels of Pizarro and his expedition; a modern
table and a set of chairs in the style which the Duke of
Anjou, Philip IV, introduced into Spain; and a large
English carpet which covered almost the whole of the
floor. The walls were whitewashed and hung with maps.
This room, at least twenty-five feet long and twenty feet
wide, was lit by a single tiny window set high in the wall.
The second room opened off it and was separated from it
by a high partition which, however, stopped short of the
vaulted ceiling. It was much smaller than the other, and
was furnished with a little iron bed hung with white
muslin curtains, an oak table, four old chairs and a faded
Gobelin carpet. The sun never penetrated this suite, which

in its shape and atmosphere was not unlike an underground cave. A profound sadness pervaded my soul as I examined the place my family had allotted me, and I felt some apprehension about my uncle and his avarice. It is easy to judge the master from the behaviour of his dependants. If Dona Carmen had given me such a lodging in my uncle's absence, she must have been quite sure that he would not have assigned me anything better. So that I would not have any doubts on that score, she had told me that the apartment, though inconvenient, was however the only one in the house available for the accommodation of friends and relations. This is characteristic of my uncle. Head of a large family, immensely wealthy, a man whose personal merit and high position bring him into contact with the best his country can provide, yet all he can offer his friends and relations is an icy cavern where you need a light in the middle of the day if you want to read! The thought made me blush for shame, and I was so upset that it was nearly dawn when I fell asleep.

Next day my cousin informed me that in accordance with custom the principal residents of the town were coming to visit me, and that courtesy required my presence in the drawing room at an early hour. But I was feeling too ill and sad to receive so many people, and to tell the truth, the chief reason for my refusal was vanity, as my face and hands were still sunburnt. Thanks to the ointment kind Madame Najarra had given me, the redness was beginning to fade, but I wanted to wait a little longer before presenting myself. The first two days my excuse was accepted, but on the third people began to talk, and M Durand, who knew the Arequipans very well, advised me to make my appearance if I did not wish to lose their goodwill. People are like this in a new country: there is always an element of tyranny in their hospitality. In Islay I had had to stay at the ball until midnight although I was dropping with fatigue; in Arequipa I had to receive the whole town three days after my arrival, although I was still suffering from the effects of the journey and the death of my grandmother. A black gown was hastily made for me and I appeared in my uncle's vast drawing room clad in deep mourning like the rest of the family, my heart even sadder than my garments.

It is the custom in Peru when women of the upper class arrive in a town where they are unknown to stay at home and receive visits for the whole of the first month, after which they return all the visits they have received. My cousin Carmen, who is a stickler for etiquette, told me how I should behave, in the belief that I attached the same importance to convention as she did and would conform to it in every detail; but in this respect the yoke of custom appeared too heavy to me, and I took it upon myself to shake it off. My cousin, who disliked receiving visits as much as I did, applauded the brisk way I dispensed with them, though she was incapable of such boldness herself.

Before I go on with my story, I think I should introduce the reader to my cousin Dona Carmen Pierola de Florez, who would have been between thirty-eight and forty when I met her. If I am to be truthful, I am afraid I have to admit that my poor cousin's ugliness amounts almost to deformity, as her face is cruelly ravaged by smallpox. But it is not God's will that His most disadvantaged creatures should be entirely deprived of charms, for my cousin Carmen has the prettiest feet, not only in Arequipa, but perhaps in all Peru, and what is even more extraordinary, although she is extremely thin, her feet and legs are plump and dimpled. Her coloured stockings are of the finest silk and she wears her skirts very short: she is right to do so, for her feet are too admirable to be hidden away. She is very fond of clothes and dresses with taste, but in a style rather too young for her age.

My cousin has a very remarkable character: she never had an education, but has educated herself and understands everything with admirable intelligence. The poor woman lost her mother when she was a child, and that

was when her misfortunes began. Raised by a strict un-
loving aunt, she was so unhappy that as her only means of
escape was marriage or the cloister, she decided to marry
the son of one of my father's sisters. He had asked for her
hand, drawn by the attraction of a rich dowry. This
cousin was exceptionally good-looking and very agreeable, but he was also a gambler and a rake who squandered his fortune and that of his wife in every kind of
debauchery. The proud Dona Carmen had to suffer every
torture imaginable during the ten years that the marriage
lasted. She loved her husband, but he brutally rejected her
devotion and lived only to gratify his senses. Several times
he left her to live openly with mistresses, and these
women would parade beneath Dona Carmen's window,
staring boldly at her and insulting her to her face. In the
early days of her marriage the young woman ventured to
complain to her husband's family or their mutual friends,
but she was told that she should stop complaining and
think herself lucky to have such a good-looking man for a
husband. People found in the ugliness of the wife and the
beauty of the husband sufficient justification for the
plundering of her fortune and the constant indignities to
which she was subjected. Such is the morality which
proceeds from the indissolubility of marriage! After that
Dona Carmen never uttered a murmur of complaint, but,
adopting an exaggerated view of human wickedness, she
banished all affection from her heart and admitted in its
place only sentiments of hatred or disdain. She sought to
deaden the pain she felt by entering society, and although
she had neither beauty nor wealth, her wit made her the
centre of an admiring circle.

After ten years of marriage, her husband, who was by
then thirty, returned to her. He had dissipated both their
fortunes, was heavily in debt and was afflicted with a
horrible malady that no doctor could identify. She received him, not with affection, for nothing could revive
this sentiment in her heart, but with the secret pleasure

people like her obtain from displaying their superiority in the exercise of a noble vengeance. Her unhappy husband paid dearly for the disorders of his life: he spent sixteen months confined to his bed suffering the cruellest tortures. All that time his wife never left him for a moment: she was his nurse, his doctor and his confessor. She had a couch placed next to his sickbed, and day and night she was there, ready to give him every assistance. She bore with admirable patience the caprices, rebuffs and despairing moods of the dying man. His long illness used up the last of my unfortunate cousin's resources, and after his death she was forced to take her only child, a daughter, and return once more to live with her aunt.

When I arrived in Arequipa she had been a widow for twelve years, leading an uneventful life and hiding her real poverty beneath an appearance of opulence. Six months of every year she spent at her aunt's place, a sugar refinery not far from my uncle's, at Camana. She intensely disliked living in the country, but she had no choice, and it was an unforeseen circumstance which had kept her in town. She and I saw it as an act of Providence, for had she not stayed in Arequipa I would have found nobody to receive me at my uncle's house.

If at first my poor cousin's unprepossessing countenance and dry manner produced a disagreeable effect on me, I soon discovered a kind of nobility and superiority in the depths of her soul which won my sympathy. From the beginning she showed me much affection and it was thanks to her that I learned Spanish so quickly. In the morning she would send for me to breakfast with her, and in the afternoon at about three o'clock I would go and dine with her. She was always intending to invite a few friends as company for me, but I preferred to stay alone with her as I found in her conversation an endless source of information on both people and things.

The day after I arrived in Arequipa I wrote to tell my uncle that I was at his house, that my health did not permit me to go to Camana to see him, and that I awaited his return with the keenest impatience. Two weeks went by and there was no reply. My cousin was as worried as I was: she was afraid my uncle's silence indicated that he disapproved of her behaviour towards me. Don Pio's enemies said he was afraid of me, while his friends said he was preparing a trap for me: some even went so far as to say that he was planning to have me arrested. From morning to night my chamber was full of busybodies telling me of their fears, their counsels, their extravagant plans. I wrote letter after letter: my cousin Carmen, M de Goyeneche and various other people wrote too. Don Pio still made no reply. At that time he was out of favour, which was fortunate for me as it gave me more support. At last, three weeks after my arrival, we received our replies, each one a masterpiece of diplomacy. Mine had the result my uncle probably intended: it was written in such a kindly tone and recalled the services my father had done him with such gratitude, that I believed I could count on his affection and his sense of justice. Every letter he wrote me during the three months I spent waiting for his return was couched in similar vein. In the end I realised that he had deceived me, that his actions bore no relation to his words; and this contradiction revealed to me all that he took so much trouble to hide.

While I was alone in my uncle's house I had no time at all to be bored: I was so busy paying or receiving visits, writing and seeing the sights that my time passed very quickly.

I had arrived in Arequipa on 13 September: on the 18th I experienced my first earthquake. This was the famous one which razed Tacna and Arica to the ground. The first tremor was at six in the morning: it lasted a full *two minutes*. I was nearly flung out of bed, but for a moment I thought I was still on board ship, so I was not frightened. My maid however sprang up immediately crying: '*Senora! temblor! temblor!*' She opened the door and rushed into the courtyard; I dashed after her, throwing my dressing-gown about my shoulders. The tremors were so violent that we had to fling ourselves upon the ground or we would have fallen. Even the bravest would have been panic-stricken to feel the earth shake and see the buildings rock to and fro. The slaves were all down on their knees praying in terror as if their last hour had come.

I returned to my chamber with my cousin right behind me, her features distorted with fear. 'Ah! Florita!' she exclaimed, 'what a dreadful *terremoto*! I'm sure that part of the town is destroyed. One day I shall be buried in the ruins of my poor old house. But you are not used to these things, my dear: sometimes we have three or four tremors in one day, and hardly a week goes by without one. It is because we are so close to the volcano.'

Dona Carmen stayed talking to me: she sat on my bed smoking her *cigaritos* and told me of the countless disasters earthquakes had caused over the years.

Towards seven o'clock there was a rumbling which seemed to issue from the very bowels of the earth. My cousin uttered a cry of fear and rushed from the room. I happened to be staring at a slight crack in the ceiling: suddenly it opened up, dislodging several enormous stones. I thought the entire ceiling was about to collapse on top of me and fled in panic. This tremor was not as strong as the other, so we went back indoors and I returned to bed: I admit I was completely shattered. My cousin sat down again beside me: her expression frightened me. 'Loathsome country!' she cried in a tone of concentrated fury. 'And to think that I am condemned to live in it!'

'If it is so loathsome, cousin, why do you stay?'

'Why, Florita? Because of the harshest of all laws, necessity! If you have no money you are a dependant, a slave, you have to live where your master puts you.'

I looked at her and said with a feeling of superiority

I was unable to hide: 'Cousin, I am poorer than you, but I wanted to come to Arequipa and here I am.'

'And what do you conclude from that?' she demanded in a resentful tone.

'That freedom is really a matter of *will*. Those to whom God has given a will strong enough to overcome every obstacle are free, whereas those whose will is weak and yields to opposition are slaves and would still be slaves even if some freak of fortune placed them upon a throne.'

My cousin did not know what to say: she felt instinctively that I was right, but could not understand what gave me the strength to speak as I did. She looked at me a long time in silence while I watched mechanically as the smoke from her cigar rose in fantastic patterns. Suddenly she got up and said angrily: 'May God forgive me, Florita, but you frighten me too, so where can I find refuge? I dare not go back home for fear that my house will fall on top of me; but by the Holy Virgin, I dare not stay here and listen to you calmly saying things which would make a monk tremble. I think you must be mad.'

'Is that so, dear cousin? Ah, don't be afraid; come and sit beside me, let me hide beneath your mantilla, and then tell me why you think I am mad.'

'Why, dear Florita, because you claim that it is sufficient to have a strong will to be free, yet you, a weak woman, the slave of laws and prejudices, the victim of a thousand ailments and so delicate that you are incapable of resisting the slightest obstacle, you dare to advance such a paradox! Ah! Florita, it is plain to see that you have not been oppressed by a tyrannical husband, dominated by an arrogant family or exposed to the wickedness of men. You are not married, you have no family, you have been free in all your actions, absolute mistress of yourself; you have had no obligations towards society, so you have never been affected by its calumnies. Florita, there are very few women in your fortunate position: most marry very young and their faculties can never develop because they are all oppressed to some extent by their masters. You do not realise how much this secret suffering paralyses the morale of even the most fortunate and gifted women; at least, this is what happens in our backward society. Is it any different for you in Europe?'

'Cousin, there is suffering wherever there is oppression, and there is oppression wherever there is the power to oppress. In Europe women are men's slaves just as they are here, and have to suffer even more from men's tyranny. But in Europe God has given more women the moral strength to free themselves from the yoke.'

I was carried away by my feelings as I spoke and my cousin was astonished at my vehemence.

'Ah! Florita, this time I admire you, you are superb when you are like this! In all my life I have never seen anyone express her feelings with so much warmth. It is generous of you to fly into a passion over the plight of women: they are indeed very wretched. But you cannot really appreciate the depths of misery in which they are condemned to live unless you are, or have been, married. Oh, Florita, marriage is the only hell I acknowledge.'

This conversation aroused such indignation in my heart that I felt myself going crimson and had to hide my head in a corner of Carmen's mantilla while I concentrated all my efforts on recovering my composure. So, I thought to myself, married women here are just as unhappy and oppressed as they are in France, and the intelligence God has given them is doomed to sterility and inertia.

The day after the earthquake I had a crowd of visitors. All the good Arequipans were curious to know my reactions, and many of them looked at me as if to say: I'll wager you don't have anything like this in France!

This earthquake completely destroyed the coastal town of Tacna, including the church, which was new and had been open for only a fortnight. Eighteen people were killed and twenty-five seriously wounded. The town of Arica suffered almost as much. The Sama region and the two departments of Moquegua and Torata were devastated, and at Locumba the ground opened and swallowed up whole houses. In all these places many people were killed or wounded. Arequipa suffered very little: the houses there are so solidly built that only a tremor strong enough to shake the whole of Peru could destroy them. The earthquake was also felt in Lima and Valparaiso but it was too slight to cause any damage.

On 24 September there was a grand procession to celebrate the feast of Our Lady of Ransom. This is the only sort of entertainment the people have, and it gives an idea of what the pagan bacchanals and saturnalia must have been like. Even in the Dark Ages the Catholic church never exposed such scandalous spectacles to the public gaze. The procession was headed by bands of musicians and dancers, all in the most ludicrous costumes: the church hires negroes and *sambos* (persons of mixed negro and Indian blood) for a small sum to take part in this religious farce and dresses them up as pierrots, harlequins and clowns, with crude coloured masks to cover their faces. There must have been forty or fifty of them, writhing and gesticulating in the most shameless and indecent fashion, arousing the excitement of the coloured women and negresses who lined the route and calling out obscenities to them. The women for their part tried to guess the identity of the dancers. This ugly rabble with its shouts and unrestrained laughter made me turn away in disgust. Then the Virgin appeared, magnificently dressed in velvet and pearls, with diamonds on her head, neck and hands. She was carried by twenty or thirty negroes and behind her walked the Bishop and clergy. Next came the monks from all the monasteries, and the official part of the procession ended with the civic dignitaries, followed by a noisy surging mass of people whose minds were far removed from any thought of prayers. It is from these festivals, remarkable for their splendour, that the Peruvians derive their chief happiness, and I fear it will be a

long time before their religion has any spiritual meaning
for them.

In the evening a Mystery play was performed in the
Plaza de la Mercred. I very much regret that I was unable
to obtain the text of this religious drama: to judge from
the little I saw and heard of it, it must be a model of its
kind. Dona Carmen has a passion for any sort of entertainment and persuaded me to accompany her, but it was
impossible to get anywhere near the stage as all the front
rows were taken by women of the lower classes who had
been waiting there since morning. People were fighting
for any little corner from which they could see. I had
never witnessed such enthusiasm. With the help of the
gentlemen who were with us I succeeded in climbing onto
a stone pillar from which I had a good view of the whole
magnificent scene. A rough stage consisting of wooden
planks mounted on barrels had been set up in front of
the church porch; the set was borrowed from the town
theatre and lit by four or five torches. At least, such was
the intention, but the moon came out to compensate for
the parsimony of the organisers, and spread its brilliant
light over Arequipa. It was a novel experience for me, a
child of the nineteenth century newly arrived from Paris,
to see a Mystery play performed before such a huge
audience, but the most instructive spectacle was not the
play but the coarseness, brutality and rags of the people
themselves, whose extreme ignorance and stupid superstition took my imagination back to the Middle Ages. As for
the play, I can say nothing about the beauty of the
dialogue as I could not hear the words distinctly, but in
essence it was like the plays performed in the Palais de
Justice for the edification of the good people of Paris in
the fifteenth century, and which Victor Hugo has brought
to life for us in his *Notre Dame*. With the help of a few
words here and there, together with the gestures of the
actors and explanations given me by connoisseurs of the
art, I succeeded in understanding the plot.

The Christians invade the territory of Islam to fight the Turks and Saracens and bring them back to the *true faith*. The Muslims have the advantage of numbers and put up a stubborn resistance; the Christians make the sign of the cross but look like being defeated for all that, when suddenly Our Lady, leaning on the arm of St Joseph and accompanied by a long line of heavenly maidens, arrives in their camp. This celestial apparition rekindles the enthusiasm of the Christians, who immediately fall upon the Muslims crying: A miracle! A miracle! The moment is propitious, for the Muslims are astounded to see among the enemy all these beautiful girls wearing yellow paper haloes and clad in all the colours of the rainbow, and are afraid of hurting them: in fact I think it is very unfair of the Christians to take advantage of them in this way. In short, the Emperor and the Sultan are beaten and unceremoniously stripped of their regalia. They choose to be Christian kings rather than dethroned potentates, so they beg Our Lady for mercy and have themselves and all their soldiers baptised. I could not help noticing that the glory for this mass conversion belonged far more to the companions of the Holy Virgin than to the soldiers of her Son. Be that as it may, the Virgin appears delighted: she appoints the Sultan Patriarch of Constantinople and the Emperor Archbishop of Mauritania and allows them to keep their temporal power. Both rulers swear upon the crucifix (which is brought in upon a silver salver) that they will pay tithes to the Catholic clergy and Peter's pence to the Pope of Rome. At a signal from the Virgin the choir of young women sing hymns and canticles to which the soldiers — Christians, Saracens and Turks — make the responses at the top of their voices. Then they all turn on the Jews who joined the Muslim army in large numbers to purchase the spoils taken from the Christians. As the Jews refuse to be converted the Christians and the new converts beat them, take their money, steal their clothes and make them dress in rags. This buffoonery was greeted with loud applause.

There follows yet more singing, during which the Sultan and the Emperor are divested of their heathen garments, and the Virgin reclothes them in the priestly robes of their new office. Then Jesus arrives, accompanied by St Matthew, and bestows his blessing on the two armies. A table is set up and all sit down in order of precedence: Jesus Christ, the Holy Virgin, St Joseph, St Matthew, the Christian generals, the Emperor and the Sultan. There are thirteen places, and a Jew who wants a free dinner slips furtively into the thirteenth seat, which is empty. Jesus has broken the bread and passed the cup to the guests when somebody notices the fraud. Immediately the Jew is snatched from his place and hanged (at least, in effigy) by the soldiers. However, the dinner continues and now attention is focused on Jesus, who in a novel version of the miracle of the wedding at Cana, changes the water into Canary wine. In fact a little negro hidden under the table smartly substitutes one for the other, while the choir of virgins sings yet more hymns. Thus ends the farce which I have attempted, no doubt inadequately, to describe.

The people were drunk with excitement: they clapped their hands, jumped for joy and shouted with all their might: Long live Jesus Christ! Long live the Holy Virgin! Long live our noble lord Don Jose! Long live His Holiness the Pope! Viva! Viva!

It is by such means that the people of South America are kept in a state of ignorance. The clergy may have supported the revolution, but they had no intention of giving up their power, and they will keep it for many years to come.

Dona Carmen, whose passion for any kind of spectacle is such that she would be quite capable of going first to church to see Christ crucified (which is always enacted during Holy Week in South America) then to the theatre to applaud the tight-rope performers, then to a cock-fight, all in the same evening: my dear cousin, I say, while she cast a disdainful glance at the common people gathered in the square, had nevertheless enjoyed the scheming of the Virgin and her soldiers as much as they had, though she took good care not to show it. She was loud in her criticism of this *nonsense*, and in her heart she was thoroughly vexed that I had been there to see it.

The Frenchmen with us were content to ridicule the play, and as far as I could see, I was the only one to be upset by it. I have always been keenly interested in the welfare of the different peoples I chance to live among, and I felt genuinely distressed at the degradation of the people here. Their happiness, I told myself, has never counted for anything in the plans of the ruling classes. If the latter had really wanted to organise a republic they would have sought to encourage the growth of the civic virtues at every level of society by means of education; but as power, not liberty, is the goal of the bunch of adventurers who take it in turns to exercise authority, the work of despotism proceeds, and in order to keep the oppressed people in a state of submission, they join hands with the priests to perpetuate superstition and prejudice among them. The country, torn with civil strife for the past twenty years, is in a deplorable condition, and one looks in vain for any hope of a better future towards the class which by virtue of its wealth occupies the first rank of society: all one finds there is the most arrogant presumption joined to the most profound ignorance, expressed in the kind of boastful language which would elicit a pitying smile from the poorest European sailor. No doubt there are exceptions among the Peruvians, but such as there are lament the plight of their country and leave it as soon as they can. True patriotism and devotion are nowhere to be found; only through even greater calamities will the political and moral education of the Peruvians be achieved. Perhaps the ever-increasing poverty will foster the love of work and thereby encourage the social virtues: perhaps once again Providence will raise up a man of iron to complete the work which Bolivar began, and lead them to liberty.

Every Sunday I was obliged to make an elaborate toilet and present myself in the drawing room at ten o'clock and receive visits until three, when dinner was served, then return to the drawing room from five until eleven in the evening. Never have I had a more tedious obligation. The ladies came to show off their finery, the men came for want of something to do, and all wore an expression of permanent boredom. As the country offers no fruitful topics for discussion, conversation is always stilted and monotonous. One is reduced to trading gossip, talking about one's health or the weather. But tedium does not kill curiosity, and I could see that all my visitors were longing to know the reason for my journey. Their caution and reserve, however, made me more careful than I would have thought possible, so that nobody knew a word of my affairs, not even my cousin Carmen, the one person in whose company I felt relaxed.

On 17 October, M Viollier, a Frenchman who worked for M Le Bris, came to tell me that the *Mexicain* had arrived at Islay and that he was going there immediately. He planned to return the following day or the day after with M Chabrié, who wished to visit Arequipa. Since leaving Valparaiso I had hardly dared to think about M Chabrié. The love I could not share, the promise I could not keep, weighed heavily on my heart. I was afraid to consider the consequences: not daring to admit to myself that Chabrié was still alive, I almost wished him dead so that I could shed gentle tears over him. How many sleepless nights I spent vainly trying to suppress my memories! But my thoughts always carried me back to the *Mexicain*: I saw Chabrié bending over me, talking about his hopes of happiness and the bliss which would be ours in California. So when M Viollier told me his news, I blushed and trembled, then went so pale that he could not help asking me if I was annoyed. 'Not at all,' I replied, 'I like Captain Chabrié very much. He has rather an abrupt manner, but he was so considerate to me during my five months of suffering that I am sincerely attached to him.' In spite of my evident agitation M Viollier suspected nothing: indeed, nobody would have believed it possible that I ever spared a thought for M Chabrié or could consent to overlook the enormous defects of his character in favour of the qualities of his heart.

That night and the following day my agitation was extreme. I invoked God's help as I felt my courage fail me. M Chabrié did not come that day, so I had one more night and day in which to strengthen my resolution and prepare myself to receive him. On the Saturday at about eight o'clock I was walking up and down my cousin's drawing room talking philosophy with her, as was our custom, when I saw Chabrié enter! . . . He came up to me, took my hands and kissed them tenderly, while big tears rained down upon them. Fortunately it was dark: my cousin, who was at the other end of the room, could see his gestures but not his tears. I took him to my chamber, where he was unable to restrain his joy, which like his grief expressed itself in tears. He sat beside me, held my hands, buried his head in my lap, touched my hair, and said in tones of love that made every fibre in my body quiver:

'Oh! my Flora! my dear Flora! at last I see you again! My God, how I longed to see you! Speak to me, dearest, I want to hear your voice; tell me you love me, tell me I am not dreaming. Oh! say it, let me hear you say it! Ah! I can't breathe!. . .'

I could not breathe either: an iron chain gripped my breast. I pressed his head against my body, but I could not find a word to say to him. We stayed like this for a long time, then Chabrié broke the silence and said: 'But why are you not weeping, Flora?'

The question made me realise that Chabrié could never understand the depth of my feelings. My silence was a more eloquent proof of my love than tears. . . . He loved me with all his heart, but his heart was very different from mine. I sighed sadly and reflected with some bitterness that it was not my fate to meet on earth an affection in harmony with the affection I felt I could give in exchange.

We did not talk for long: M Viollier came for Chabrié, who was staying with M Le Bris for the six days he was in Arequipa. Both men left: they were exhausted, having made the journey at great speed. M Miota and Fernando had remained in Congata.

Next day, Sunday, I could not say a single word to Chabrié as I was surrounded with people until midnight. He came to see me on Monday and I let him unfold his plans, which were the same as they had been at Valparaiso, except that now he wanted me to marry him immediately, so that everybody would know he was marrying me for love, as I had not yet received any hopeful sign from my uncle. I had not foreseen this new demand, which increased the difficulty of my position. I did not know what to say to him, and I was so worried I nearly went out of my mind.

That evening, as I did not wish to be left alone with him, I took him to a house where there was music-making: he sang to please me, but he was in such a bad humour that everybody noticed it. On Tuesday he showered me with reproaches for having made him lose an evening when we had so little time to settle our affairs. The expenses of the *Mexicain* were about 120 francs a day, of which Chabrié contributed one third. M David wrote me letter after letter begging me to send Chabrié back at once, while that gentleman declared that he would not leave until we were married.

Chabrié's obstinacy put me in the cruellest dilemma I have known in all my life. I used every argument I could think of to make him see reason, but all he said was: 'If you love me, give me proof; if you are happy to marry me, why wait? I shall have to leave you again soon, and in my profession I might die at any time — perhaps I shall never see you again, so why not enjoy life while we can?'

As you can imagine, this made me exert all my influence to make Chabrié realise that our interests as well as our happiness depended on waiting until we had settled our separate affairs before getting married. But I do not know what demon had taken possession of his wits; my words, my prayers, my most emphatic arguments, all were unavailing. Chabrié had been cruelly deceived several times before and this had made him distrustful; besides, jealousy had robbed him of the power to reason.

I spent Wednesday night in the most painful indecision, not that I hesitated to sacrifice my affection for Chabrié to his happiness, but I did not know what reason I could give him for refusing to marry him. I was convinced now that if I told him the truth he would seize upon it as a further reason for hastening our union, so that he could protect me and ensure for me the repose I needed so much. On board I had thought otherwise: I had believed that if I told him I was married, I would drive him away, and perhaps at the time this was true; since then, however, his love had completely taken possession of him. If I was wrong in this supposition, if my marriage proved an obstacle he dared not surmount, then I could not confess it to him without compromising a secret it was important not to divulge; his indignation against me for having made him believe that I was not married would have passed all bounds, as indeed I was later to have proof.

The conviction that if I accepted Chabrié's love I would reduce him to misery and eternal regret at having left his family and his country to exile himself with me on the coast of California restored my courage and made me rack my brains for some means of estranging him from me for ever. I knew he was a man of strict integrity, so this was where I decided to attack him. Ah! I had need of God's help to pursue such a plan, for its execution demanded superhuman strength; in undertaking to make Chabrié renounce his love, I risked losing his esteem as well as his love, and these had been my sole consolation for eight months. Well, then! I had the necessary courage, but only God knew the magnitude of my sacrifice.

On Thursday evening Chabrié hurried to see me, as I had promised him the previous day that I would give him a definite answer, so the moment he entered he asked me what was to be his fate.

'M Chabrié, this is my decision: if you love me as much as you say, prove it to me by doing as I ask. You know that my certificate of baptism is not sufficient proof of my legitimacy; I must have another document confirming that my mother was married to my father; if I cannot produce it my uncle will not give me a penny. Well, you can give me a million. Undertake to obtain a marriage certificate for me from some old missionary in California: we can antedate it, and for a hundred piastres we shall gain a million. On this condition I give you my heart and my hand.'

The poor man sat dumbfounded, his elbow resting on the table. He looked at me without speaking, like an innocent man who has suddenly been condemned to execution. I paced up and down the room seeking to avoid his glance, suffering a thousand deaths at the agony I was causing a man for whom I felt the tenderest affection. At last he said in a tone of profound indignation:

'So, when I want to marry you as you are now, with no money, and with a child; when I am ready to give up everything for you, everything, you set conditions on your love . . . and what conditions!'

'Do you hesitate, M Chabrié?'

'Hesitate, mademoiselle? Oh no! as long as this old heart beats in my breast, I shall never hesitate between honour and infamy.'

'But where is the infamy in my proposal, monsieur,

when I ask you to help me recover what in all justice belongs to me?'

'I am not the judge of your rights. You want to make me your instrument, to serve you in your ambitious plans: this is how you repay my love . . .'

'If you loved me, M Chabrié, you would not hesitate a moment to do what I ask, and you refuse me.'

'But Flora, my dear Flora, do you know what you are saying? Is there a fever burning in your brain, or has ambition made you forget everything else? You are asking me to do something dishonourable: ah, Flora, I love you so much that I would sacrifice my life for you; with you, I would endure poverty and never complain, but do not ask me to debase myself, for by the love I bear you, I will never consent to such a thing.'

This was exactly the response I expected from him! With such a man I could have lived in the middle of a desert and still been blissfully happy! What delicacy! What love! I felt my defences crumbling; I made one last effort, and adopting a tone of scathing irony I proceeded to inflict further torture on a self-esteem which my proposal had already pierced to the depths. Chabrié became so angry that he overwhelmed me with the most bitter reproaches, the most terrible maledictions, and finally abandoned himself so completely to the violence of the grief which this latest betrayal had caused him that for a moment I thought he would do me some injury.

At last he left me, and I collapsed, utterly exhausted. I never saw him again. His last words to me were: 'I hate you as much as I loved you. . . .'

It had become so urgent to make Chabrié stop pursuing me, to put an end to his love, that I made him my strange proposal for want of a better, without stopping to consider that it was really too implausible for me to hope that Chabrié would take it seriously. Afterwards I wondered how he could have thought me so lacking in common-sense as to imagine it would be possible to regularise my mother's marriage by means of a certificate forged in California. If I had been capable of resorting to forgery, surely I would have conceived the idea in Europe, not in Arequipa. Was it not impossible to carry out in any case? Where in California could one expect to find a priest who might once have been attached to a church in one of the towns on the Spanish border where my mother had lived? And how could anyone supply the necessary legal formalities, stamps, and so on? Only in Spain would such a plan have any chance of success. If Chabrié had been calm enough to think for ten minutes, he would easily have seen that this was just a subterfuge on my part, a pretext for severing our relationship; but he was so violently agitated that he was not amenable to reason.

He left next day for Islay. Before leaving Arequipa he wrote me a letter containing these words: 'I tell you once more, so that your last hours may be peaceful, your daughter will find in me a *friend* who will teach her to love her mother's memory.' This assurance made me feel very secure. The letters I wrote to Chabrié after our rupture confirmed him in this frame of mind. Six weeks after his departure from Arequipa he left Lima for California and I had no more news of him until his return to France, three months after mine.

The origin of the town of Arequipa is shrouded in myth; however, in Cuzco there is a chronicle containing traditional Indian lore which states that in about the twelfth century of our era, Maita-Capae, ruler of the City of the Sun, was driven from his throne and wandered in his flight through forests and over mountain peaks with only a few companions. On the fourth day, tormented by fatigue, hunger and thirst, he halted at the foot of a volcano. Suddenly, yielding to a divine inspiration, he planted his spear in the ground and cried: *Arequipa*, which in the *Quichua* language means: *Here I stop*. Then he turned and saw that only five of his companions had followed him; nevertheless he put his trust in the word of his God and stood by his resolve. Around his spear, on the flanks of a volcano surrounded on all sides by desert, men built their dwellings.

Although Arequipa is sixteen degrees south of the Equator, it has a temperate climate because of its height above sea level and its proximity to the mountains which enclose it. It is situated in a tiny valley of ravishing beauty which cannot be more than five miles long and three miles wide and is watered by the river *Chile* which rises at the very foot of the volcano. The noise of the river in its course recalls the Gave in the Pyrenees, but it has a curious feature: its bed is wide in some places yet very narrow in others, and while it consists for the most part of huge jagged stones or shingle sometimes it reveals a stretch of sand smooth enough for the feet of a young girl to walk upon. The Chile is a raging torrent in the rainy season but nearly alway dries up in summer. Wheat, maize, barley, alfalfa and vegetables are cultivated in the valley. There are few country mansions though: in Peru people are too busy plotting to want to live in the country.

The town occupies an extensive site which from the heights of Tiavaya looks larger still; up there only a narrow strip of land seems to separate the town from the foot of the mountains; up there the mass of white houses, the multitude of domes gleaming in the sun against the various greens of the valley and the uniform grey of the mountains produce on the spectator an effect he would have thought beyond the power of earthly things to convey.

The volcano of Arequipa is one of the highest mountains in the chain of the Cordilleras; it is completely isolated, and perfectly conical in shape. Its unrelieved greyness gives it a gloomy air, its summit is nearly always covered with snow. Sometimes it emits smoke, particularly in the evening, and I have often seen flames mingled with the smoke. When there has been no smoke for a long time, the people expect an earthquake. My cousin Althaus has climbed to the summit of the volcano, visited its crater, and descended as far as the third chimney. He has some notes and some extraordinary drawings about this expedition, and I am sorry I cannot pass them on to the reader. He made the ascent with ten Indians armed with hooks. Only five were strong enough to follow him to the top: three dropped out on the way and two fell to their death. It took three days to reach the summit and they could stay there only a few hours as the cold was so intense. The descent was even more difficult: none of them escaped serious injury and Althaus was very nearly killed. The volcano (it is known by no other name) is 12,000 feet above sea level, and its nearest neighbours, which stand some distance away, one on either side, are more gigantic still. One is called *Pichain-Pichu* and the other *Chachaur*: both are now extinct.

When Francisco Pizarro discovered Arequipa he made it one of the seats of government and established a bishopric there. At various times earthquakes have been the cause of appalling disasters: those of 1582 and 1600 almost completely destroyed the town, and those of 1687 and 1785 were hardly less serious.

Arequipa has wide and well-paved streets which intersect at right angles. Each has a gutter running down the middle, and the principal streets have pavements made of large white flagstones. When Don Pio was Prefect he had several new pavements made and the old ones repaired. The streets are quite well lit as every householder has to put a lantern outside his door, on pain of a fine. The town square is spacious: the cathedral occupies the north side, the town hall and the military prison are opposite, and large private houses stand on the other two sides. With the exception of the cathedral, all these buildings have arcades which contain shops of various kinds. The square is used for markets, festivals, parades, and so on. The bridge over the river Chile is a crude construction which does not look strong enough to withstand the torrent which rushes beneath it at certain seasons of the year.

Arequipa contains many convents and monasteries, all of which possess very beautiful churches. The cathedral is vast, but it is dark and ponderous in style; Santa-Rosa, Santa-Catalina and Santo Francisco are remarkable for the prodigious height and beauty of their domes. In all the churches there are grotesque wood or plaster figures representing the idols of Peruvian Catholicism, with perhaps a few paintings so crudely executed as to make the saints they represent look indescribably ludicrous. In this respect the Jesuits' church is an exception, for here the faithful can offer up their prayers to a more decorous collection of saints. Before Independence, all these churches were richly furnished with candlesticks, railings and altarpieces of solid silver and ornaments of gold, both metals used with more extravagance than taste. But religious faith no longer protects these treasures: already several presidents and party leaders, having in their quarrels emptied the coffers of the republic, have not scrupled to despoil the churches and melt down their treasures to pay the soldiers and gratify the vices of the generals. The precious ornaments which have so far been respected may yet suffer the same fate: during the recent war between Orbegoso and Bermudez there was talk of robbing the statues of the Virgin of their jewels.

Arequipa has a hospital, a madhouse and an orphanage, all three, for the most part, very badly maintained. I shall have occasion elsewhere to speak of my visit to the hospital. I also visited the foundlings and was no happier with the treatment they receive than I was with the care of the sick. It is pitiful to see these poor little creatures, naked, thin, in a deplorable state. The obligations of charity are thought to be satisfied if the children are given just enough to sustain their miserable existence; what is more, they receive no education or training, so any who survive become beggars, the inevitable consequence of this criminal neglect. The way these unfortunate victims gain admission to the hospice struck me as rather ingenious: it is a box shaped like a cradle, accessible from the outside, so the wretched mother can abandon her child without being obliged to show herself to anyone within — a dispensation which often leads to crime.

The houses, solidly built in fine white stone, have only one storey, because of earthquakes, and the ceilings are vaulted. They are in general spacious and commodious; they have a wide gateway in the middle of the facade, and all the windows are barred and unglazed. Houses are built with three courtyards: the first contains the main reception room, the bedrooms and offices, the second, where the garden is, contains the dining room (an open gallery appropriate to the climate), the chapel, the wash-house and various storerooms, and the third, at the back, contains the kitchen and the slaves' quarters. The walls of the houses are between five and six feet thick, and the rooms, despite their vaulted ceilings, are very lofty: a few are papered half-way up, but the rest are bare and white-washed. This vaulting makes the rooms resemble cellars, and their unrelieved whiteness is monotonous. The furniture is massive: beds, chests, tables, chairs, seem made to stay for ever in one place. The mirrors have metal frames, the hangings lack taste. English carpets have been so cheap for some years that everybody covers the floor with them; not one room has a wooden floor.

The Arequipans are very fond of food yet they do not cultivate the pleasures of eating. Their cuisine is detestable: the food is bad and the culinary art is still primitive. The valley of Arequipa is very fertile, yet the vegetables are poor. The potatoes are not floury, the cabbages, lettuce and peas are hard and tasteless. The meat is dry, and the poultry is as tough as if it had come out of the volcano. Butter and cheese are brought from a distance and never arrive fresh: the same is true of fruit and fish, which come from the coast. The oil used for cooking is rancid, the sugar unrefined, the bread heavy: in short, nothing is good.

This is the sort of thing they eat: breakfast is at nine and consists of rice with onions (they put onions, raw or cooked, in everything) and roast mutton so unappetising that I could never eat it, then chocolate. For dinner at three o'clock they have *olla podrida* (which is known as *puchero* in Peru). This is a conglomeration of ill-assorted ingredients: beef, fat pork and mutton boiled with rice, seven or eight kinds of vegetables and all the fruit that comes to hand — apples, pears, peaches, plums, grapes, and so on. The sight, smell and taste of this barbarous concoction is as offensive as an orchestra playing out of tune. Next come crayfish served with tomatoes, rice, raw onion and pimento; various kinds of meat with grapes, peaches and sugar; fish with pimento; salad with raw onion, eggs and pimento, the latter being used in all their dishes, together with a number of other spices which burn your mouth. Only a totally insensitive palate could endure them. Water is the usual drink. Supper is at eight and consists of the same sort of dishes as dinner.

There is as little feeling for refinement at table as there is for refinement in the culinary arts. In many households today there is still only *one glass* for all the company, and the plates and cutlery are dirty. This is not just the fault of the slaves: like master, like servant. The slaves of English masters are very clean. It is good form to select a choice morsel from your own plate and have it passed on the end of a fork to a favoured guest. The Europeans were so disgusted by this custom that it is falling into disuse. But one is not often invited out to dinner as everything is so expensive, and it is now the fashion to invite people to evening parties. Every Sunday there was a family dinner at my uncle's to which close friends were invited, and in the evening tea, chocolate and cakes were served. The only things I really enjoyed in Arequipa were the cakes and other dainties made by the nuns; thanks to my numerous relations I never ran out of them all the time I was there, so I was able to partake of some delicious little snacks.

The Arequipans are very fond of all kinds of spectacles and flock to them with equal enthusiasm whether they are theatrical or religious. They need such diversions because of their total lack of education, which also makes them very easy to please. The theatre is made of wood and so badly built that it lets in the rain; it is too small for the population, so often one cannot get in. In any case the company is very bad: it consists of seven or eight actors, rejects from the theatres in Spain, supported by two or three Indians. They perform every kind of piece: comedies, tragedies, operas. They mutilate Lope de Vega and Calderon and murder music so that it sets your nerves on edge, all to the applause of the audience. I went to this theatre four or five times: they were playing tragedy, and I observed that for want of proper cloaks the actors were draped in old silk shawls.

Cock-fights, tight-rope dancers, Indians performing feats of strength: all these spectacles draw the crowds. One French acrobat and his wife made *thirty thousand piastres* in Peru.

The Peruvian church exploits popular taste to increase its hold over the people. Quite apart from the great processions which mark all the solemn festivals, not a month goes by without some sort of spectacle in the streets of Arequipa. Sometimes it is the Franciscans going round in the evening collecting for the dead, sometimes it is the Dominicans parading in honour of the Virgin; next comes a procession for the Infant Jesus, then it is the turn of all the saints — it is never ending. I have already described one of them, so I will not weary the reader with another. The processions for the saints are not as grand, but they are just as grotesque, and the indecent antics which so delight the people are every whit as scandalous. All have one thing in common: the good monks always ask for money, and the people always give it.

It is during Holy Week that the wildest orgies of Peruvian Catholicism take place. In every church in Arequipa they make a great pile of earth and stones and plant it with olive branches to represent Calvary. Here on Good Friday they enact the Passion of Our Lord, his arrest, flagellation and crucifixion, to the accompaniment of continual chanting. At the moment of Christ's death, the candles are extinguished; darkness reigns, and it is easy to imagine what goes on in every corner of the crowded church, given the loose morals of the populace ... but God is merciful, He has given his ministers the monks power to grant absolution. The second scene is the descent from the cross: a mob of men and women, white, black and brown, rush upon the hill uttering heart-rending cries; they uproot the trees, scatter the stones and expel the soldiers, then they seize the cross and take down the body; blood pours from the cardboard Christ and the howling of the mob redoubles. The people, the priests, the cross, the olive branches: all these together create a scene of utter chaos you would never expect to find in any place of worship, and which nearly always ends in people getting hurt, sometimes seriously.

In the evening the people throng the streets on their way to church to make the stations of the cross, intoning prayers as they go. The more devout fall upon their knees and kiss the earth; others beat their breasts or pile rags upon their heads; some go barefoot carrying the cross on their backs, others stagger beneath the weight of paving stones. In every house superstitious zeal spurs these fanatics to even greater follies. They look for guidance to the supernatural, never to their own conscience.

At mass on Sundays the men remain standing and talk and laugh among themselves, or stare at the pretty women on their knees in front of them, half-hidden in their mantillas. The women themselves are easily distracted from the service; they never have a prayer book. Sometimes they examine what their neighbour is wearing, or speak to their black maidservants stationed behind them.

Sometimes they can even be seen lying on their mat, sleeping or making conversation.

The monks who conduct the mass are invariably shabby; the poor Indians who help them are barefoot and half naked. The music is always frightful: there are two violins and a kind of bagpipe as well as the organ, and they are all so out of tune, and the singing they accompany is so ragged, that it is impossible to stay a quarter of an hour without feeling irritable all day. At least in Europe the fine arts lend lustre to the sterility of the ritual. But in Peru the church is just a meeting-place and very little else.

All things reflect the degree of civilisation a people has attained. In Arequipa the amusements of Carnival are no more decent than the farcical antics of Holy Week. Some people make a living all the year by blowing eggs. At Carnival time they fill the shells with paints of different colours — pink, blue, green, red — and seal the opening with wax. Ladies dress themselves all in white, fill a basket with these eggs, and sit on the roofs of their houses throwing them at the passers-by. The latter, whether on foot or horseback, are armed with the same missiles and retaliate: but to make the game more fun, the eggs can be filled with ink, honey, oil, or other quite disgusting things. Several people have lost an eye in this novel form of combat: I had two or three pointed out to me, but in spite of these examples the Arequipans preserve a passionate enthusiasm for the sport. Young women display the numerous stains on their dresses and are proud of these strange marks of gallantry. The slaves too share in the fun: they throw flour at each other, as this is more economical — in fact many other people do the same. In the evening everybody goes off to balls where the most indecent dances are performed. Many people are in bizarre fancy dress, but there is nothing particularly Peruvian about their costumes. These entertainments continue for a whole week.

The population of Arequipa, including the suburbs, is

between thirty and forty thousand people, about a quarter of them white, a quarter black or half-caste, and half Indian. In Peru, as in the whole of South America, European origin is the supreme *title of nobility*; in aristocratic parlance, 'white' means anyone with no negro or Indian ascendants, and I saw several ladies who passed as white, although their skin was the colour of gingerbread, because their fathers were born in Andalusia or Valencia. So the free population forms three classes drawn from three distinct races: European, Indian, Negro, the last-named including half-castes from all three and known as *coloured*. As for the slaves, whatever their race, the loss of their liberty makes them all equal in misfortune.

In the past four or five years there have been many changes in the customs and habits of Peru. Nowadays the influence of Paris is paramount, and only a handful of rich and ancient families refuse to accept its rule: withered old trees which survive, like the cells of the Inquisition, only to show how far society has progressed. The costume of the upper classes is no different from that in Europe; men and women dress the same as they do in Paris. Ladies follow fashion in the strictest detail, save that they go bareheaded, and that, in obedience to custom, they resume the full severity of Spanish costume, including the mantilla, when they go to church. French dances are replacing the fandango, the bolero and the native dances which decency condemns. The vocal scores of our operas are sung in every drawing-room, and people have even started to read novels. In a little while they will stop going to mass unless they can listen to good music. People in easy circumstances spend their time in smoking, reading the newspapers and playing faro. The men ruin themselves gambling, the women in buying clothes.

In general the Arequipans have an abundance of natural wit, a great facility for expressing themselves, a good memory, a happy disposition, noble manners; they take life as it comes and are born intriguers. The women, like the women of Lima, struck me as being far superior to the men; they are not as pretty as their sisters in Lima, they have different ways, and their character is different too. Their proud and dignified manner is impressive, and at first sight you might think them cold, but when you know them better, their subtle minds and refined sentiments, enshrined in that grave exterior, acquire a new value and impress you all the more. Unlike the ladies of Lima, whose zest for intrigue and pleasure impels them to go out all the time, they stay quietly at home and keep themselves busy. They make their own clothes and achieve a perfection which would astonish our French milliners. They dance with grace and decorum, love music and are often accomplished performers: I know four or five whose fresh melodious voices would be admired in any Paris drawing-room.

The climate of Arequipa is not healthy: headache, dysentery, nervous complaints and above all, colds, are very common. The inhabitants also suffer from the delusion that they are always ill. This is the excuse they make for their perpetual travelling: it is their restless imagination, combined with their lack of education, that accounts for this passion for movement. Only a change of scene can give them food for thought, new ideas, fresh emotions. The ladies in particular come and go between the coastal villages like Islay, Camara and Arica, where they bathe in the sea, and the mineral springs, of which there are several in the vicinity of Arequipa renowned for their properties, especially the springs at Ura, where the water is green and scalding hot. Nothing could be dirtier or more uncomfortable than these resorts where the upper classes go to take the waters, yet they are very popular, and people are willing to spend a great deal of money to stay three weeks or a month at one of them.

The women of Arequipa seize eagerly upon any occasion for travel, no matter whether it is to Cuzco or Lima, Bolivia or Chile, and no amount of expense or fatigue can deter them. It is to this taste for travel that I am tempted to attribute the preference young women give to foreigners. By marrying a foreigner they hope to realise a cherished dream and see the country where he was born, France, Italy or England; and this prospect lends such unions a charm they might otherwise not have possessed. The idea of travel makes the French language much in vogue among the ladies; many learn it in the hope that they may need it some day. In the meantime they derive much pleasure from reading some of our good books, and the development of their intelligence compensates for the monotony of the life the country has to offer. Every well-bred man knows French as well.

The *Pantheon*, a beautiful cemetery of recent construction five miles from the town, occupies a vast site on the slope of a hill facing the volcano. From a distance nothing could be more melancholy and bizarre than the appearance of the high, white, jagged walls which surround it. Inside, three rows of niches have been hewn out of the thickness of the walls; the coffin is placed inside one of these niches and the opening sealed with a stone, upon which is engraved in letters of gold, upon plaques of marble or bronze, an inscription to commemorate the *illustrious marshal*, the *celebrated general*, the *venerable curé*, and so on. Elsewhere more modest epitaphs enumerate the many virtues of the dead, for like every other cemetery in the world, this one contains none but good fathers, beloved wives, loving mothers, etc. Thus the intense feeling of the moment dictates our words, and we exaggerate in the dead the virtues we failed to recognise in the living. The poor lie in a common grave which is sealed in the same way when it is full. As for the Protestants, they are not allowed to be buried here. It is only a few years since they stopped burying people in the churches: some Arequipans are unhappy about this and buy a place in one of the convent churches at enormous expense. This is how it happens that my grandmother's tomb is in Santo-Domingo; with money one can dispense as easily

with the requirements of the law in this country as with
the requirements of religion; the latter however are less
expensive.

When well-to-do people die in Arequipa, it is not only
their heirs who rejoice but the monks as well, as they
profit from the occasion to sell their habits at high prices
to shroud the corpse. It is considered good form to be
buried in a monk's habit, so the good brethren nearly
always possess new habits which form a striking contrast
with the rest of their costume. Immediately after death the
body, no matter what its sex, is clothed in one of these
habits and laid on the deathbed, with the face uncovered,
for three days, during which visits of condolence are paid.
The most distant relations act as chief mourners: that is to
say, they stay in the chamber and receive the visitors, all
of them in mourning, who as they enter greet the assembled relatives on their dais with due solemnity, then retire
to a corner or pray beside the corpse. Bearers carry the
body to church, and likewise, after the ceremony, they
take it outside the town, whence it is conveyed to the
cemetery on a cart.

There are no carriages in Arequipa: in former times
important people were carried around in sedan chairs.
There was one at my uncle's which my grandmother used,
and which my uncle still uses when he is unwell. It is like
the chairs they had in France before the Revolution
Nowadays everybody goes by horse or mule; donkeys are
used only to carry loads in the mountains, where the
Indians use llamas.

The llama is the beast of burden of the Cordilleras, and
the Indians use it to trade with the valleys. This graceful
animal is very interesting to study. Of all the animals to
have had dealings with man, it is the only one he has
never been able to debase. The llama will not consent to
being beaten or maltreated. It will make itself useful only
on condition that it is *asked* and never *ordered*. Llamas
always travel in flocks and the Indian who leads them

walks a long way in front. If they feel tired, they stop, and so does he. If the halt is prolonged, the anxious Indian, seeing the sun declining, at last decides to beg them to go on. He takes up his position fifty or sixty paces away, adopts a humble attitude, stretches out his hands affectionately towards them and gazes tenderly at them, meanwhile uttering in the softest voice imaginable and with a patience I never wearied of admiring: ic-ic-ic-ic-ic-ic. If the llamas feel inclined to resume their journey, they follow the Indian in good order and at a steady pace, covering the ground quickly as they have long legs. But when they are in a bad humour they do not even turn their heads in the direction of the voice so patiently and lovingly calling them. They remain motionless, packed close together, some standing, some lying, looking at the sky so tenderly and sadly that one would really believe these astonishing animals were conscious of another life, a better existence. Their long majestic necks, shining silky coats and timid supple movements give them an expression of nobility and sensitivity which commands respect. This must be so, as the llama is the only animal in the service of man which he dares not strike. If by some rare chance an Indian is angry and tries to obtain from the llama by force or the threat of force what the creature is unwilling to do of its own free will, the moment it realises that it has been treated roughly, it raises its head with dignity, and making no attempt to run away (for the llama is never tethered or hobbled) it lies down and turns its gaze towards the sky; big tears fall in abundance from its beautiful eyes, sighs issue from its breast, and in the space of half an hour or three-quarters of an hour at the most it expires. Happy creatures, who seem to accept life only on condition that it be sweet!

As llamas offer the only means of communication with the Indians of the mountains, they are very important for trade, but one is tempted to think that the almost superstitious reverence in which they are held is due to something more than a sense of their usefulness. I some-times saw twenty or thirty of them blocking one of the busiest streets in the town; everybody who came by would give them a timid glance and then retrace their steps. One day about twenty came into our courtyard and stayed there for *six hours*; their Indian was in despair and our slaves were unable to get on with their work, but no matter, everybody put up with the inconvenience these animals caused, and nobody dreamed of casting an angry glance in their direction. Even the children, who have no respect for anything, *dared not touch the llamas*.

When the Indians want to load their llamas, two of them approach the animal, stroke it and cover its head so that it will not see them place the burden on its back; if it were to notice, it would drop dead on the spot; they have to do the same when they unload it. Should the load exceed a certain weight, the animal would immediately throw itself upon the ground and expire. These animals are very frugal: a handful of maize lasts them three or four days. Yet they are very strong, climb nimbly up the mountains, endure cold, snow, and every kind of fatigue. They live for a long time: an Indian told me he had one that was thirty-four years old. No other man save the Indian of the Cordilleras would have enough patience or gentleness to make use of llamas. It is doubtless from this extraordinary companion Providence has given the Peru-vian native that he has learned to die when asked to do more than he is willing to perform. The moral strength necessary to escape oppression through death, so rare in our species, is very common among the Indians of Peru, as I shall often have occasion to remark.

The reader can hardly have failed to perceive that life in Arequipa is extremely boring. It was especially so for me, as I am so active; I could not reconcile myself to the monotony. Only at the house of M Le Bris did I find any distractions. Every time a stranger arrived in Arequipa he would send me a brief description and ask me if I wished to meet him. But then there arrived from Lima one of my cousins by marriage, M d'Althaus, the most unusual man I have ever met in all my life. From our very first meeting we were friends. Althaus is German, but speaks French to perfection, having spent a good part of his life in France. He has been a soldier since the age of seventeen, serving as an officer of engineers in both the French and Allied armies. In his eyes soldiering is the only profession worth considering; he loves war for its own sake and joins whichever side he judges the more skilled.

After the events of 1815 he remained in the service of Germany; he had a high rank and good pay, but peace did not suit him, he needed the opportunity to exercise his art, so he resigned his commission, left his family (who loved him dearly) and like a true adventurer came to Peru in search of combat. There he had remained for fourteen years, taking part in every engagement without suffering a single scratch.

In 1825 Althaus came to Arequipa as a member of Bolivar's staff and stayed with my uncle Pio whom he knew well. There he met my cousin Manuela de Florez, the orphan daughter of one of my father's sisters. He fell in love with her, gained her love in return, and after some demur obtained consent to the match from my uncle, who was her guardian. Althaus married my cousin in 1826. At the time of my visit they had three children, two sons and a daughter.

Althaus was careful to avoid speaking to me about the purpose of my journey, preferring to leave such matters to Don Pio, who had long been accustomed to dealing with all the affairs of the family. He had administered my grandmother's estate for forty years, and when the time came to divide her property, Althaus, simple soldier that he was and little versed in such matters, was no match for my uncle. He came off badly, complaining among other things that all the best land of the Camana estate went to my uncle, while the worst was left for Manuela and the daughter of my cousin Carmen.

My uncle had by now left Camana and gone to Islay to take the waters. It was quite clear to me that he was delaying his return to Arequipa in order to show me that he was not afraid of me. For three months I had been staying in his house and waiting for him. At last he announced that he was leaving Islay and invited me to come and meet him, if this was convenient for me, at his country house, where he planned to break the journey.

So at last I was going to meet this uncle upon whom rested all my hopes, the man who owed everything to my father: his education, his advancement, and all his subsequent success. What sort of welcome would he give me? What would I feel when I saw him? My heart beat violently at the thought: I had lavished so much love upon him in my youth, I had suffered so much when my mother told me he had abandoned me, that I could never think of him without feeling the keenest emotion.

On 3 January 1834 at about four in the afternoon I set out on horseback accompanied by my dear cousin Emmanuel, kind M Viollier and Althaus, my three closest friends, and followed by a crowd of people who had come out of curiosity rather than concern for me or respect for Don Pio. Our destination was the lovely country house which my uncle always refers to as his *chacra*, the local word for a simple hut, and which is situated about four miles from the town. As we drew near the house, Emmanuel and Althaus galloped ahead to announce me. Soon afterwards I saw a horseman approaching at full speed; I cried out: 'There is my uncle!' I set spurs to my horse and in a moment I was at his side. What I felt then is difficult to put into words. I took his hand, and pressing it lovingly I said: 'Oh, uncle, how I need your affection!' 'My daughter, it is all yours: I love you like my own child; you are more like my sister, for your father was a father to me. Ah! my dear niece, how happy I am to see you, to look upon your features which are so like my brother's.' He drew me towards him, I leaned my head against his chest, at the risk of falling off my horse, and stayed thus for quite a long time. My face was wet with tears when I withdrew; were they tears of joy or sorrow? I do not know. My emotions were too strong and too confused for me to analyse the exact cause. The other gentlemen joined us, I dried my tears, made an effort to regain my composure, and we went on without speaking. As we entered the courtyard, my aunt, who is also my cousin, as she is Manuela's sister, came up and welcomed me graciously enough, yet I thought I detected a great coldness in her heart. I kissed her three daughters and her son, and all four struck me as being equally cold. My cousin Manuela was quite different: she threw herself into my arms, kissed me tenderly, and with tearful eyes and trembling voice she said, 'Ah! cousin, how long I have waited to see you! Ever since I learned of your existence I have loved you; I admire your courage and I weep for your sorrows!'

We stayed in the country for nearly two hours. I walked in the garden with my uncle and never tired of listening to him: he speaks the most beautiful French and I was enchanted by his wit and kindness.

Towards seven o'clock we set out for Arequipa. My uncle rode his lovely spirited Chilean mare; the skill and grace with which he handled her showed that he had learned to ride in Andalusia. Once again I was at the head of this large cavalcade, and my uncle, on my right, kept up a constant flow of friendly conversation.

When we reached the house we found my cousin Carmen busy looking after all the visitors who had come to welcome Don Pio and his family home. She had had a splendid supper prepared, to which my aunt invited the whole company. Some accepted; the rest remained to smoke and chat. I stayed a long time with my uncle: his conversation had an irresistible attraction for me.

However, we had to retire for the night, and although it was so late, I could hardly bear to drag myself away. My uncle had bewitched me, and while I enjoyed the happiness of being near him, I did not dare to reflect on what awaited me at his hands, I was so completely under his spell.

IX

Don Pio de Tristan and his family

My uncle does not look European: like everything else in nature, he has come under the influence of the sun and the climate. Yet our family is of pure Spanish blood, and, what is most remarkable, all its numerous members look alike. All, that is, except my cousin Manuela and my uncle, and they are totally different. Don Pio is only five feet tall, slender and fine-boned, but with a very strong constitution. He has a small head and his hair has hardly started to turn grey. His skin is sallow, his features delicate and regular, his eyes blue and sparkling with wit. He has all the agility of the inhabitant of the Cordilleras: he was sixty-four at the time, yet more active and nimble than a Frenchman of twenty-five. From behind you would take him for thirty, and from the front, forty-five at the most. He combines the grace of the Frenchman with the obstinacy and cunning peculiar to the mountain-dweller. He has an extraordinary memory and there is nothing he does not grasp with amazing facility. His manner is mild, friendly and full of charm; his conversation is lively, and if sometimes he permits himself a pleasantry, it is always in good taste. This attractive exterior is all of a piece: everything he says and does, right down to the way he smokes his cigar, reveals the man of distinction whose education has been exceptionally thorough; and it is surprising to find so finished a courtier in the military man who has spent twenty-five years of his life among soldiers. My uncle has the rare gift of speaking to each individual in language he can understand, and people are so fascinated by the charm of his conversation that any grievance they might have against him is quite forgotten.

But to all these brilliant qualities, which make Don Pio de Tristan one of the select few ordained by Providence to lead others, must be added one overriding passion which even his ambition is powerless to subdue, and that is avarice. Avarice is responsible for his cruellest actions, and his efforts to conceal so unworthy a failing sometimes force him to act in a very generous manner. This may confuse chance observers, but it cannot deceive those who know him best.

It was not long after his return from Spain that my uncle married his niece, Manuela's sister. My aunt is called Joaquina de Florez; she must without a doubt have been the most beautiful woman in all the family. When I met her she would have been about forty and still very good-looking; her numerous pregnancies (she had had eleven children) rather than the passage of time had caused her beauty to fade. Her big black eyes are admirable for their shape and expression, and her smooth golden skin and teeth as white as pearls give her a very striking appearance. Her early education was neglected, but my uncle took her in hand, and now the pupil is a credit to her teacher. Joaquina's great gift is to persuade everybody, even her husband, shrewd as he is, that she knows nothing, that she is concerned only with her children and her household. Her great piety, her humble and submissive air, the kindness with which she speaks to the poor, the interest she shows in the unimportant people who greet her in the street, all make her seem a modest woman without ambition. I felt an instinctive dislike for Joaquina from the first. I have always distrusted people whose gracious smile is not in harmony with their look, and my aunt offers a perfect example of this discordance to the experienced eye, in spite of the pains she takes to match the tone of her voice to the smile on her lips. Her strategy is the admiration of all who

know her, for in Peru nothing is esteemed more than
duplicity. Beneath a semblance of humility Joaquina con-
ceals a boundless ambition. She loves the world and its
pomp, she has a passion for gambling, she takes a sensual
pleasure in food and drink. She spoils her children to stop
them from bothering her, and as a consequence they are
very badly behaved. The parents have given themselves up
body and soul to their ambition and their avarice, so they
have no time at all for their children, and although Arequipa offers some opportunities for education, and there
are teachers of drawing, music and French in the town, as
far as I could see my uncle's children knew nothing and
showed no talent of any kind. Yet the eldest was sixteen
at the time, and the others were twelve, nine and seven.

Joaquina's sister Manuela is quite unlike her in every
way: her charm is natural, she is the model every woman
envies and tries to emulate. Manuela spares neither
trouble nor expense to keep abreast of fashion; she has
the best dressmaker in permanent residence to make her
copies of the outfits illustrated in the fashion magazines:
copies so exact that often when I saw my cousin I thought
she had stepped straight out of Martinet's window in the
rue du Coq. Such slavish imitation would not suit everybody, but Manuela is so graceful that on her everything
looks charming.

Manuela, like my uncle Pio, differs from the rest of the
family in character as well as looks. Her love of spending
money is nothing short of reckless. Luxury and elegance
are necessities for her: she would be genuinely miserable
without her cambric nightgowns trimmed with lace, her
fine silk stockings, her beautifully made satin shoes. Her
house is maintained in splendid style, her slaves are well
dressed and her children are the best turned out in the
whole town, especially her little girl, who is an absolute
darling in her frills and finery.

Manuela has none of the traditional Spanish gravity.
She has a passion for every kind of amusement: plays,

balls, parties, outings and visits, are her favourite occupations, but they are not enough to absorb her energies. She finds time to take an interest in politics, to read all the newspapers, to keep up to date with everything that is happening in her country and in Europe; she has even learned French in order to read the newspapers published in France. What is more, she maintains a regular and voluminous correspondence with her husband, who is nearly always away, and with many other people too; she writes very well and with an amazing facility. In addition to all these gifts she is genuinely good-hearted: she is very generous and has a sensitivity rare in Peruvian women. From the portrait I have painted of her, it may seem surprising that she should have chosen as her husband a soldier like Althaus, who would seem to have little in common with his dainty, fragrant, elegant wife. But in fact they make a good pair. Manuela loves her husband very much, is not in the least alarmed by his blunt ways, and carries out all his wishes notwithstanding. For his part Althaus loves his wife, and proves it by the consideration he shows her: he leaves her absolute mistress of the household, buys her everything he thinks will please her, and delights in all the adornments which enhance her beauty. The example of this marriage proves that people of contrasting temperament sometimes get on better than those who are alike.

The first few days after my uncle's arrival were spent in talking: I never wearied of listening to him. He told me all the family history and regretted that fate had prevented him from knowing me sooner; in short, he spoke to me so affectionately that I forgot his previous conduct and thought I would be able to rely on him to treat me fairly. But alas! I was soon to be disillusioned. One day when we were talking about family matters, my uncle seemed anxious to know what had made me come to Peru. I told him that as I had neither family nor fortune in France, I had come to seek aid and protection from my grandmother, but that when I reached Valparaiso and learned of her death, I had transferred my hopes of justice and affection to him.

This reply seemed to make my uncle uneasy, and when he began to speak I was petrified with astonishment and grief. 'Florita,' he said, 'where business is concerned I recognise only the law and I set aside any special circumstances. You ask me for justice, but this must depend on the documents you have brought with you. You show me a certificate of baptism which describes you as a legitimate child, but you do not produce your mother's marriage lines, and state records confirm that you were registered as illegitimate. This entitles you by law to one-fifth of your father's estate: accordingly, as his executor, I sent you an account of the property he left, which, as you saw, was barely enough to enable me to settle the debts he had contracted in Spain, long before he ever went to France. As for our mother's estate, Florita, you know that illegitimate children have no legal right to the property belonging to the ascendants of their father or mother. So until you can produce an authentic document to prove that your mother was married to my brother, you can claim nothing from me.'

My uncle continued in this vein for more than half an hour, pacing up and down his study while I sat on a sofa watching him.

'Uncle,' I said, 'do you really believe I am your brother's daughter?'

'Of course I do, Florita. You resemble him too closely for there to be any doubt.'

'Uncle, the marriage of your brother and my mother was common knowledge and was only dissolved by death. It was solemnised by a priest, as you know, and I admit that it was not invested with the formalities which human laws prescribe: I told you as much from the first. But can you in good faith use this omission as a pretext for taking bread from the orphan's mouth? Do you think I would have had any difficulty in obtaining a certificate regularising my mother's marriage from a Spanish church? Had I done so you would have tried in vain to refuse me my father's share of the inheritance. Before I left, several Spanish lawyers advised me to arm myself with such a document; what is more, they told me how to get one. But I rejected their advice, uncle, because I believed in your love, and because I wanted to owe any fortune I might obtain to your justice and nothing else.'

'But, Florita, I do not understand why you persist in thinking me unjust. Am I responsible for your money? Have you the right to claim a sou from me?'

'Very well, uncle; since you stick to the letter of the law, you are right. I know that as a natural child I have no claim on my grandmother's estate, but as the daughter of that brother to whom you owe everything, haven't I the right to your special consideration? Well, uncle, I appeal to that. I do not ask you or your fellow beneficiaries for the 800,000 francs which each of you has had as his share: I ask you for only one-eighth of that sum, just enough to enable me to live an independent life. My needs are very limited, my tastes are modest, I do not love the world or its luxuries. With an income of five thousand francs I shall be able to live a free and happy life anywhere I choose. This gift will fulfil all my desires, uncle, and I want it to come *from you alone*. I shall bless you for it, and my life will not be long enough for me to express my gratitude.'

While I was speaking I had drawn closer to him; I took one of his hands and pressed it to my heart. My voice was choked with tears; I looked at him with an ineffable mixture of tenderness, anxiety and gratitude, trembling in expectation as he considered his reply.

Then with an impatient gesture he broke the silence.

'But, Florita, do you realise what you are asking? Do you really think I can give you twenty thousand piastres? It's an enormous sum! Twenty thousand piastres!'

I cannot explain the effect this curt response produced

on me: I can only say that my mood of sympathy was immediately replaced by an access of indignation so violent that I thought it would kill me. For a while I paced the chamber unable to speak. Then I stopped before my uncle, gripped him by the arm, and said in tones he had never heard me use before: 'So, Don Pio, you deliberately and heartlessly reject the daughter of that brother who was a father to you, to whom you owe your education, your fortune, and everything you are today. And in return for all you owe him, you, who have an income of three hundred thousand francs, condemn me to a life of misery; you have a million of mine, yet you abandon me to poverty, you force me to despise you; you, whom my father taught me to love, you, my only relation, the sole repository of all my hopes. You inhuman, dishonourable, faithless man, I hereby reject you in my turn. I am not of your blood, I leave you to the reproaches of your conscience. I want nothing more to do with you. I shall leave your house this evening and tomorrow the whole town will know how ungrateful you are to the memory of the brother whose name you cannot mention without tears, how cruel you are to me, and how basely you have betrayed the trust I was foolish enough to place in you.'

I left his study and returned to my great vaulted chamber. I was in a state of exasperation and distress beyond the power of words to convey. I wrote immediately to M Viollier, and when he came I asked him to find me a lodging, adding in confidence that I did not wish to stay with my uncle a moment longer. He begged me to wait two days, as M Le Bris would be returning from Islay then.

My uncle had gone straightway to tell the whole family of my hostile intentions. Althaus was charged to act as peacemaker and I told him about the scene I had just had with my uncle. 'It doesn't surprise me,' he said, 'and after all you know about him, you must have been expecting something of the kind. But my dear Flora, before you make a scandal and bring even greater troubles upon yourself, let us see if it is possible to settle things. If you have rights, neither Manuela nor I will contest them. The property can be redivided: we shall each have our own share and that will be the end of it. Don Pio and Margarita's uncle (Margarita is my cousin Carmen's daughter) have two very crafty lawyers, but you could choose Dr Valdivia, who is certainly a match for them. If you still want to leave your uncle's house, you can have ours, and even if we end up on different sides, we shall still be good friends.'

Manuela came with similar offers of help and did her best to comfort me.

That night I could not enjoy a moment's rest. I was feverish and could not stay in bed: I even went out into the courtyard to take the fresh morning air. How I suffered! My last hope destroyed! 'Oh! uncle, uncle!' I cried, 'who can make you understand how much your accursed avarice condemns me to suffer? But no, you feel nothing, your only pleasure is to contemplate your gold. Well, I hope you go blind!'

The next day I went to see the President of the Court of Justice and told him in confidence what my position was. He told me that when my uncle received my first letter, he had asked his advice, and he had told Don Pio not to worry about any claims his brother's daughter might make, because she had the right to only one-fifth of anything left by her father. However, the President persuaded me to consult one of the best lawyers so that I would have no cause to reproach myself later. I consulted two, and both were of the opinion that I had a case, though they admitted the outcome was uncertain, especially against Don Pio, in a country where justice could be bought. My uncle was the most interested party, since in addition to his own share he had had a further third share on behalf of his wife, not counting a separate bequest of a hundred thousand francs which my grandmother had made Joaquina. He was the sort of man who would sacrifice a quarter of it, or even half, if necessary, in order to win his case. The two lawyers could not understand my conduct any more than the President could. 'That letter, mademoiselle,' they said, 'that unfortunate letter was your ruin; if only you had come with a paper stating that your mother was married to your father, that would have been accepted here as an authentic marriage certificate, and you would have overcome every difficulty that anybody could put in your way.' I dared not tell these gentlemen that I had counted on the *affection, the gratitude and the justice* of my uncle; they would have thought me *mad*, and I preferred to be thought *stupid*.

However, my uncle did not want me to leave his house; it is his way to settle every conflict amicably, as far as possible, and he knows from experience how he excels at negotiations. He therefore wrote to ask me if I would agree to a family meeting: that is, with him, Althaus, and the old doctor who represented Carmen's daughter Margarita. I had not been able to bring myself to see him since the scene I have just described. My meals were served in my chamber, and I was still determined to leave. However, I yielded to the persuasions of Althaus and betook myself once more to my uncle's study. What pain it was to see him again, this man who forced me to despise him, yet for whom I felt the keenest affection! He was more gentle and friendly to me than ever: before these two witnesses he described how he had behaved towards me. Althaus and the old doctor confirmed that when my grandmother's property was divided, it was at the solicitation of Don Pio that I had been granted the fifteen thousand francs she had left me.

These two gentlemen also told me that it was to the generosity of my uncle *alone* that I owed the allowance of two thousand five hundred francs I had been receiving for the past five years. I was touched by these marks of my uncle's affection; my eyes filled with tears. He noticed this, and fearing that my pride might be hurt at receiving this sum free of charge every year, he was quick to point out to them that this was not a *gift* on his part but a *debt* he was discharging. 'For,' he added, 'even if certain irregularities in the marriage of her mother and my brother deprive Florita of the rights of a legitimate child, she still has the incontestable right, as a natural child, to a living allowance; I undertook to pay her this myself, and I beg her still to accept me as her adviser.' After a long conversation, in the course of which my uncle managed to persuade every one of us, even me, that he loved me like his own child and that his behaviour towards me had never been anything but loyal, generous and full of gratitude for everything he owed my father; after he had made me cry and even succeeded in *moving Althaus*, he asked me, in the most affectionate manner, to forget all that had passed between us, and to consent to remain in his house as his daughter, his friend, his wife's friend, the second mother of his children, and all this with so much charm and sincerity that I promised him everything he wanted. Then Joaquina came to finish what my uncle had so successfully started, and the two *enchanters* so bewitched me that I renounced all thoughts of a lawsuit and entrusted myself, not to their justice this time, but to their promises.

I submitted because of my children's interests. If I brought my uncle before the courts, if I made a scandal, I would alienate him for ever; I stood little chance of success against a man of his influence, and in losing the lawsuit I would also lose the protection he could give my children. Of course if I had had only myself to consider, I would not have hesitated for a moment; as I based my claims on my certificate of baptism, in a country where this is practically the only proof of legitimacy, I would have been tempted to regain the ground that my imprudent letter had lost me; and if I were not recognised as a legitimate member of the family, I would have severed all connections with such unnatural relations and rejected with indignation the pittance they gave me to prevent me from dying of hunger. But I was not free to act in this way: I had to swallow my pride and not risk losing help which, though insufficient, was indispensable to help pay for the education of my children; unless, that is, I were given some hope of winning the lawsuit or coming to an agreement. But to embark on a lawsuit I needed money, a great deal of money. When I left Bordeaux, M Bertera, out of generosity and the concern he felt for me, gave me letters of credit for 5,000 piastres (25,000 francs) on the account of M de Goyeneche of Arequipa, and when I reached Valparaiso I found a letter from M Bertera containing a further letter of credit for 2,000 piastres (10,000 francs) so I had more than enough money to cover the legal costs; but if I were unsuccessful, as there was good reason to fear, I would be deeply in debt to M Bertera and in no position to repay him.

I had also to consider how frail I had become. The prolonged suffering of my five months at sea had weakened my constitution, and from the moment I set foot on Peruvian soil I had been unwell. The volcanic air of Arequipa, the food which disagreed with me, the violent shock of my grandmother's death, the separation from Chabrié, and last of all the cruel disappointment caused by my uncle's ingratitude, had so drained me of strength that I feared I would not live very long. My end seemed near, and this conviction made me calm. I thought that in this circumstance my only duty was to my children, and above all to my daughter, who would be alone in the world. I hoped that perhaps the sad spectacle of my death would have the power to move my uncle, and that in my last moments of agony I might be able to make him promise to take my children under his protection and guarantee them a means of existence which would put them beyond the reach of poverty.

At this point political events intervened to complicate

my position and make my success in a lawsuit even more doubtful. My uncle had returned to Arequipa on 3 January, and on 23 January news reached us of the revolution in Lima. President Bermudez was overthrown, although he had the support of the former president Gamarra, and Orbegoso was recognised as his successor. The news made a great stir in Arequipa. The majority declared in favour of Orbegoso, and General Nieto was appointed commander-in-chief of the local forces; in short, a government was improvised in twenty-four hours, and without pausing to consider the probable consequences of such a decision, Arequipa broke away from the departments of Junin, Cuzco, Ayacucho and several others. The revolution had thrown the whole town into a state of panic: nobody who felt his own fortune in danger could spare a thought for the problems of anybody else. Before the crisis the peculiarities of my position had captured the general interest, but as soon as the Arequipans had worries of their own, they stopped worrying about mine. The lawyer Valdivia threw himself into the fray in the hopes of making his fortune, and informed me that he could no longer take any part in my affairs. I had little confidence in any of the other lawyers, but as it happened they would have nothing to do with me either, as they were afraid of compromising themselves with Don Pio. My uncle would probably return to power; this prospect robbed me of any hope that my judges would be impartial. A new future took shape before my eyes, and I felt that it would be mad — wicked, even — to continue to resist so obvious a sign of Providence. I bowed my head before the power of the destiny which had weighed on me since my birth, and like the Muslim I cried: God is great! . . . I abandoned all thought of a lawsuit and all hope of a fortune, knowing full well that I could expect nothing from the generosity of my uncle, nothing from the reproaches of his conscience. I wrote him the following letter:

I came to you for fatherly affection, uncle, not to settle accounts. My hopes have been disappointed. Armed with the letter of the law, you have calmly robbed me one by one of any claims to kinship with the family in whose bosom I came to take refuge. You have not been held back by respect for the memory of a brother who was dear to you; you have been unmoved by pity for the innocent victim of her progenitors' culpable neglect. You have rejected me and treated me like a stranger. Such acts, uncle, can be judged only by God.

If in the first flight of my justified indignation I desired to set before the tribunal of men the spectacle of these wrongs, after a few days of reflection I felt that my failing strength would not permit me to endure the anguish which the scandal of such a lawsuit would cause me. I know, uncle, that not everybody would be affected in this way, and that there exist persons base enough to stand up in court and shamelessly reveal the crimes of their father and mother, as well as their brother, in their desire for a handful of gold. As for me, the thought alone is enough to make me ill. The fact that the legitimacy of my birth was contested gave me a burning desire to be recognised as legitimate so as to cast a veil over the offence of my father, whose memory remains sullied by reason of his failure to provide for his child. But once I had examined the means which would have to be employed in order to reject my demand, I repeat, uncle, I recoiled in horror. For you would have to demonstrate, in effect, that your brother was a dishonourable man and a criminal, that he had the wickedness to deceive a defenceless young woman whose misfortune ought rather to have made her respected in the foreign land where she had sought refuge to escape the revolutionary axe, and that, taking advantage of her love and lack of experience, he cloaked his perfidy in the farce of a clandestine marriage; you would also have to prove that your brother abandoned the child God gave him to poverty, insult and the scorn of a barbarous society; and while in fact he *commended his daughter to you in his dying words*, you would have to dishonour his memory and accuse him of deliberate and culpable negligence. Oh! if ever I were compelled to bring him before the courts, I would renounce my claim. I feel I have the courage to bear poverty with dignity, as I have done up to now; at this price, my father's spirit may rest in peace.

You have invited me to continue to live in your house. I consent, on condition that I am not required to be cheerful, and that my misfortunes are accorded the respect which is their due. Never will you hear me complain or see me show any sign of discontent.

FLORA DE TRISTAN.

I confess that after sending this letter I felt comforted; my proud nature demanded the satisfaction of letting the whole family know how I felt. My uncle showed it to them: Joaquina was the only one to take offence. Her husband persuaded her that I should be forgiven because I was distressed and overwrought; he set an example of indulgence by not uttering a word of reproach at the harsh words I had addressed to him. That evening Don Jose, the chaplain of the house, came to tell me, as if in confidence (though it was plain he had been ordered to do so), that the family was considering providing me with the means to purchase a little property where I could live in a style appropriate to my station.

My cousin Carmen, Manuela, Althaus, Don Juan de Goyeneche — everybody, in fact, except M Le Bris — strongly criticised my behaviour, not just towards my uncle, but even more towards my aunt. 'You chose the wrong way to go about it if you wanted to get something out of them,' they told me. 'If you were unwilling to take the matter to court you should have cultivated your uncle, flattered Joaquina, and waited patiently until you could give Don Pio the opportunity to make a public display of his great generosity towards you. Instead of that you touch them on their most sensitive spot, you expose their meanness to the whole world; so how can you expect anything from them now but a hatred which will be all the more dangerous for being hidden?'

They were right: anybody else in my place would have managed to get a hundred thousand francs out of my uncle as well as the gracious protection of Joaquina, but that person would not have had my frankness and pride, or shared my invincible disgust for the trade of the flatterer. If my uncle had had the nobility of character to give me a hundred thousand francs, I would have accepted so generous a gift with the keenest gratitude; but when, in order to obtain this sum, I saw myself compelled to compromise my independence, I preferred to remain poor, because I set too high a value on my freedom of thought and the individuality God gave me to exchange them for a little pile of gold, the mere sight of which would have excited my remorse.

Althaus told me that in front of all the family my uncle had undertaken to guarantee me the allowance of 2500 francs he was paying me. I conveyed my thanks to him without relying too much on his word, but reserving the right to remind him of it when I needed a little help for my children. By now I felt I had plumbed the very depths of despair, and I must say, if only for the consolation of the afflicted, that once I had reached this point I found an inexpressible pleasure in my pain, a heavenly joy I had never dreamed could exist. A superhuman power transported me into higher realms from which I could see the things of the earth in their true light, stripped of the deceptive glamour in which men's passions clothe them. Never at any period of my life have I been more calm: if I could have spent my life in solitude with books and flowers, my happiness would have been complete.

X

The Republic and the three Presidents

It would be difficult for me to explain to my readers the causes of the revolution which broke out in Lima in January 1834 and of the civil wars which followed. I was never able to understand how the three claimants to the presidency could justify their claims to their supporters. The explanation my uncle gave me was not very intelligible, and when I asked Althaus he just laughed and said: 'Florita, ever since I have had the honour of serving the republic of Peru I have never yet seen a president whose claim was not extremely questionable. . . . Sometimes there have been as many as five all claiming to be legally elected.'

To put it briefly, this is what I was able to grasp. The wife of President Gamarra, seeing that she could no longer keep her husband in power, had one of her creatures, Bermudez, nominated as candidate by her supporters, and he was elected president. Her opponents alleged, I do not know for what reasons, that the nomination of Bermudez was null and void, and on their side they appointed Orbegoso. Then the trouble broke out.

I remember that on the day the news arrived from Lima, I was feeling unwell and was lying fully dressed upon my bed talking with my cousin Carmen about the emptiness of worldly things; it must have been about four o'clock. Suddenly Emmanuel burst into the room with a bewildered air and said: 'Have you heard what has happened? The messenger has just brought news of a terrible revolution in Lima! A frightful massacre! People here are so shocked that they have all gathered of their own accord in the cathedral square. General Nieto has been put in command of the department. Nobody knows who to listen to or what to believe. My father has sent me to see my uncle Pio.'

'Well,' said my cousin calmly, shaking the ash from her cigar, 'go and tell all that to Don Pio de Tristan; it's the sort of news that concerns him, seeing that he can expect to have to pay whoever wins or loses. But what does it matter to us? Isn't Florita a foreigner? And as for me, I haven't a sou left, so why do I need to know whether they are cutting one another's throats for Orbegoso, Bermudez or Gamarra?'

Emmanuel left us. Not long after, Joaquina came in.

'Holy Virgin! Sisters, have you heard about the latest disaster to strike our country? The town is in revolt; a new government is being set up and the scoundrels in power are bound to extort money from the unfortunate landowners. My God! what a calamity!'

'You are right,' said Carmen, 'in such circumstances one is almost happy not to be a landowner, for it is hard to have to give one's money to wage civil war when it could be used to help the needy. But what do you expect? That's the disadvantage of being rich.'

Then came my uncle and Althaus. Both were visibly worried: my uncle, because he was afraid he would have to part with his money, Althaus because he hesitated to declare himself for either side. Both however had a great deal of confidence in me, and in their perplexity they asked my opinion.

My uncle approached me first and said with perfect frankness: 'My dear Florita, I am very worried, do give me your advice; you see everything so clearly, and you are really the only person with whom I can discuss such serious matters. This Nieto is a scoundrel, a spendthrift, a weakling who will let himself be led by the lawyer Valdivia, a very capable man but a born intriguer and a rabid revolutionary. These brigands will hold all of us

landowners to ransom: God knows how much they will
want. Florita, I have had an idea: if I go along early
tomorrow morning and offer these robbers two thousand
piastres, and at the same time suggest that they exact a
levy on all the other landowners, don't you think that
will make me appear to be on their side so that perhaps
they won't ask me for so much? My dear child, what do
you think?'

'It's an excellent idea, uncle, only I think the sum you
are offering is not large enough.'

'But, Florita, do you think I am as rich as the Pope?
What! won't they be satisfied with ten thousand francs?'

'My dear uncle, bear in mind that their demands will be
relative to people's wealth. If you, the richest man in the
town, give only ten thousand francs, their takings will not
amount to very much, and I have an idea they intend to
sweep the board.'

'What makes you think that? Do you know something?'

'Not exactly, but everything points that way.'

'Ah, my Florita, tell me all about it. I can never get a
word out of Althaus, and young Emmanuel is sulking.
They are both very fond of you, though, so try to see that
they keep you informed. I am going back now; I shall
give out that I am ill, for in times like these I dare not say
anything; one word would be enough to compromise me.'

My dealings with Valdivia had made me a judge of his
character: when I learned that he was a member of the
new government, I took it for granted that the landowners would be exploited; that was what made me speak
with such assurance to my uncle.

When he had gone Althaus approached me in his turn
and said: 'Florita, I do not know what to do. Which of
these three rascally presidents should I support?'

'Cousin, you have no choice. Since Orbegoso is recognised here, you must march under his flag and take your
orders from Nieto.'

'That is just what makes me so angry. Nieto is an ass, presumptuous like all fools, and bound to come under the thumb of that glib lawyer Valdivia, whereas on the side of Bermudez there are a few soldiers I would not mind having as comrades-in-arms.'

'Yes, but Bermudez is in Cuzco and you are in Arequipa. If you refuse to join Orbegoso and Nieto they will strip you of your rank, hold you to ransom and harass you in every way they can.'

'That's exactly what I am afraid of. How long does Don Pio think this government will last? I haven't asked him because he has lied to me so often that I no longer believe anything he says.'

'But you can believe what he *does*, cousin; what ought to decide you is that Don Pio thinks this government will last long enough for him to offer them money. Tomorrow he is going to take Nieto four thousand piastres.'

'Has he told you that?'

'Yes, dear friend.'

'Oh! that alters things. You are right, cousin. When a politician like Don Pio offers four thousand piastres to Nieto, a poor soldier like me had better accept the place he is offered as chief of staff. Tomorrow before eight o'clock I shall go and see the general. A plague on the trade! To think that I should be forced to serve under a man I would not have accepted as a corporal when I was an officer in the army of the Rhine! . . . Ah! you gang of robbers, if I can get myself repaid half of what you owe me for all I have done for you — and which you are quite incapable of appreciating — I swear I shall leave your accursed country and never set eyes on it again.'

Now that he had got into his stride Althaus let fly against all three presidents: the old one, Gamarra, the new one Orbegoso, and the one in command of the military, Bermudez. But he soon saw the comic side of the situation and had some amusing and original observations to make on it.

After Althaus had left me my thoughts took a more serious turn. I could not help pitying the plight of Spanish America. In no part of it has there yet been established a government sufficiently stable to protect the persons and property of its citizens. But the day ordained by Providence will arrive at last, and these peoples will be united beneath the banner of labour. Then, remembering the calamities of the past, let them execrate the men of blood and pillage! Let them reject the medals, crosses, stars and all the other decorations their former masters thrust upon them as so many badges of infamy! Let them learn to esteem only knowledge and talent employed to promote the happiness of mankind!

The next day my uncle came to see me first thing in the morning when I was still half asleep. 'Dear Florita,' he said, 'forgive me for disturbing you so early. I have been thinking about what you told me, and I am afraid that two thousand piastres may not be enough, but four thousand is an enormous sum!'

'Yes, but Althaus told me yesterday that they were only taking the money as a loan.'

'Ha! so they too use grand words! They talk of loans — the shameless rascals! Bolivar called his exactions *loans* as well, yet who has ever thought to repay the twenty-five thousand piastres the illustrious Liberator took from me when he came here? It was the same when General Sucre took our money, yet I never saw the ten thousand piastres he borrowed from me again. Ah! Florita, such barefaced impudence puts me in a rage. To come here and rob people by force of arms, and then add insult to injury by describing the sums stolen as *loans* — well, that surpasses everything for sheer effrontery!'

'Uncle, what time is it?'

'Eight o'clock.'

'Then I advise you to leave, as I know they are going to publish the list of contributions at ten.'

'Are they really? Then I have no time to lose; I'll settle

for four thousand piastres.'

So, I thought, this is how fate redresses the balance: the money refused me by iniquity is seized by force. If I believed in divine retribution, would I not see this as an example?

My uncle returned well satisfied.

'Ah! Florita, I did well to take your advice. Would you believe it, those rascals have already made their list! The general received me very cordially, but that Valdivia gave me a look as if to say: "You are bringing us your money because you are afraid we might have asked you for more, but you will gain nothing by it." Fortunately I am as clever as he is.'

At ten o'clock the town crier read out the *bando* (proclamation). Never in all my life have I seen such agitation! When Althaus came to see me he was laughing like a madman. 'Ah! cousin,' he cried, 'how lucky you are not to have any money! Those who have are looking really sorry for themselves and I should hate to see anyone as nice as you pulling such a long face. Well, I am chief of staff to General Nieto now, and already it has saved me eight hundred piastres. The good doctor Valdivia had put Manuela Florez von Althaus down on his list for that modest sum, but as in these happy times everything is done in the name of the military authorities, the aforesaid *bando* arrived at my headquarters, and before signing it I thought it might be a good idea to read through the names of the victims. When I came to my illustrious spouse I crossed her out immediately, then I stormed off to complain to the general. I told him I found it extraordinary that my wife was down for eight hundred piastres when neither his own wife nor the wife of any other member of the supreme government was down for as much as a *real*. Valdivia began to say something about "the niece of Don Pio" but I cut him short. "There's no niece of Don Pio here," I said, "only the wife of Colonel Althaus, and if dog is going to eat dog, why, I'll be damned if I don't throw off this skin and cry with another pack!" As I uttered these words in my gentle voice I clattered my sabre and jingled my spurs so fiercely that the monk picked up his pen and crossed out my wife's name. Seeing that he was beaten he turned pale, pursed his lips, and looked at me as if he was trying to find out what made me so confident; but just the same as at Waterloo, I was firm as a rock, and looking him straight in the eyes I said to him, "Comrade, in this business each of us has his own job: yours is to draw up *bandos* for extorting money from the townsfolk, and mine is to see that they are carried out. I think that in these circumstances my sword will be as useful as your pen." The comrade understood, and I assure you, Florita, that my little display of military manners, as you would call them, was most effective.'

Towards midday my cousin Carmen came in with an expression of intense joy. 'Florita,' she said, 'I have come to fetch you; get up, my dear, you really must come and sit in my window to watch what is happening in the street of Santo Domingo; such things ought to go in your journal. You can wrap yourself up in your cloak and cover your head with your big black veil; I shall put a lot of rugs and cushions on the window ledge. You will be as comfortable as if you were in bed, and we shall have a royal time. Do hurry, Florita; every moment we are missing something.'

Carried away by her insistence, I settled myself at her window. Carmen was right: there were some interesting things to see.

My cousin is filled with that concealed malice common to those who do not dare to engage in open warfare with the society which oppresses them; she eagerly seizes every opportunity of taking her revenge, so now she was accosting everyone who passed and enjoying herself by twisting the knife in their wounds.

'What a load you have there, Senor Gamio! Where are you taking all those bags of money? It looks like enough to buy a nice little *chacra* for each of your daughters.'

'Why, Dona Carmen, don't you know they have had the wickedness to make me pay six thousand piastres?'

'Really, Senor Gamio? Ah! that is shocking: the head of a family, a man so law-abiding, so thrifty that he goes without necessities in order to add to his pile of money-bags; it's a monstrous injustice!'

'Yes, you know how I have gone without to make my fortune; well, the fruits of all my sacrifice have gone at a single stroke — they are taking everything I have!'

'And do you think you will be let off with what you have there, Don Jose?'

'What, Dona Carmen? Surely you don't think they will take any more?'

'Don Jose, we live in times when honest people are not free to speak; we can only commend our souls to the Holy Virgin and pray for the unfortunate folk who have money. . . .'

Senor Gamio, tearful and trembling with fear, left Carmen's window with despair in his heart. The next to pass by was Senor Ugarte, a man as rich as my uncle but very much meaner. In ordinary times Ugarte goes about in blue stockings, worn-out shoes and a patched coat; today, driven to desperation by what is perhaps the most powerful of all emotions, the agony of the miser, he had put on the oldest rags he could find, regardless of their colour, in the belief that this would mislead people into thinking he was poor. I could not repress a burst of laughter at the grotesque figure he cut, and was forced to hide my head beneath my veil, while my cousin, more accustomed to controlling her emotions, entered into conversation with this poor old rich man who would have been taken for a beggar, though he has a fortune of five or six millions.

'Senor Ugarte, why break your back carrying those heavy sacks? Have you no negro or donkey to save you the trouble?'

'What can you be thinking of, Dona Carmen, expecting me to trust a negro with so much money? Just help me put it down on your window sill; there's ten thousand piastres there, Dona Carmen, and nearly all in gold!'

'Oh! Never mind the colour, Senor Ugarte; if you have piles of gold and silver quietly tucked away in some dark corner, it is hard to give them to people who will make them circulate.'

'Give them! Say rather that they stole them! For as surely as the Virgin and her blessed Son are in Heaven, if it weren't for the fact that they had threatened to put me in prison, and that while I was there my wife would have robbed me of my money, I would sooner have been burned alive than give them as much as a sou! My poor money! My only consolation! They are taking it away from me!'

In a paroxysm of grief the demented old man began to weep as he contemplated his sacks, like a mother in the presence of her dead child. My cousin went back into the drawing-room so that she could laugh in comfort. As for me, I felt sorry for the poor wretch; I thought his mind must be affected, and madness arouses my deepest compassion and concern. But then I saw that he was nothing but the vile slave of gold, and I felt the most profound contempt for him. My cousin, who had returned to the window, offered him a cigar, knowing that this was the best way to bring him to his senses; Ugarte never offers anybody a cigar; on the contrary, he always forgets his and relies on the charity of others — it saves him a few coppers, after all.

'Here's a fine Havana cigar, Senor Ugarte, contraband goods, it's worth two sous.'

'Thank you, Senora, that's a real gift. It's such a pleasure for me to smoke a good cigar, but you know that the price is beyond me.'

'Alas, Senor, with a quarter of what is in one of those sacks you could buy cigars as big as the towers of Santo

Domingo, but now you will never be able to afford a good cigar for the rest of your life.'

'You are right, Dona Carmen, but what is worst is the injustice of it all: to tax me ten thousand piastres, a poor man like me without a coat to his back! My enemies say I am rich – me, rich! Holy Virgin! Just because I have two or three little properties which cost me more than they bring in; it is common knowledge that for six years I have not received a piastre from my farmers. What little ready money I had has been lent to people who never pay it back, so that often my wife hasn't enough to go to market.'

'And yet, Senor, since ten o'clock this morning – and it is still only midday – you have somehow managed to find these bags of gold in some corner . . .'

The poor idiot looked at my cousin with an air of terror.

'Who told you that?'

'Nobody you know. People know everything here; they even say that you have a cask full of gold in your cellar.'

'Holy Virgin, what a wicked lie! By St Joseph, my enemies will drive me mad.'

He took hold of his sacks in a frenzy, trembling in every limb, and staggered off as fast as his burden permitted.

'Carmen, you are very cruel; because of you that poor wretch will go right out of his mind.'

'A fine loss that will be to the country! Isn't it revolting to see a millionaire covered with rags hoarding up his money so that he cannot enjoy it and robbing the poor of a chance to work? There are five or six enormously wealthy men in this town, and it is hard to say which of them looks the shabbiest; they are like so many leeches forever sucking up gold and silver from society and never giving anything in return.'

Carmen's anger was justified. In countries where money is the reward for labour and where the establishment of banks dealing in paper currency puts money within the reach of anyone prepared to work, the miser is merely the object of public ridicule; but in backward countries where gold has retained all its power, the miser is a public enemy who prevents money from circulating and makes work either difficult or impossible because of his exorbitant demands. So it is not surprising that the masses who are exploited by the greed of a few should rejoice and give their active support to the military leaders who squeeze the rich, because it is the suffering of the many that has filled the coffers of the few.

As we finished our reflections on the avarice of Senor Ugarte, Don Juan de Goyeneche approached, looking so ill that I thought he was going to collapse. Carmen invited him in.

'I am going to see Don Pio,' he said. 'I hope he will be able to lend me some money, or God knows what will happen to our family. You ladies probably know that these people (Dona Carmen, there's no danger of our being overheard? Look out of the window and see if anybody is listening) these people have had the impudence to ask our venerable brother the Bishop for twenty thousand piastres! My sister has to pay five thousand and I have to pay six: that's thirty-one thousand gone from our fortune at a single stroke! To say nothing of the forty thousand that went to Bolivar and the thirty thousand that went to General Sucre. Ah! Florita, what would I not give to be in the place of our brother Mariano, peacefully enjoying his income in Bordeaux! Today is not the first time I have repented of having bought the property he had here, and since this revolution started I have regretted the madness which made me chain myself to this country more than ever.'

'Cousin, what you need is a little philosophy. The wheel of fortune turns up winning tickets and losing ones: you cannot always be lucky. Your father came to this country with nothing and amassed a fortune. Your brother Don Manuel is Count of Guaqui today and they say he has twenty millions; all that wealth comes from Peru. Do you really think, Don Juan, that if your father had stayed in Spain one of your brothers would be a bishop and the other a grandee?'

Don Juan got up, seeing that he could not expect the least consolation from Carmen, who detested him. 'I shall go and see if Don Pio is willing to lend me any money,' he said, and took his leave.

Carmen insisted that I return to the window, but the spectacle of avarice in the grip of oppression was repugnant to me; it showed me humanity in too contemptible a light, so I resisted her entreaties.

'At least, Florita, come and see our neighbour Hurtado; the dear old soul has loaded his six thousand piastres onto his donkey like the philosopher he is; let's see what he has to say to us.'

I allowed myself to be persuaded, curious to know what the old philosopher thought as he gave up his money.

'Bravo, uncle Hurtado! At least you are not bent double carrying your sacks to the town hall yourself.'

'Carmen, the philosopher should bend only to wisdom. It is my donkey's fate to carry burdens, and I do not see why gold and silver should be an exception and be carried only by men, when far more useful metals like iron, copper and lead are carried by beasts of burden.'

'Neighbour, I see that you are paying up with a good grace, which is easy enough for anyone like you who has discovered an Inca tomb, but for less fortunate mortals like Don Pio, Juan de Goyeneche, Ugarte, Gamio and the rest, it is not so simple.'

'Yes, Carmen, you are right in a way, but my treasure trove is true wisdom, which is more durable than the tomb of the richest of the ancient Incas.'

'Uncle Hurtado, you are making me lose my temper again; it is always the same each time I talk to you. You are going to tell me that it is your wisdom that has provided you with the means to buy the seven or eight houses you own in town, your country estate, your sugar refinery; that it is with your wisdom that you have raised your eleven children, had them all educated, given your daughters dowries; that it is in your wisdom you find the wherewithal to maintain your daughter, the nun at Santa-Catalina, in a luxury that scandalises the entire community, to make donations to all the convents, to build a church in the village where your estate is situated. For the love of Christ, don't talk to us about your wisdom; at that price, everybody would be wise.'

'Yes, if everybody were capable of wisdom; but I look around me in vain for a wise man, I see only fools ... Good-bye, neighbour ... Dear mademoiselle Florita, come and visit me now that you are better. I still have a lot of interesting things to show you. You have all the qualities necessary to attain wisdom, my dear, that is why I like talking to you so much.'

And he went away, leaving Carmen to rage at the contrast between her poverty and his wealth.

I should explain that people here say of anybody who has unaccountably acquired a fortune that he possesses a *tomb*, because the ancient Peruvians were buried with their treasures, and because at the time of the conquest they hid their wealth in the tombs. Everybody in Arequipa is convinced that old Hurtado has discovered such a *tomb*, and that this is what feeds his enormous expenditure. As for me, I believe that like the old man in La Fontaine's fable, he has found his reward in his work, or as he puts it, in his wisdom. There is no doubt that intelligent labour is the best human wisdom. This venerable old man is thrifty without being mean; his range of knowledge is extensive and far surpasses that of the rest of the populace. He has worked hard for the whole of his long life and succeeded in all his numerous enterprises. It seems to me that this is sufficient explanation of his wealth and that there is no need to resort to stories about the miraculous discovery of a *tomb*. What is more, if fate has been kind to Hurtado, we should rejoice at his good fortune, since he makes such a noble use of his wealth. But people are jealous of men whose intelligence sets them above the rest; when they cannot discredit their success, they attribute it to a miracle rather than to superiority.

My uncle sent for me and I returned home. In spite of the letter I had written to the family, Don Pio still trusted me completely; he spoke to me of his secret worries and consulted me on everything with a frankness and friendliness I found difficult to understand. Did he fear my hostility and was trying to disarm me? I am tempted to think so. Through my connections I could be of some service to him, and when a person can be useful to him, however humble that person may be, Don Pio has a special gift for making use of him.

Recent events had completely changed the atmosphere of the town: calm, monotonous and intolerably boring before the revolution, it was now extraordinarily lively and in a state of perpetual noise and bustle. The government which had been formed in the name of Orbegoso had to use the money it had taken from the landlords to raise an army strong enough to resist the forces of Bermudez. I knew everything that happened at headquarters, as in his need to ridicule his illustrious superiors, Althaus told me everything down to the smallest detail. The arrogance and inefficiency of these men was beyond imagination. Emmanuel, on his side, confided to me everything that Althaus was not in a position to know, so that I was better informed than anybody else.

If Nieto and Valdivia had been equal to their task and had husbanded their resources they should certainly have been able to meet the needs of the moment by means of the colossal sums they had extorted from the unfortunate landowners; but money easily won is easily spent, and there was no folly or extravagance these two men did not commit. If a vessel arrived at Islay, the general gave orders for the immediate purchase of any sabres, rifles, powder, shot, cloth, etc she might have on board. As you can imagine, with Nieto behaving in this fashion, the coffers were soon empty. Valdivia was no wiser, though he did not forget his own interests. He founded a newspaper in Arequipa which cost a great deal to produce, with himself as editor-in-chief, at a salary of a thousand piastres a month, in addition to the payments he received for the articles he contributed.

A month had elapsed since the publication of the famous *bando* when one day Althaus came to see me laughing so much he could not speak.

'What now, cousin? Another blunder by the generalissimo, I'll be bound. Tell me quickly so that I can laugh with you.'

'Let me tell you then, dear friend, that this morning our amiable and provident general said he would like me to inspect what he calls his magazine, in other words the little chapel next door to the prison, which up to now I have been forbidden to enter. They had good reason to make such a mystery of it; guess, dear child, what I found inside?'

'How should I know? Sabres? Rifles?'

'Yes, sabres, but you would never guess how many; there were two thousand eight hundred which they have just bought, when I defy Nieto to recruit any more than six or eight hundred men to serve under him! There are also eighteen hundred rifles, and what rifles! Ah! there is no danger of their killing their brothers with these rifles made in Birmingham. They cost only twenty-two francs; that's not much to pay for a bit of genuine English workmanship! But a harmless beanpole would be a more formidable weapon than ten of these rifles; and as for the sabres, ho! they would be excellent for cutting turnips. I won't mention the piles of blue cloth, the colour French grenadiers wear, and the thousands of sword-belts and shoulder-belts I discovered in a corner — but no sign of a cartridge-pouch anywhere. I'll be damned if I don't think the carrier pigeons must have taken news of the revolution in Lima to the French and English sea captains for those jokers to come and unload all their rubbish onto us. You might think that these weapons were arranged in some sort of order to keep them from going rusty — not a bit of it! Everything was piled up anyhow in the old chapel, which lets in water on all sides. Well, all you good people of Arequipa, you should be happy now; they may have taken your money, but at least you have the satisfaction of seeing it put to good use!'

'Althaus, you really ought to give these people your advice; you can see that their ignorance and imprudence has put them in a situation where they do not know which way to turn.'

'Give them my advice? Ah, Florita, it is clear that you do not know yet what the people here are like; they are presumptuous fools who think they were born knowing everything. The first few years I was in America I was like you, it upset me to see them making so many mistakes; I used to tell them straight out that if they did things a different way it would be better. Do you know what happened to me? I made implacable enemies of all these idiots; they distrusted me and kept me in the dark about everything — as they did about the arms, for instance — and if it were not for the fact that they need my knowledge, they would have got rid of me long ago. I had a lot to suffer from them at first, but eventually I managed to hold my own, and now I don't worry any more, I let them muddle along and content myself with making fun of them.'

'But Althaus, what you have just told me is very alarming and could have disastrous consequences for the people of Arequipa. If Nieto keeps buying all this rubbish from the European captains, he will have to raise a fresh levy, and from the way they go about things, there will never be an end to it.'

'That is exactly what will happen; the brazen monk Valdivia is already preparing his second *bando*. This time Don Pio will not escape, Ugarte and Gamio will be squeezed dry, but their chief target is the bishop and his household. Ha! all you good citizens, so you wanted a republic! All right, my friends, now you are going to see how much it costs!'

Althaus proceeded to ridicule this particular system of government; he was an absolutist at heart, the *Baron von Althaus*, and what he had seen of republicanism was hardly likely to make him change his mind.

The cities of Spanish America, separated one from another by vast tracts of wild and uninhabited territory, still have few common interests. One would have thought that their most urgent need was to be provided with a form of municipal government in keeping with the intellectual development of their respective populations; and to be united in a confederation based on the relations already existing between them. But in order to free themselves from Spain it had been necessary for them to raise armies, and as always happens the power of the sword prevailed. If there had been more contact between the peoples of the different republics, they would have discovered where their common interests lay, and Spanish America would not have been the scene of constantly erupting wars over the past twenty years.

For Independence, that historic achievement, has not lived up to expectations. England expended enormous sums of money in order to bring it about, but ever since Spanish America became independent, the motive which has been exploited to encourage its peoples to throw off the Spanish yoke for good has not been the love of political freedom, which they were too backward to desire, nor the wish for economic independence, which most of them were too poor to enjoy, but the hatred nurtured by the sight of the preferential treatment which the Spaniards received.

When one considers the wonders freedom has worked in North America, one is astonished that the South should still be a prey to political upheavals and civil wars, until one looks a little closer at the difference in their climate and in the moral outlook of their peoples. In South America needs are simple and easy to satisfy. The distribution of wealth is still very unequal, and begging, the inseparable concomitant of Spanish Catholicism, is almost a profession. Before Peru became independent huge fortunes were made out of public office, trade (especially contraband) and above all, mining, but very few people owed their wealth to the cultivation of the land. The masses were covered in rags and their lot has not improved to this day. In British America, on the other hand, morals and customs evolved under the influence of liberal political and religious ideas, and communities lived close together. The climate was exacting and the people retained the industrious habits of Europe. As wealth could be acquired only by cultivating the land or engaging in legitimate trade, it was fairly equally divided.

It is somewhat surprising that the wealthy classes did not obey the dictates of prudence and leave South America when the Spanish government left, as it was obvious that they would be the victims of all the subsequent upheavals. In fact their wealth has fed the wars, and these will never end until there are no more fortunes to be plundered. The exploitation of the mines is declining daily: as a consequence of the wars several of them have been flooded. When tranquillity is restored and the people have to devote themselves almost entirely to cultivating the soil, this civilising work will gradually inspire them with ideas of order and liberty.

When the news of events in Lima reached Arequipa, the men who declared the town for Orbegoso were not moved by concern for the public good, or by the conviction that this president was any better than his rivals. What they saw was the opportunity to seize power and make a fortune, and they were quick to profit from it. Valdivia, who exerted a great influence on General Nieto, induced him to take command of the military throughout the whole department; as for himself, he assumed control of the civil administration and distributed all the posts to his minions. These two men, or rather, Valdivia alone, managed everything for the three months which preceded the arrival of the opposing army led by San-Roman.

As Althaus had told me, Valdivia published his second *bando* a month after the first; this time my uncle was taxed six thousand piastres. He complained bitterly, but he had to pay *that very day*; the *bando* decreed that defaulters would be imprisoned. The bishop was taxed thirty thousand piastres! His brother and sister each had to pay six thousand. Ugarte was down for ten thousand; this brought on a fit of madness and his wife had to remove him to the country. Poor Gamio very nearly died of shock. The only person to show a spark of character was one of my cousins, a woman called Gutierrez; she flatly refused to pay, and nobody could make her. The whole town was so outraged that Nieto no longer dared show his face in public, while the bold Valdivia, who had for some time been dressing like an ordinary citizen, judged it prudent to resume his monk's habit, which still retained some influence with the populace. As for the landowners, he cared little for their resentment. After raising this second levy, which was no better employed than the previous one, they requisitioned first the horses, then the mules, and finally even the *donkeys*. All these exactions broke the spirit of the unfortunate Arequipans; they bore them unwillingly but lacked the courage to resist. The crowning blow fell when Nieto ordered them to report for military service. The Peruvian people are *anti-militarist*: they all abhor the profession of soldier. The Indian even prefers to kill himself rather than serve. My uncle told me that during his twenty years of campaigning a considerable number of his Indians threw themselves into rivers or jumped off precipices rather than suffer the life of a soldier. So at first the Arequipans refused point-blank to answer the general's call to arms, but then Valdivia resorted to persuasion, and in a series of articles in his newspaper he exploited their vanity and ignorance so cleverly that all the young men enrolled of their own free will.

The turbulent activity of the town, my numerous relations, my intimate conversations with my uncle, Althaus and Emmanuel, all gave me a varied and busy enough existence, but there was nothing in it to engage my heart, and a terrifying emptiness, an unspeakable sadness, took possession of me. I realised too late that, driven by despair, I had yielded too easily and recklessly to my imagination when I came to Peru in search of a happiness which I could find only in the sweet emotions I was no longer permitted to feel. Still young, and passing as unmarried, I might have hoped to win the love of a man who was willing to marry me in spite of my lack of fortune. I may even say, without fear of contradiction, that several gentlemen in Arequipa made their sentiments sufficiently clear to leave me without any doubts on that score. Had I been free I would gladly have shared the affection and gratefully accepted the protection of one of them, but I felt the weight of my chains, even at the immense distance which separated me from the master to whom I belonged. I had to stifle the finer feelings God had given me and appear cold, indifferent, and sometimes thoroughly ungracious. Candid to a fault, I felt the need to pour out my sorrows, but when I would have liked to weep upon the bosom of a friend, I was forced to shut myself away and live under constant constraint. I declare that when I left France I had no idea of the tortures the role of *demoiselle* would impose upon me: at least on board, my sufferings had been eased by my affection for Chabrié; but when I broke with him, I vowed that never again would I entertain that kind of friendship for anybody, as it became too dangerous, both for me and for the object of my affection.

I was not living: to live is to love, and I was not conscious of my existence, apart from the needs of my heart, which I was unable to satisfy. If my thoughts turned towards my daughter, I perceived the danger here too, and laboured unceasingly to banish her from my mind, I was so afraid of betraying myself by mentioning her. Ah! how difficult it is to forget eight years of your life, especially when you are a mother! ... Joaquina's youngest child was the same age as my daughter; she was a charming, mischievous little thing, and her childish prattle reminded me of my poor Aline; at the thought, my eyes would fill with tears ... I fled from her innocent games and gained my room in a state of suffering only a mother can understand. Ah! wretched woman, I said to myself, what have you done? Grief has made you cowardly, unnatural; you have left your daughter in the care of strangers, perhaps she is ill, perhaps dead! Then my imagination exaggerated her danger as well as my guilt, and I fell into a fever of despair.

Everything around me only added to my grief. I no longer spoke to the children, I would rather not have seen them. I became so cold towards my uncle's children that the poor little things no longer dared to speak to me or even look at me. This house where my father had been born and which should have been mine, but where I was regarded as a stranger, touched a raw spot in my heart; the sight of its masters was a constant reminder of the callous way I was being treated. The thought of France only recalled my past sufferings ... I did not know where to fly or what would become of me: I saw no refuge anywhere on earth. My hopes of an early death receded as my health improved. A sombre melancholy took possession of me; I grew silent and meditated sinister designs. I held life in aversion: it had become an intolerable burden. It was then that I had to struggle against the violent temptation to make an end of myself. I have never approved of suicide: I have always looked on it as the act of a coward. Yet I had a hard struggle to overcome my disgust for life, my thirst for death: an infernal spectre was forever showing me all the misfortunes of my past life, as well as all those yet to come. I spent eight days and nights in the grip of death; I felt its icy hands upon my body. At last I emerged from this long debate and allowed the infernal power to take possession of my mind.

I resolved that I too would enter the arena, and having been for so long the dupe of society and its prejudices, I would try to exploit it in my turn. I am in the midst of a society in revolution, I told myself; let us see what role I can play, what instruments I can use.

At that time, while I did not believe in Catholicism, I believed in the existence of evil. I had not understood God, His omnipotence, His infinite love for the beings He creates; my eyes had not yet opened. I did not see that joy and sorrow are inseparable, that one inevitably brings the other, and that this is how human beings progress; all must pass through certain stages of development, all are blind agents of Providence with their mission to fulfil. To deviate from this course is to show a lack of respect for divine power.

I thought that it depended on our will to fit ourselves for any role in life. Up to then I had felt only the needs of the heart: ambition, greed, and other passions I looked on as the figments of a disordered mind. I had always aspired to a life animated by tender affections, to a condition of modest comfort; but both were denied me. Enslaved to a man (whom I have already described) in an age when all resistance was vain; born to parents whose union was not legally recognised, I was forced when still very young to renounce for ever any hope of love or a life free of poverty. Isolation was my lot: I could not take my place openly in society, my father's fortune went to an uncle who was already a millionaire. My cup of bitterness overflowed and I rose in open revolt against a social order which sanctioned the enslavement of the weaker sex, the spoliation of the orphan; and I resolved to join the other ambitious intriguers, to rival the monk Valdivia in boldness and cunning, to be as singleminded and ruthless as he was.

From that moment hell entered my heart; it is always thus when we stray from the path mapped out for us by Providence. It is futile to try to change our nature; I think there can be few to whom God has given a will stronger than mine, yet despite my determination to become hard-hearted and ambitious, I could not succeed. This did not make me any less persistent in the plan I had formed, not only to enter politics but to play an important part. I had the example of Senora Gamarra to encourage me; the fate of the republic was in her hands. Gamarra and his wife had overthrown Orbegoso only so that they might rule in the name of Bermudez; Senora Gamarra dictated policy and commanded the troops; in fact the real struggle for power lay between her and the monk. It would be necessary for me to supplant him and rally the supporters of Orbegoso to my side; for in such an enterprise only the power of the sword could ensure success. It vexed me exceedingly to have to rely on another when I felt capable of action myself, but I would have to find a soldier whose character and influence were strong enough to be of service to me, then inspire him with love, fire him with ambition and use him to risk the final throw. I began to make a serious study of the officers who came each evening to visit my uncle and Althaus.

However I had not managed to suppress my nature to such an extent that my principles did not revolt against the career on which I was determined to embark. When I was alone I was assailed with ominous reflections. I imagined all the victims who would have to be sacrificed in order for me to seize power and retain it. In vain did I foster the illusion of all the good I planned to do; a secret voice asked me how I could be so certain of success as to risk murder, and whether the people whose death I was plotting were responsible for the misfortunes of my position.

If after a night of such agonising reflections I arrived at a state of relative calm, a word from Althaus or Emmanuel was enough to revive my determination and the conflicts of the night began all over again. It was impossible for me to escape the discussion of politics; at my uncle's it was the sole topic of conversation. Carmen was the only one who avoided the subject as much as she could. When I did not know how to escape the inner torment which consumed me I would seek her out and beg her to join me in an excursion of some kind. I shall always be grateful to Carmen for her inexhaustible kindness towards me; she yielded to my entreaties, although outings were irksome to her. There is no public promenade in Arequipa, so women are not in the habit of going out; the care they take of their feet is an additional reason for their sedentary habits, as they are afraid that walking makes the feet larger.

Our favourite excursions were to the flour mill by the river. Sometimes we went inside and then I loved to examine the primitive machinery which is so backward in comparison with ours. On other occasions we visited the chocolate mill next door and admired the progress of civilisation as we watched the cocoa beans and sugar being blended to make chocolate. The machinery here has been imported from England: it is very fine and is worked by water power. The manager held me in particular regard because I showed a genuine interest in the machinery and listened attentively to his explanation of how it worked. I never left without a small supply of very good chocolate and a charming bouquet.

When the river was low enough for us to cross, either on foot, jumping from stone to stone, or carried by our negresses, we climbed the hill which dominates the valley and rested at the summit. Sitting beside Carmen, cross-legged like Orientals, as is the custom in Peru, I found an inexpressible charm in staying there for hours, plunged in sweet reverie, or chatting with Carmen while she smoked her cigar. Whenever she mentioned the misfortunes of her country, my sufferings redoubled. It was obvious to me that if a person gifted with a strong and generous soul were to succeed in gaining power, the troubles would cease and a prosperous future would open up for this unfortunate country. I thought again of all the good I could do if I were in the place of Senora Gamarra, and I became all the more determined to try to attain it.

Among the military men who visited my uncle and Althaus, I met only one who fulfilled my requirements, and although I also found him the most repugnant, I would not have hesitated for a moment to seek to inspire him with love, so convinced I was of the sanctity of the role I could have played; but I am forced to conclude that God was reserving me for another mission, as this officer was married. When I became convinced that nowhere in Arequipa was there a man capable of serving my purpose, I was forced to abandon my plans. However, I had one remaining hope, and to this I clung: I resolved to go to Lima. I announced to my uncle and all the family that I wished to leave for France, but that as I wanted to see the capital city of Peru, I would embark at Lima. This news took everybody by surprise; my uncle seemed keenly affected and tried hard to make me change my mind, without however offering me a more independent position than the one I enjoyed in his household. Althaus was genuinely upset and his wife was beside herself with grief. But the two people in the family most affected were Carmen and Emmanuel. As for me, I cannot describe how much it grieved me to leave Carmen; the others did not need me, whereas I had become necessary to her. But then my uncle begged me at least to wait and see how the political situation turned out before I left, and to this I consented.

By dint of money and rhetoric the monk had succeeded in raising the following forces:

Infantry	1000 men
Cavalry	800 men
Battalion of Immortals	78 men
(the flower of Arequipa's youth)	
Chacareros	300 men
(labourers from outside town)	
Total force	2178 men

In addition to this there was a national guard of between three and four hundred veterans kept in reserve for the defence of the town.

In order to create a warlike impression, General Nieto had set up a camp; he thought it would accustom his soldiers to the hardships of war if he made them leave their barracks. This camp, very badly placed from the strategic point of view, was about three miles from Arequipa, and as it adjoined a village, it had the serious disadvantage of being surrounded by *chicherias* – these are taverns where they sell *chicha*, an intoxicating drink made of crushed fermented maize. The general established his headquarters at the house of a Senor Menao. Althaus had tried to dissuade him from setting up camp on this particular site, pointing out that as it was the rainy season the soldiers' health would suffer and this would lead to enormous expense, but the presumptuous general paid no heed to these considerations, or to the wise counsel his chief of staff gave him as to the most suitable place to camp. Nieto fancied that this martial display created an effect and made him look a great leader. He also yielded to the foolish vanity of parading his authority in the camp and before his large circle of officers. He loved to be seen in public, followed by his glittering retinue; there was constant activity between the town and the camp, and we found the daily performances of this comedy vastly entertaining. The general, mounted on a fine black horse, put on all the airs of a Murat, he had such a variety of rare and splendid uniforms. Valdivia, often in his monk's habit and always on a white horse, was cast as the Peruvian Lafayette, while the crowd of officers, covered in gold and smothered in plumes, were no less ridiculous.

Thanks to Althaus and the complaisance of the general, a horse was put at my disposal whenever I wished to visit the camp; the townsfolk had no horses left, having been forced either to surrender them or hide them away. My uncle alone had kept his Chilean mare, because she was so mettlesome that none of the officers cared to ride her, and in the middle of a body of cavalry she might have caused accidents. Visiting the camp was a favourite outing for me; I went with my uncle, Althaus, or Emmanuel, who was now an officer. The general always gave me a cordial welcome, but Valdivia, seeming to sense how much I despised him, greeted me coldly. He listened attentively to everything I said, while appearing not to do so, and never took part in the conversation. I knew from Emmanuel that my visits were viewed with displeasure and that some of the gentlemen resented the fun Althaus and I had at their expense, but how could I help laughing at them when they were so ridiculous! Nieto had only eighteen hundred men to provide for, as the *Immortals* and the chacareros were stationed elsewhere, yet he was taking up more space than a European general would need for an army fifty thousand strong. On a hillock to the left of Menao's house he had built a redoubt and armed it with five light guns. It was the first time I had seen toy artillery like this and they reminded me of drainpipes. As it happened, this redoubt was dominated by a position which nature herself had fortified, and where the enemy could entrench himself unhindered should he come by that route. As in any case Arequipa is in open country and can be approached by ten different ways, it was difficult to foresee which the enemy would take.

The infantry, camped in several lines next to the redoubt, looked thoroughly wretched: the unfortunate soldiers were sleeping in little tents which could not be properly fastened and were made of cloth so thin that it gave them no protection against the frequent rains of the season. The cavalry, commanded by Colonel Carillo, was quartered on the other side of the redoubt and took up far more space; the horses were a good distance apart in one long line, and the general made me gallop from one end to the other. Things were no better ordered here than they were in the infantry: it was quite pitiful. At the very end of the camp, behind the soldiers' tents, were quartered the *rabonas* with their jumble of cooking-pots and children. Here there were clothes drying and women busy washing or sewing, all making a frightful commotion with their shouting, singing and conversation.

The *rabonas* are the camp-followers of South America. In Peru each soldier takes with him as many women as he likes: some have as many as four. They form a considerable troop, preceding the army by several hours so that they have time to set up camp, obtain food and cook it. To see the female avant-garde set out gives one an immediate idea of what these poor women have to suffer and the dangerous life they lead. The *rabonas* are armed; they load onto mules their cooking-pots, tents and all the rest of the baggage, they drag after them a horde of children of all ages, they whip their mules into a gallop and run along beside them, they climb high mountains, they swim across rivers, carrying one or even two children on their backs. When they arrive at their destination, they choose the best site for the camp, then they unload the mules, erect the tents, feed the children and put them to bed, light the fires and start cooking. If they chance to be near an inhabited place, they go off in a detachment to get supplies; they descend on the village like famished beasts and demand food for the army. When it is given with a good grace they do no harm, but when they are refused they fight like lionesses and their fierce courage overcomes all resistance. Then they sack the village, carry their loot back to the camp and divide it among themselves.

These women, who provide for all the needs of the soldier, who wash and mend his clothes, receive no pay and their only reward is the freedom to rob with impunity. They are of Indian race, speak the native language, and do not know a single word of Spanish. The *rabonas* are not married, they belong to nobody and are there for anybody who wants them. They are creatures outside society: they live with the soldiers, eat with them, stop where they stop, are exposed to the same dangers and endure far greater hardships than the men. When the army is on the march it is nearly always on the courage and daring of these women four or five hours ahead of them that it depends for its subsistence, and when one considers that in leading this life of toil and danger they still have the duties of motherhood to fulfil, one is amazed that any of them can endure it. It is worth observing that whereas the Indian would rather kill himself than be a soldier, the Indian women embrace this life *voluntarily*, bearing its fatigues and confronting its dangers with a courage of which the men of their race are incapable. I do not believe it possible to adduce a more striking proof of the superiority of woman in primitive societies; would not the same be true of peoples at a more advanced stage of civilisation if both sexes received a similar education? We must hope that some day the experiment will be tried.

Several able generals have sought to find a substitute for the service the *rabonas* provide and prevent them from following the army, but the soldiers have always revolted against any such attempt and it has been necessary to yield to them. They are not at all sure that the military administration would be able to provide for their needs, and that is why they refuse to give the *rabonas* up.

These women are horribly ugly, which is understandable when one considers the kind of hardships they endure. In fact they have to withstand extremes of climate ranging from the burning sun of the pampas to the icy summit of the Cordilleras, so their skin is burnt and wrinkled, their eyes red-rimmed; their teeth, however, are very white. Their only clothing is a little woollen skirt which reaches only to their knees, and a sheepskin cover with a hole in the middle for their head to go through, while the two sides cover their chest and back; their feet, arms and head are always bare. They seem to get on fairly well together, though their jealous scenes sometimes lead to murders; as there is nothing to restrain their passions, such happenings should occasion no surprise. There is no doubt that if an equal number of men were freed from all control and forced to lead the life of these women, murders would be far more frequent. The *rabonas* adore the sun but do not observe any religious practices.

The military headquarters had been transformed into a gaming-house; the large main room on the ground floor, divided in two by a curtain, was occupied on one side by the general and the superior officers, and on the other by the junior officers. In both parts they were playing faro for enormous stakes. The Peruvians are great gamblers: Colonel Morant once lost thirty thousand piastres in a single night. Althaus, wishing me to see the officers of the republic in their true colours, took me at eleven o'clock one evening to Menao's house; we did not go in, but looked through the window without being observed. Ah! What a sight met our eyes! There were Nieto, Carillo, Morant, Rivero and Ros, cards in hand, sitting round a table with a pile of gold in front of them; the table was littered with bottles and glasses full of wine or spirits. The players' faces reflected the greed or fury of the gambler in its most concentrated form; they all had cigars in their mouths, and the feeble light which penetrated the smoke-laden atmosphere gave their faces an infernal look. The monk was not playing; he was slowly pacing the room, and every now and then he stopped in front of the players, folding his arms and looking at them as if to say: What hope have I, with instruments like these! We stayed a long time observing the scene; nobody saw us, the slaves were asleep, the brave defenders of the fatherland were absorbed in their game, the monk in his thoughts. On the way back, we deplored the practice of gambling — for his part, Althaus preferred chess — and feared for the fate of a country at the mercy of leaders such as these.

In the last days of March we heard from Lima that President Orbegoso himself was preparing to come and take command of the army in the department of Arequipa. Nieto was in despair: he said the president would rob him of the glory he anticipated from his encounter with San-Roman. The conceited general did not dream of revolting openly; he had insufficient influence to assume leadership of his faction and act entirely on his own account; however, in his desire to prevent what he regarded as an affront, he resorted to a plan which showed the level on which his mind worked. He had a confidential letter written, in secret, to some individual, and took care that it should fall into the hands of San-Roman. The letter said that Nieto's army was in a wretched condition, had no arms or ammunition, and was quite incapable of putting up a fight. After the dispatch of his missive the general hoped each day to see the enemy army arrive, and his impatience knew no bounds.

For three months the famous San-Roman's imminent attack on Arequipa had been the only topic of conversation; during the first two, the name of this leader had the same effect on the population as the mention of a bogeyman has on little children. Orbegoso's supporters pictured him as a bloodthirsty monster capable of slitting the throats of the poor Arequipans for his amusement and putting their town to fire and sword to satisfy his party's desire for vengeance: these and a thousand similar charming habits were laid at his door.

If the townsfolk rather enjoyed telling stories about San-Roman to frighten one another and indulge that taste for the miraculous which always tends towards extremes, others, such as the general, the monk, and their subordinates, had a strong interest in making these rumours believed.

All the hopes of the two parties depended on their armies, which were preparing to stake everything on a single throw. Victory meant complete success, defeat irreparable ruin. Orbegoso's party, weak in every respect, had nothing left to rely on except the valour of the Arequipans, and all eyes turned to them. Senora Gamarra, on her side, knew that the authority of the government she had established could not be maintained as long as there was armed resistance; that to be mistress in Lima she must first be mistress in Arequipa; and that if, with the three battalions she had left, she could capture the town, Orbegoso would not be able to hinder her return to the capital. So it was obviously important for the military leaders, the civic authorities and all who had an interest in supporting Orbegoso to spread among the people exaggerated ideas of the calamities in store for them if San-Roman should triumph, so that they would be roused to defend themselves to the last man. Every day the monk wrote and circulated unsigned handbills declaring that San-Roman had promised his troops that they could sack the town. The descriptions of the massacres, rapes, and other atrocities they contained inspired in the timid inhabitants a terror verging on despair. Thus the monk achieved his ends, for despair lends courage even to the most craven. The general harangued his troops, the prefect and the mayor issued proclamations, and even the monks in the various convent churches yielded to pressure and preached resistance unto death.

All these harangues and sermons produced the intended

result. In the first month following the insurrection, fear of the sudden arrival of San-Roman, who commanded the three best battalions, excited acute alarm and prompted enthusiastic organisation of the defences. In the second month, the Arequipans, taking confidence from their preparations and from anticipation of the triumph which the monk promised them as a reward for their valour, grew accustomed to the idea of the approaching struggle, and awaited the enemy with firm resolve, but in the third month, their impatience knew no bounds! San-Roman's delay seemed to prove that he was afraid of them; their courage increased, and as always happens when people have no experience of war, they passed straightway from abject terror to a bravado which made all reasonable folk justifiably apprehensive. They began to fear victory as much as defeat, if such cowardly braggarts were to come out on top. From that moment onwards I realised that whatever the outcome, the country was lost: whether Nieto or San-Roman were triumphant, extortion, ruin and pillage would ensue.

On 21 March Althaus told me: 'Florita, it seems that at last the general has some accurate information: San-Roman will be here tomorrow or the day after. Would you believe it, up to now, in spite of the vast sums of money we have paid out to spies, we have not been able to obtain a single reliable report about what is happening in the enemy camp? The general doesn't want me to have anything to do with it, sensible advice is a blow to his pride, so he hides as much as he can from me.'

For the past two days the troops had been back in barracks, as they were so exhausted from the hardships and privations they had suffered during their pointless stay in the camp. It might have been supposed that after receiving information he judged to be so reliable, the general would have sent them out again immediately either to occupy the same positions as before, or to take up new ones to suit the changed circumstances; that he would have taken all the necessary precautions to avoid being surprised by the enemy, to prevent confusion among his troops and alarm among the people; that everything, in short, had been foreseen, and every measure taken to guard against the disorders which could result from either victory or defeat. Such would have been the conduct of any commander with a grain of commonsense, but none of these concerns entered Nieto's head, and leaving everything unsettled, without even troubling to deploy his troops, he went off to Tiavaya with the other officers to celebrate Holy Week. The next day, about four in the afternoon, a spy arrived in great haste to announce that the enemy was at Cangallo: then everything was in an uproar! On one side, they rushed off to find Nieto, on the other, the Immortals assembled, the troops turned out in disorder, the chacareros refused to march, and the dignitaries at the town hall committed one blunder after another.

What happened that night and the next would be incredible to a European, so I will not go into details, but I believe the confusion was such that if San-Roman had been aware of it he could have seized the town that very day and quartered his troops there without a fight: nobody was in any state to fire a single shot to prevent him. That would have ended the war in three hours flat. It is regrettable that he did not do so; much bloodshed would have been spared and many irreparable evils avoided.

XI

The Convents of Arequipa

— ❧ —

As I have already said, Arequipa is one of the Peruvian cities which contains the largest number of monasteries and convents. From the calm religious atmosphere surrounding most of these institutions one might be led to think that if peace and happiness inhabit the earth, it is within the shelter of these hallowed walls that they reside. But alas! it is not in the cloister that the heart disillusioned with the world will find repose. There only feverish agitation is found, captive but not stifled, seething like the lava concealed inside the volcano.

Before I had even penetrated inside one of these convents, each time I passed before their porches, always open, or along their great black walls thirty or forty feet high, I felt my heart constrict; I experienced so profound a compassion for the unfortunate victims buried alive beneath this mass of stone that my eyes filled with tears. During my stay in Arequipa I often went to sit on the roof of our house, and from this spot I loved to let my gaze wander from the volcano to the charming river flowing at its foot, from the smiling valley to the two magnificent convents of Santa-Catalina and Santa-Rosa. My thoughts were particularly drawn to Santa-Rosa, for it was in its gloomy cloisters that a most moving drama had taken place, with a beautiful but unfortunate young girl as its heroine. She was a relation of mine and I loved her out of sympathy, though as I was forced to bow to the fanatical prejudices of the world around me I could see her only in secret. When I arrived in Arequipa two years had elapsed since her escape from the convent, yet the sensation the event had produced was still fresh, so I had to be very careful not to show how interested I was in this victim of superstition; had I behaved in any other way it would not have helped her, I would only have risked exciting the fanaticism of her persecutors even more. All that Dominga (that was the young nun's name) told me of her strange story gave me the keenest desire to see the interior of the convent where the poor girl had languished for eleven years. She was only sixteen when an access of spite and wounded self-esteem drove her to renounce the world. The foolish child had cut off her hair with her own hands, and, casting it down at the foot of the cross, had sworn in the name of Christ that she would take God as her spouse. The story of the *monja* (nun) made a great stir in Arequipa and in all Peru; I think it sufficiently remarkable to warrant a place in my narration. But before telling my readers about the sayings and doings of my cousin Dominga, I ask them to follow me into the interior of Santa-Rosa.

In ordinary times these convents are inaccessible: nobody may enter without the permission of the Bishop of Arequipa, and since the escape of the nun such permission has always been refused. But in this time of crisis all the convents offered refuge to the anxious population. My aunt and Manuela judged it prudent to take shelter in one of them, and I profited from this circumstance to find out exactly what convent life was like. Santa-Rosa was always in my thoughts, so I tried to persuade my relations to go there in preference to Santa-Catalina, which was their choice. I had a good deal of trouble to overcome their objections; however, I succeeded. Towards seven o'clock that evening we made our way to the convent, having first taken care to send a negress to announce us.

I do not think there has ever existed, even in the most monarchical of states, an aristocracy more arrogant and more shocking in its distinctions than that of Santa-Rosa, which struck me with astonishment the moment I entered. To see the members of this large community in procession, all clad in the same uniform, you would think that the same equality existed in all things; but enter one of the courtyards and you are surprised at the arrogance of the titled woman in her relations with the woman of plebeian origin, the disdainful tone the white adopts towards the coloured and the rich towards the poor. We were met at the door by a solemn deputation of nuns who conducted us with all due ceremony as far as the cell of the Superior, who was ill in bed and had sent them to welcome us. We stayed quite a long time with this venerable lady. After the good nuns had satisfied their curiosity about current events and had shyly asked me a few hesitant questions about European ways, we retired to the cells which had been prepared for us.

Santa-Rosa is one of the largest and wealthiest convents in Arequipa. It is very well laid out, with four cloisters, each of which has a spacious courtyard in the middle. Broad stone pillars support the somewhat low arched ceiling of these cloisters; the nuns' cells are ranged all round the sides. They are entered by a little low door. Inside they are large and the walls are kept very white. Each cell is lit by a casement with four panes which opens onto the cloister, like the door. The furniture consists of an oak table and stool, an earthenware jug and a pewter goblet. Above the table hangs a large crucifix; the Christ is in bone yellowed and blackened with age, and the cross is of black wood. On the table are a death's-head, an hourglass, a book of hours and sometimes other books as well. At the side, hanging on a large nail, is a scourge made of black leather. Nobody except the Mother Superior is permitted to sleep in her cell; the other nuns use theirs only for solitary and silent meditation. They eat together in an immense refectory, dine at midday and sup at six. While they eat, one of their number reads passages from sacred books. The nuns all sleep in dormitories, of which there are three at Santa-Rosa.

These dormitories are L-shaped and are built without a single window to let in the daylight. A sepulchral lamp placed in the angle throws barely enough light to illumine the space of six feet around it, so that the two sides of the dormitory are always in total darkness. Entry to the dormitories is forbidden, not only to visitors but even to the servants, and if you manage to slip inside at dusk and venture beneath the cold and sombre vaults of their long aisles, you would think from the objects all around you that you had descended into the catacombs. These places are so dismal that it is difficult to repress a shudder of fear. The *tombs*, as the nuns' sleeping-places are called, are set on a platform on either side of the dormitory, about twelve or fifteen feet apart, and look just like the tombs you see in the crypts of churches. They are hung with black woollen cloth of the kind used as draperies at funerals. Inside they are from ten to twelve feet long, five to six feet wide, and about as much in height. They are furnished with a bed made out of two massive oak planks set on four iron posts, upon which is a coarse pallet filled with wool, straw, ashes, pebbles, or even thorns, depending on the degree of sanctity of the owner. I must say that in all three of the cells I entered I found that the pallets were filled with straw. At the end of the bed is a small black wooden piece of furniture which serves as table, prayer-desk and cupboard. Here too there is a large figure of Christ hanging on the wall, with a death's-head, a book of prayers, a rosary and a scourge arranged beneath it. It is expressly forbidden under any circumstances to have a light in the *tombs*. When a nun is ill, she goes to the infirmary. To think that my poor cousin Dominga slept in one of these places for eleven years!

The life these nuns lead is very hard: they rise at four in the morning to go to matins, and there follows an almost uninterrupted sequence of compulsory religious observances until noon, when they repair to the refectory. From then until three they enjoy some repose, but after that prayers are resumed and continue until the evening. They are also obliged to take part in the processions and other ceremonies associated with the numerous religious festivals: such is a glimpse of the austere régime of life in the cloisters of Santa-Rosa. The nuns' sole recreation is to walk in their three magnificent gardens, where they cultivate beautiful flowers with the greatest assiduity.

When they enter the Carmelite order the nuns of Santa-Rosa take a vow of poverty and silence. When two of them meet, one must say: 'Sister, we must die,' to which the other gives reply, 'Sister, death is our deliverance', and they must not say another word. For all that, these ladies are extremely talkative, but only when they are working in the garden, or in the kitchen supervising the servants, or when they have some duty to perform in one of the bell-towers; and whenever they can they pay one another long visits in their cells. To ease their conscience they observe a deathly silence in the courtyards, in the refectory, in the church, and above all in the dormitories, where the sound of a human voice has never been heard. I would certainly not count these minor infringements a crime: I find it quite natural that they should seek the opportunity to exchange a few words after long hours of silence; but for the sake of their own happiness I could wish that they would confine themselves to talking about the flowers they grow, the excellent cakes and preserves they make, the magnificent processions and rich jewels of their Madonna, or even to speak of their confessor. But unfortunately in all their conversations, evil-speaking, lying and slandering predominate: it is difficult to imagine all the petty jealousy, base envy and cruel spite they harbour towards one another. They are no more rigorous in their observation of the vow of poverty. According to the rule, none of them is allowed more than one maid to serve her; however, several have three or four slaves living in the convent, and each nun has in addition a slave outside to run errands, buy her anything she wants, and keep her in touch with her family and the outside world. In this community there are even nuns with a considerable fortune who make rich gifts to the convent and its church, send frequent gifts of fruit, delicacies of every kind, or little things made in the convent to their acquaintances in the town; and sometimes they send gifts of greater value to people of whom they are particularly fond.

Santa-Rosa is considered one of the wealthiest convents in Peru, yet the nuns there seemed more unhappy than those in any of the other convents I was able to visit, and other people confirmed my impression that it has the strictest and most austere régime. However I must say that the Mother Superior received me with some ceremony. She was sixty-eight years old at the time, and had been at the head of the community for eighteen years. She must have been very beautiful, for her face is noble and everything about her testifies to the great strength of her will. Born in Seville, she came to Arequipa at the age of seven. Her father sent her to Santa-Rosa to be educated, and she has never left it since. She speaks remarkably pure and elegant Spanish and is as learned as any nun can be. All the questions she asked me about Europe showed that the Superior of Santa-Rosa had concerned herself a great deal with the political events which have convulsed Spain and Peru for the past twenty years. Her political opinions are as exalted as her religious ones, and her fanaticism exceeds the bounds of reason. A single remark of hers is sufficient to convey the workings of her mind. 'Alas! my dear child,' she told me, 'I am too old now to undertake anything, my life is over; but if I were only thirty, I would go with you; I would go to Madrid, and there, even if I had to give up my fortune, my illustrious name, and my very life, I swear to you, by the death of Jesus Christ upon the cross, I would restore the Holy Inquisition.' Her discourse was always pitched in this high key: speaking of Dominga, she said, 'That girl was *possessed of*

the devil; I am well contented that the devil should have
chosen my convent for preference, as this example will
rekindle the faith; for to you, my dear Flora, I will
confide a part of my troubles: each day I see that faith,
which alone can foster a belief in miracles, growing
weaker in the hearts of our young nuns.' It seemed to me
that Dominga's escape was hardly likely to produce the
result the Superior expected, but would tend rather to
encourage imitation!

The three days we spent inside this convent had proved
so wearisome to my aunt and my cousins that whatever
the risks they might run in leaving, none of them wanted
to stay any longer. As for me, I had gathered much
information during so short a stay and I had not been at
all bored. The grave nuns accompanied us as we left with
the same formalities they had observed on our arrival. At
last we stepped across the threshold of the massive oaken
gate, bolted and barred like the gate of some citadel, and
no sooner had it closed behind us than we all began to run
down the long wide street of Santa-Rosa, crying, 'God!
what happiness to be free!' All the ladies were weeping,
the children and the slaves were dancing in the street, and
I confess that I was breathing more easily.

The day after we entered Santa-Rosa, Althaus had sent
word that it was a false alarm; the Indian who had
brought the news was in the pay of San-Roman, who
would probably not arrive for a fortnight. We therefore
thought it safe to return home, but that very evening there
was another alert, and this time my relations retired to
Santa-Catalina. It appeared certain that San-Roman was at
Cangallo. His presence at so short a distance from Arequipa — only ten miles — made the danger imminent, and
the moment the news spread, the disorder in the town and
in the camp was no less than on the previous occasion:
there was a call to arms, they rang the tocsin, and masses
of people took refuge in the convents, which by now were
more like furniture repositories, as for the past fortnight

people had been transporting all their movables there, and their empty houses looked as if they had been pillaged. As for me, I had my trunks taken to Santo-Domingo with my uncle's things. It was midday when news came that San-Roman was at Cangallo, and he was expected to appear at about six or seven o'clock. The roof-tops swarmed with people looking out in every direction but they waited in vain: the enemy had called a halt.

Althaus returned from the camp and said to me: 'Cousin, it is quite true this time that San-Roman is at Cangallo, but his soldiers are exhausted and I am certain that they will stay there three or four days to recuperate.'

'So you do not think they will come today?'

'I do not think they will be here for four or five days, so you can join Manuela. In any case, you will see the battle from the towers of the convent just as well as from the roof of your uncle's house.'

I followed his advice and went to Santa-Catalina to rejoin my relations.

So here I was once again inside a convent, but what a contrast with the one I had just left! What a deafening noise, what joyous cries when I entered! *'La Francesita! La Francesita!'* I heard on all sides. Hardly was the gate open than I was surrounded by at least a dozen nuns all speaking at once and laughing and jumping for joy. One pulled off my hat, another took my comb, a third tugged at my leg-of-mutton sleeves, because, they said, such things were *indecent*. Yet another lifted up my skirt from behind, because she wanted to see how my corsets were made. One took down my hair to see how long it was, another took hold of my foot to examine my boots from Paris; but what excited the most wonder was the discovery of my drawers. The dear girls are very naive, and, without a doubt, their questions were far more indecent than my clothes! In short, they turned me this way and that like children with a new doll. I must have been there a good quarter of an hour, expecting any moment to be suffocated in the press. I was bathed in perspiration and so deafened by the noise that I no longer knew where I was. At last the Mother Superior arrived to welcome me. She is cousin to the Mother Superior at Santa-Rosa, so both are related to our family in the same degree. At her approach the noise abated a little and the crowd parted to let her through. By this time I was feeling really ill. The good lady saw this; she scolded her nuns severely and told the black servants to go away. Then she took me to her large and beautiful cell, where she made me sit down on soft cushions and had a tray of the finest Parisian work-manship set before me, on which were a selection of excellent cakes made in the convent, Spanish wines in exquisite crystal decanters, and a superb gilded glass, elegantly cut and engraved with the arms of Spain.

When I was feeling a little better, she insisted on accompanying me to the cell intended for my use. Oh, what a love of a cell! and how our smart Parisiennes would like it for their boudoir! Imagine a little vaulted chamber fourteen to sixteen feet long and ten to twelve feet wide, the floor entirely covered with a beautiful English carpet in a Turkish design; a little gothic door in the middle and little windows to match on two sides, with curtains of cherry-coloured silk with blue and black fringes; on one side a little iron bed with a mattress covered in English twill and cambric sheets trimmed with Spanish lace; on the other a divan also covered in twill, with a rich tapestry from Cuzco over it; beside the divan, cushions for visitors and pretty tapestry-covered stools. At the far end there was an alcove containing a marble-topped console which served as an altar, and on it stood several vases of natural and artificial flowers, branched silver candlesticks with blue candles, and a small mass-book bound in purple velvet and fastened with a little gold clasp. Above the console there hung a fine oak carving of Christ, and above that a Virgin in a silver

frame, flanked by St Catherine and St Teresa. A charming
rosary with tiny beads had been wound around the head
of Christ. As a final elegant touch there was a table
covered with a rich cloth in the middle of the room, and
on it stood a large tray containing a tea set with four cups,
a cut-glass carafe, a glass and everything necessary for
refreshment. This charming retreat belonged to the
Mother Superior herself, and in spite of all my protestations she insisted that I should install myself there. She
was particularly friendly towards me because I came from
the country *where Rossini lived*. The kind lady stayed
quite late and we spoke chiefly of music, then of events in
Europe, in which the nuns took a keen interest. Then she
retired, surrounded by a flock of nuns, who all love her as
their friend and mother.

  In ten years of travel I have often had to change
lodgings and beds, but I do not remember ever feeling
such a delightful sensation as when I slept in the charming
little bed of the Mother Superior of Santa-Catalina. I was
childish enough to light the two blue candles on the altar,
then I took up the rosary and the pretty prayer-book and
read for a long time, pausing from time to time to admire
the collection of objects which surrounded me or to
breathe in the sweet fragrance of my lace-edged sheets.
That night I almost wished to become a nun. The next
day I rose very late, as the indulgent Mother Superior had
told me there was no point in getting up at six to go to
mass, as we had had to do in Santa-Rosa, and that I need
not even go at eleven if my state of health did not permit
it. The first day was spent in paying visits to the nuns; all
wanted to be the first to see me, touch me, speak to me,
and they asked me questions about everything. How did
people dress in Paris? What did they eat? Were there any
convents there? But they particularly wanted to know
what the music was like. In each cell we found plenty of
company: everybody spoke at once and there was much
laughter and wit. Everywhere we were offered a variety of

cakes, fruit, preserves, sweets, syrups and Spanish wines: it was an unending succession of banquets. For the evening the Mother Superior had arranged a concert in her little chapel, and there I heard a very good recital of the most beautiful passages from Rossini, performed by three pretty young nuns no less devoted to the fine arts than their Mother Superior. The piano was the work of the most skilled craftsman in London and had cost the Mother Superior four thousand francs.

Santa-Catalina belongs to the Carmelite order too, but, as the Mother Superior observed to me, *with many modifications*. Yes, I thought, with *enormous* modifications. . . .

These ladies do not wear the same habit as the nuns of Santa-Rosa: theirs is white, very full and trailing on the ground. On ordinary days they wear the Carmelite veil, but for grand and solemn ceremonies it is black. I do not know if their order requires them to use only woollen material, but I *do* know that of all their garments, only the habit is made of wool, and that is of the finest texture, silky and dazzlingly white. Their bonnet is of black crêpe so prettily pleated that I longed to take one away as a curiosity; its graceful shape lends their faces a particular charm. The veil too is of crêpe, and they wear it lowered only in church or during ceremonies. We may also assume that these good ladies dispense with the vows of silence and of poverty, for they are very good at talking and nearly all of them spend a great deal of money.

The convent church is large and the interior is very ornate but somewhat shabby. The organ however is very fine, and the nuns devote special attention to the choirs and everything else which has to do with the music of the church.

The plan of the convent is very odd: there are in fact two buildings, one called the old convent, the other the new. The latter consists of three elegant little cloisters containing small but light and airy cells. In the middle of

the courtyard there is a flower-bed and two beautiful
fountains which keep the place fresh and clean. The
outside of the cloisters is covered with vines. From here a
steep street leads to the old convent, a veritable labyrinth
of lanes and alleys bisected by one main thoroughfare
which has to be climbed almost as if it were a ladder. All
these byways are due to the disposition of the cells, which
are in effect small individual dwellings, each of original
design. For the nuns who live in them they are more like
country houses in miniature. I saw some with courtyards
big enough for keeping poultry: this was where the
kitchen and the slaves' quarters were situated, then came a
second courtyard with two or three rooms opening off it,
and finally a garden and a little *retiro*, the roof of which
formed a terrace. The nuns here have not lived a com-
munal life for more than twenty years: the refectory is
abandoned, the dormitory too, though for form's sake
each nun still has a bed there, which is white, as the rule
prescribes. Neither are they required to observe the
numerous religious practices which take up so much of
the nuns' time at Santa-Rosa. On the contrary, when they
have finished their conventual duties they have plenty of
leisure, which they devote to looking after their households, their clothes, their charitable works and their
diversions. The community has three enormous gardens
where only maize and vegetables are grown, as each nun
grows flowers in the garden attached to her cell. All in all
they lead a very industrious life: they do all kinds of
needlework, take in and teach boarders, and maintain a
free school for poor girls. Their charity has a wide range:
they give linen to the hospitals, provide young girls with
dowries, and make daily distributions of bread, maize and
vegetables to the poor. The revenues of this community
are enormous, but these ladies spend in proportion.

The Mother Superior was at that time seventy-two and
had been removed from office on several occasions by
the priests who control the convent, but the exceptional

goodness of her character, which was what made them reject her, always caused her to be reappointed by the nuns, who have the right to elect their Mother Superior by ballot. This lovable woman, the opposite in every way of her cousin at Santa-Rosa, was so slender, so delicate, that she almost disappeared beneath her long and ample habit. I would never have thought it possible that a woman of her advanced age and fragile constitution could be so active and lively. I told her of the sentiments the Mother Superior at Santa-Rosa had expressed; she shrugged her shoulders with a pitying smile and said with the conviction of the true artist: 'For my part, my dear child, if I were only thirty, I would go with you to Paris to see the sublime masterpieces of the immortal Rossini performed at the Opera; one note of that genius does more for the moral and physical welfare of humanity than the hideous autos-da-fé of the Holy Inquisition ever did for religion.'

At Santa-Catalina each lady did almost as she pleased: the Mother Superior was too kind to oppose their wishes in any way. The aristocracy of wealth, which reigns everywhere, even in the heart of democracies, was the only one of which I was aware in this convent. The nuns of Santa-Catalina were quite advanced. There were three among them who were the acknowledged queens of the community. The first, placed in the convent at the age of two, was about thirty-two or thirty-three when I was there; she belonged to one of the richest families of Bolivia and had eight negresses or *sambas* to serve her. The second was a young woman of twenty-eight, tall and slender, with the kind of bold and vivacious beauty found in women of Barcelona: she was in fact of Catalan origin. This charming creature, an orphan with an income of forty thousand francs, had been at the convent for five years. Finally the third, a lovable woman of twenty-four, good, bright and cheerful, had been a nun for the past seven years. The eldest, Margarita, was the convent pharmacist, the second, Rosita, was the porter, while as for the youngest, Manuelita, she was too scatterbrained to be entrusted with any duties.

Ever since we arrived, each of the three friends had evinced a keen desire to hear from our lips a true account of what had happened to poor Dominga; the rumour was running through the convent that they were planning some similar and no less gruesome escapade themselves. Rosita was about the same age as Dominga and took a lively interest in her, as she had known her well when they were both children. My cousin Manuela, who asked for nothing better than to tell this story, perhaps for the twentieth time, gladly offered to satisfy the nuns' curiosity.

Manuelita received us in her pretty little lodging in the old convent. The dinner was one of the most splendid and certainly the best served of all the meals to which I was invited during my stay in Arequipa. We had fine Sèvres porcelain, damask table-linen, elegant silver, and enamel-handled knives at dessert. When the meal was over, Manuelita graciously invited us to adjourn to her *retiro*. She closed her garden gate and told her chief negress that on no account were we to be disturbed.

Manuelita's retreat was not as pretty as the Superior's but it was more unusual. As I was a foreign visitor I was given the place of honour on the divan, while the three nuns grouped themselves around me, Rosita cross-legged on the floor, Manuelita by my side, where she amused herself arranging my hair in a thousand different ways, and Margarita complacently admiring her plump white hand as it toyed with her big ebony rosary. My cousin, as the principal actress, sat facing us in a large antique armchair with a foot-stool beneath her feet.

She began by explaining what had made Dominga become a nun: 'Dominga was lovelier than any of her three sisters; at fourteen her beauty was already sufficiently developed for her to inspire love. She attracted a young

Spanish doctor, who, learning that she was rich, set out
to make her love him, which was not difficult, as she was
of an age when love is tender and trusting. He asked for
her hand in marriage, to which her mother agreed, but
fearing that her daughter was still too young, she wished
the marriage to be deferred for a year. This Spaniard, like
nearly all the Europeans who land on these shores, was
dominated by cupidity: he wanted to attain great wealth,
and as the possession of Dominga seemed to him a sure
means of acquiring it, he exploited the innocent credulity
of this child. Hardly had a few months elapsed than he
renounced her for a widow without qualities of any kind
but of course far richer than Dominga. He did not show
the slightest concern for the profound distress his abandonment would cause her. His lack of faith cruelly
wounded Dominga's feelings: her projected marriage had
been publicly announced to all the family, and her pride
was unable to support such an outrage. In her despair she
saw no other refuge save the cloister; she declared to her
family that God was summoning her and that she had
determined to enter a convent. All her relations joined
together in an attempt to shake her resolution, but she
was equally indifferent to their protestations and their
entreaties: in fact the only result of their opposition was
to make her all the more determined to enter the strictest
Carmelite convent of them all. After a year's novitiate,
Dominga took the veil at Santa-Rosa.

'It seems,' continued my cousin, 'that in her religious
enthusiasm Dominga was happy for the first two years of
her stay, but then she began to weary of the relentless
moral exaltation, and when at last she reflected on the fate
she had chosen, she shed bitter tears. She dared not
confess her sorrows to the family who had so strongly
opposed her decision, and, besides, how would it have
helped her? You ladies know that regret is futile; once a
person has entered one of your retreats, she does not
come out again.'

Here the three nuns exchanged glances, and there was a tacit understanding in their look that did not escape either of us.

'The unhappy Dominga locked her sorrows away in her heart and resigned herself to suffering until death should put an end to her woes. But one day towards the end of her third year, when it was her turn to read in the refectory, Dominga found the hope of her deliverance in a passage from St Teresa which described how the devil tempted a nun of Salamanca to place the body of a dead woman in her cell so that the whole community would believe that she was dead, and she would have time to make her escape.

'What a ray of light for the young girl! She too would be able to escape from her prison, her tomb, by the same means as the nun of Salamanca. From that moment hope re-entered her heart and she was no longer anxious; her active imagination gave her hardly enough time to think of ways in which to realise her plan. She no longer found the austere practices and exacting duties a burden, because she saw the end of her captivity in sight. She gradually changed her behaviour towards the other nuns as she sought out opportunities of getting to know them better. She made a special effort to become friendly with the porters, whose term of office lasts for only two years at Santa-Rosa. At each change she endeavoured to ingratiate herself with the new porter. She was very kind and generous to the negress who ran her errands outside the convent in order to ensure her unlimited devotion. However eight years elapsed before she could realise her plan.

'In the end, feeling that she could hold out no longer, she decided to confide in one of her companions whom she liked better than the rest, and who had just been appointed porter. Her trust was well-founded, and once she was sure of the help and silence of the porter, Dominga thought of nothing but how to obtain what she needed for the execution of her design. She had to confide in her negress, for without the help of this slave it would be impossible to succeed. They could communicate only through a grille in the parlour, and whatever Dominga said could be heard by one of the silent nuns always coming and going, always on the alert. Here then is the plan she had conceived and which she was bold enough to disclose to her negress, while offering her a large reward to compensate her for the risks she would have to run.

'The negress was to procure the body of a woman and bring it to the convent at nightfall; the porter would open the gate and show her where to hide the corpse, then at dead of night Dominga would come and fetch it, place it upon her bed, set fire to it and make her escape while both corpse and *tomb* were consumed by the flames. It was not until long after she had entered into her mistress's plan that the negress was able to bring the body. It would have been dangerous to ask at the hospital, which in any case would have consented to give one only to a surgeon, and that for a specified purpose, seeing that there is no school of medicine in Arequipa. It was next to impossible to obtain the body of a woman who had died at home, so it is certain that had it not been for the good offices of a young surgeon who was let into the secret, Dominga's friend would have finished her two years as porter before the slave had been able to obtain the means of making everybody in the convent believe that her mistress was dead. But one dark night the negress managed to overcome her terror as she thought of the promised reward, and loaded onto her shoulders the body of an Indian woman who had died three days before. She gave the agreed signal at the convent gate, the porter opened it, trembling all over, and without a word the negress deposited her burden in the place the porter pointed out to her. Then the slave posted herself round the corner of the street of Santa-Rosa to await her mistress.

'In the evening the porter bolted the gate but omitted to

lock it, then she took the key to the Mother Superior as the rules prescribed and retired to her *tomb*. Towards midnight, when she thought the nuns must all be sound asleep, Dominga emerged from her own *tomb* where she left her little dark lantern, and went to fetch the corpse. It was a heavy burden for the delicate limbs of the young nun; but is there anything the love of freedom cannot do? Dominga picked up her ghastly burden as easily as if it had been a basket of flowers. She put it down upon her bed and clothed it in her habit; and when she had dressed herself in a complete set of garments with which she had had the foresight to provide herself, she set fire to her bed and fled, leaving the gate of the convent wide open. The porter, who as you can imagine, was not asleep, quickly bolted the gate behind her, and in the confusion caused by the fire, she managed to retrieve the key from the Mother Superior's cell and lock the gate as usual. Everybody was convinced that Dominga had burned herself. The remains were unrecognisable, and were buried with the ceremony usually observed when a nun dies. Two months later the truth began to emerge, but the nuns of Santa-Rosa did not want to believe it, and even when everybody else was convinced that Dominga was alive, the good sisters still maintained that she was dead and that all the talk about her escape from the convent was a malicious lie. They were not convinced until Dominga herself settled the matter by demanding that the Mother Superior return her dowry, which amounted to ten thousand piastres.'

My cousin stopped speaking, and once again the three nuns exchanged glances, but this time with an air of complicity that enabled me to guess what was in their thoughts. When we left them they were plunged in a reverie we felt it would be indiscreet to disturb. I said to my cousin, 'I am prepared to wager that before two years are up those three nuns will not be here.'

'I think so too,' she replied, 'and I am glad. Those three

women are too beautiful and too lovable to live in a convent.'

We left Santa-Catalina next day: we had been there for six days, during which the nuns had done their utmost to make our stay as agreeable as possible. Splendid dinners, delicious informal meals, walks in the gardens, and visits to every interesting spot inside the convent: the kindly nuns omitted nothing which would give us pleasure and enable us to enjoy every recreation the convent permitted. We were escorted to the gate by the whole community. There were no formalities whatever, but their affection was so genuine and so moving that we all wept together and felt really sad at parting. It was quite unlike our departure from Santa-Rosa: in fact, I had such happy memories of Santa-Catalina that before I left Arequipa I went back several times to chat with my old friends in the convent parlour. They showered me with little gifts and asked me to send them some of Rossini's music from France.

XII

Battle of Cangallo

We left Santa-Catalina on Tuesday 1 April: my aunt, worried about her husband and her household and unable to curb her impatience, was anxious to return home. Besides, everybody said that San-Roman, alarmed at the size and impressive appearance of Nieto's forces, would not dare to advance any further, but would remain at Cangallo until Gamarra had sent him reinforcements from Cuzco. The general shared the opinion of the populace and, still worrying lest Orbegoso should arrive, he chafed at the slow progress of the enemy but took no measures to make ready for him; the monk, in his broadsheet, was already singing songs of victory, while the wits of Arequipa were composing ballads in honour of Nieto, Carillo and Morant and lamenting the fall of San-Roman, all this in a farcical and exaggerated style which reminded me of the Paris street singers after the July Days of 1830.

That same Tuesday, a feast-day, the troops were paid, and in order to ingratiate himself with the soldiers Nieto gave them leave to enjoy themselves, a favour of which they took the fullest advantage. They went off to the taverns to drink *chicha*, sang all the songs I have mentioned above at the tops of their voices, and spent the whole night in drunkenness and disorder. They were doing no more than follow the example of their leaders, who for their part had gathered together to drink and gamble. They were so sure that San-Roman would not dare to advance before he had received reinforcements that they made no preparations and took no precautions; the same negligence prevailed at the outposts.

On Wednesday 2 April, while the defenders of the fatherland were still sleeping off the wine of the previous night,
it was suddenly learned that the enemy was approaching,
and everybody climbed onto the housetops. It was two
o'clock in the afternoon; the sun was burning and a dry
wind made the heat even more intolerable as it swept
across the roofs of the houses blowing dust into the faces
of the watchers. Only a person of my intrepid nature
could have borne to remain there long. My uncle called
from the patio that I would be blinded by the sun, that I
was waiting in vain, that San-Roman would not come that
day, but I took no heed of his advice. I had settled myself
on top of the wall; I had taken a big red umbrella to
protect me from the sun, and, armed with a telescope
made by Chevallier, I felt very comfortable. As I contemplated the valley and the volcano I let my mind
wander and forgot all about San-Roman until I was
suddenly reminded of the reason for our being there by a
negro who called out to me: 'Here they come, madame!' I
heard my uncle coming up; and training my telescope in
the direction the man was pointing, I clearly saw, high on
the mountain next to the volcano, two black lines, fine as
a thread, winding their way through the desert in a series
of unbroken curves, like flocks of migrating birds.

At sight of the enemy the whole town uttered a cry of
joy. Conditions under Nieto and the monk had become
so intolerable that people were willing to pay any price to
escape from them. There was great rejoicing in Nieto's
camp as well; officers and men resumed their drinking
and songs of victory, celebrating the funeral of all those
they were going to *crush* and *annihilate*. Towards three
o'clock Althaus came galloping into the courtyard, and as
he saw that we were all on the roof, he called to me
urgently to come down. I did so, promising my uncle to
tell him if there was any news.

'Ah! cousin,' cried Althaus, 'never have I been in such a
critical situation; no doubt about it, they are all mad out

there. Would you imagine it, all those wretches are drunk; not one officer is in any state to give an order, and not one soldier is capable of loading his gun. If San-Roman has a good spy, we are lost; in two hours he will be master of the town.'

I went up and told my uncle the ominous news. 'I was expecting this,' he said. 'These men are totally incompetent; their cause will be lost, and perhaps it will not be a bad thing for the country.'

San-Roman's little army took nearly two hours to come down the mountain. It took up its position to the left of the volcano on the hill called *La Pacheta*, which dominated Nieto's defences, and was in fact the position Althaus had predicted the enemy would occupy. San-Roman extended his lines to give an illusion of greater numbers, but it was perfectly plain that they were only two deep. He drew up in a square the whole of his cavalry, which amounted to only seventy-eight men: in short, he did all an able tactician could do to make out that he had four times as many troops. The *rabonas* lit a multitude of fires on top of the hill and spread out their gear with so much noise that they could be heard shouting from the bottom of the valley.

But once in view, the two armies were afraid of one another, each being convinced of the superiority of the other. If San-Roman's display of military skill made Nieto fear that his elegant Immortals would be no match for the seasoned troops of his adversary, San-Roman, for his part, perceiving the great numerical superiority of Nieto's forces, began to fear he had been rash, and this made him lose his head. Although a good soldier, San-Roman was no wiser or less presumptuous than Nieto; from the reports of his spies, he thought he was marching towards an easy victory; he even believed it could be won without a fight. Several of his officers told me later that when they left Cangallo in the morning they were all so confident of entering Arequipa the same evening that they had no thought of anything but their personal appearance, so that they would be ready to visit the ladies as soon as they arrived. The soldiers, just as confident, had thrown away what remained of their food, overturned the cooking-pots, and cried: 'Here's to the soup at the barracks in Arequipa!'

However, in spite of all their efforts to make it appear that they were busy cooking, the *rabonas* had nothing, not even a cob of maize, to offer their companions, and to crown their misfortunes, they had camped in a place where there was not a drop of water. When San-Roman realised his predicament he gave himself up to despair and wept like a child, as we heard later, but fortunately for his cause he had three young officers, Lieutenants Torres, Montaya and Quirroga, who took command, restored the morale of the soldiers, calmed the rebellious murmuring of the *rabonas*, and set an example of the resourcefulness which every soldier in such circumstances ought to possess by cutting down with their sabres the prickly pears which grow abundantly in the mountains, and chewing them to quench their thirst, after which they distributed them to the soldiers and the *rabonas*, who all accepted them meekly and fed upon them without daring to utter a word of objection. But the officers knew very well that this measure could not keep their men satisfied for more than a few hours, and they decided to risk battle, preferring to die by the sword rather than of thirst. Lieutenant Quirroga asked his soldiers whether they wished to retire without a fight, to flee ignominiously in full view of the enemy and return to Cangallo, thereby exposing themselves to the risk of dying of hunger and thirst in the desert like mules; or whether they wished to make Nieto's braggarts, who were incapable of standing up to them despite their superior numbers, feel the strength of their arms; and the soldiers, who in any other circumstances would have turned tail and fled at the mere sight of such a large force opposing them, acclaimed this warlike speech and demanded battle.

It was nearly seven o'clock in the evening; I had just returned to my post on the roof. Both camps were quiet, and considering how late it was, we assumed that the battle would not take place until dawn next day. Suddenly I saw a figure which I took to be a standard-bearer detach itself from San-Roman's square, immediately followed by the whole of his cavalry; and at the same time Nieto's dragoons, led by Colonel Carillo, advanced to meet them. The two troops galloped furiously to the charge, and when they came within range, there was an exchange of musket fire, followed by another; the battle had begun. I was now aware of a great commotion in both camps, but the smoke became so thick that it hid the scene of carnage from our view. Then night fell, and we remained in complete ignorance of all that passed.

Towards nine o'clock a man arriving from the battle-field passed by the street of Santo-Domingo; we stopped him and he told us that all was lost, that Nieto had sent him to bid his wife retire immediately to the convent of Santa-Rosa. He added that there was frightful disorder among our troops; that Colonel Morant's artillery had fired on our dragoons, taking them for the enemy, and that a great number had been killed. The news spread through the town and everybody was in the grip of panic; all those who had thought they could stay in their homes, terrified at their own courage, now hastened to leave them. They were rushing about like madmen, loaded with their silver dishes and chamber pots of the same metal; one woman clutching a casket of jewels, another a *brasero*, while negresses and *sambas* carried off piles of their mistresses' gowns and carpets. It was probably the first time these black and white countenances had openly expressed all the vileness of their souls. The Indian threatened, the white cringed, the slave refused to obey, his master dared not strike him. Calm amid the chaos, I contemplated with a disgust I could not repress this panorama of all the worst passions of our nature. I spoke to my *samba* just as I always did, and this girl, who was drunk with joy, obeyed me because she saw that I was not afraid. My aunt and I had no wish to enter any more convents, so my cousins went off alone with their children. The tumult of the dreadful scene I have just described was followed by the silence of the desert; in less than an hour the entire population was crammed into the convents, monasteries and churches. I am sure there were not twenty houses still inhabited.

Our house had become the general meeting-place, first because of the security offered by its proximity to the church of Santo-Domingo, and next because it was hoped that Althaus would manage to get news through to Don Pio. We were all gathered in my uncle's study, an immense vaulted room giving onto the street; there was no light, so as not to attract the attention of passers-by, only the glow of the cigars which that evening were never extinguished. It was a scene worthy of Rembrandt's brush. Through the thick haze of smoke which filled the room one could make out the broad and stupid faces of four Dominican monks with their long white habits, heavy rosaries with black beads, and clumsy shoes with silver buckles, with one hand shaking the ash from their cigar, the other toying with their scourge. My aunt was sitting in a corner of one of the sofas, her hands clasped, praying for the dead on both sides. As for my uncle, he came and went from one end of the room to the other, talking and gesticulating in an animated manner. I was sitting on the window-sill wrapped in my cloak, enjoying the double spectacle offered by the study and the street. That night was an education for me. Peruvian society has a character all its own; its taste for the exaggerated and the miraculous is extraordinary. I could not say how many frightening stories I heard that night, embroidered with every kind of falsehood and related with a dignity and aplomb which amazed me, though from the calm indifference with which they were received it was plain that not one of the listeners believed a word of them.

But the story-telling was abandoned each time any news, whether true or false, arrived from the camp. If a wounded soldier, dragging himself off to the hospital, reported that the Arequipans had lost the battle, there immediately arose throughout the room a chorus of recrimination against that *coward*, that *scoundrel*, that *imbecile* Nieto, and loud praise for the *worthy*, the *brave*, the *glorious* San-Roman. The good monks of Santo-Domingo addressed to heaven their heartfelt supplications that the dog Nieto should be killed, and began to plan the brilliant reception they would give the illustrious San-Roman. A quarter of an hour later another soldier happened to pass by shouting, 'Long live General Nieto! Victory is ours! San-Roman is crushed!' Then there was wild applause: the good fathers clapped their hands and cried, 'Oh, the brave general! What courage! What talent! May that wretched Indian, that *sambo* San-Roman be damned!' My uncle was afraid of being compromised by these impertinent chatterboxes, as ludicrous as they were contemptible; but in vain did he employ all his eloquence to silence them, for it is in the nature of people here to be just as pitiless in their abuse as they are extravagant in their praise.

Towards one o'clock in the morning Althaus sent one of his aides to tell us that there had been no action since eight the previous evening, that the enemy, intimidated by their numbers, had not dared venture at night into unknown territory, that because of Morant's fatal mistake we had already lost thirty or forty men, including one officer, and that an alarming disorder reigned in our camp. My cousin sent me a pencilled note in which he said he considered the battle as lost.

At about two o'clock, feeling very tired, I retired to my room, but as at this stage I was anxious not to miss anything, I begged my aunt to wake me as soon as it began to grow light.

At four in the morning I was on top of the roof: as the sun rose I admired the magnificent spectacle which the domes and towers of the numerous convents and churches presented to my view. The mass of human beings gathered there formed one single whole. There were men, women and children of every hue from black to white, all dressed according to their rank in the various costumes of their respective races, yet at that moment all were equal, because the same thought was in every mind. From all those thousands of breasts arose one single heart-rending cry which moved me to tears. There was no need for me to turn my head towards the battlefield, I could tell that the fighting had begun. That great cry of grief was followed by a deathly silence: the tense attitude of the watchers showed how concentrated their attention was. Suddenly a second cry went up, and from its tone and the gesture which accompanied it I was reassured as to the fate of the combatants. I turned and saw signs of great activity in both camps. I begged my uncle to lend me his telescope, and then I saw officers hurrying from one camp to the other firing pistol-shots in the air, then General Nieto, followed by his officers, went to meet a group of officers from the enemy camp. I saw the two sides mingle in mutual embraces, and this convinced us that San-Roman had just surrendered and that everything would now be settled.

As we were wondering what was happening, Althaus entered the courtyard at full gallop shouting at the top of his voice: 'Ho, you up there, come down quickly, I have important news for you!' I was first down the ladder and reached the courtyard before any of the others. I fell upon his neck and embraced him tenderly for the first time; he was not wounded, but, good God! what a state he was in! Always so immaculate before, he was now covered with mud, dust and blood. His features were unrecognisable;

his eyes, red and puffy, were starting out of his head; his nose and lips were swollen; his skin was broken and bruised, his hands were black with gunpowder and his voice so hoarse that what he said was almost unintelligible.

'Ah! cousin,' I said, my heart wrung, 'I did not need to see you in this state to make me loathe war; after what I saw yesterday I think there is no punishment too cruel for the men who cause it.'

'Florita, I'm no match for you today, I can't speak; but for pity's sake don't dignify by the name of *war* a farcical shambles in which not one of those greenhorns knew how to aim a gun. Just look at me! Anyone would think I was a burglar! And to put me in an even better humour, my dear wife has hidden everything away down to my last shirt!'

Althaus made the best of things, gulped down four or five cups of tea, ate a dozen slices of bread, and then began to smoke, managing at the same time to grumble about his wife, laugh and joke as usual, and tell us everything that had happened since the previous evening.

'Yesterday,' he said, 'the engagement was only a *skirmish*, but what inextricable confusion it caused! Luckily the Gamarrists took fright and withdrew. It took me all night to restore a bit of order on our side. This morning we were occupying the battlefield and expecting the enemy to attack at any moment with all the advantage of his position, when instead of that we saw him send somebody to parley who demanded to speak to the general in the name of San-Roman. Nieto, forgetting his dignity and not stopping to think, was all for accepting the invitation there and then; the monk was against it, and the others too. To cut the discussion short, I said: "As chief of staff, it's up to me to go," and without waiting for a reply I galloped off towards the messenger, but he announced that San-Roman wished to speak to the general in person, so as this was all I could get out of him,

I went back to the general and said: "If you want my opinion, the only conversation you'll have with him will be bullets: they're always understood." The idiot took no notice of my advice, he wanted to do the generous thing, see his old comrade, his brothers-in-arms from Cuzco; the monk ground his teeth, foamed with rage, but there was nothing for it but to yield to the man he had been hoping to use for his own ends. Nieto shut him up with these words: "Senor Valdivia, *I* am the only leader here." The furious *padre* gave him a look which said: "If ever I get my hands on you, I'll squeeze the life out of you." All the same, not wanting to throw in his hand, he resigned himself to following the tender-hearted Nieto. At this very moment, together with two journalists, Quiros and Ros, they are in conference with the enemy; but as for me, now that I've eaten and cleaned myself up a little, I'm going back to the camp, where I propose to sleep until someone comes and tells me whether we are to fight or kiss and make friends.'

The news Althaus gave us spread rapidly through the town and into all the convents. People thought that the interview between the two leaders would bring peace; this hope alone was enough to make everybody happy. The Arequipans are essentially indolent: the cruel agitation they had suffered during the past day and night had quite exhausted them, and they eagerly seized upon the opportunity to recuperate. I was certainly feeling tired myself; I went to bed after giving my *samba* orders not to wake me until the enemy was actually in the courtyard. It was now Thursday 3 April.

Towards six in the evening I was still fast asleep when Emmanuel and my uncle entered.

'Well?' my uncle asked him. 'What news do you bring us?'

'Nothing positive; the general stayed with San-Roman from five in the morning until three this afternoon, but on his return he said nothing about this long conference except that he thought that everything would be settled. We knew from what one of the aides told us that the meeting of the two leaders was very touching; they both shed floods of tears over the misfortunes of the country and the loss of the officer Montenegro; they stood over his body and swore by his memory an oath of *union* and *fraternity*. The whole day was spent in exchanging flowery speeches. The Gamarrists are playing the innocent, they are gentle as lambs; while Nieto, more soft-hearted than ever, has allowed San-Roman to send his men and horses to water at the spring of Agua-Salada; he has even sent them food and is treating them like brothers.'

Emmanuel persuaded me to visit the camp; my uncle was very willing to accompany me, and off we went. I found the little taverns and Menao's house almost completely destroyed, and the camp in the greatest disorder. From the look of it you would have thought it had been taken by the enemy; the fields of maize were ruined, the poor peasants had been forced to flee, and their cabins were full of the *rabonas*. At headquarters the handsome officers, usually so elegant, were dirty, with red eyes and hoarse voices; most of them were sleeping on the ground like the soldiers. The quarters of the *rabonas* had suffered most: in the confusion Morant's artillery had scored a hit and wrought havoc there. Three of the women had been killed and seven or eight seriously wounded. I did not see the general or Valdivia; they were sleeping.

On our return my uncle said to me: 'Florita, I do not like the look of this. I know the Gamarrists, and they are not the sort to give up. San-Roman has some good men on his side; Nieto is no match for them in finesse. If I am not mistaken there is a trap hidden beneath this show of cordiality.'

The next day Nieto went to see San-Roman again and sent him wine, meat and bread for his troops. People were expecting the general to issue a proclamation informing the army and the townsfolk about the result of these meetings, but two o'clock came, and still no proclamation appeared. Then voices were raised against this man who had been appointed supreme head of the department by popular acclaim, who for three months had done as he pleased with the fortune, life and liberty of its inhabitants, and who had repaid their trust by giving himself the airs of a president, or rather a *dictator*.

This conduct raised the exasperation against Nieto to its highest pitch: the entire population of thirty thousand souls, forced to abandon their normal routine to cower in monasteries and churches, was impatient to know how things stood. The small number of people remaining in their homes, as we had done, were extremely uncomfortable, as everything was hidden away in the convents: there was no linen, cutlery, chairs, or even beds. But if we suffered from all these privations, the thousands of poor wretches crammed into the convents suffered very much more, for they were short of clothes and had no means of preparing food. Men, women, children and slaves were compelled to live together in very little space, so their situation was appalling.

Apart from these material sufferings, the people experienced real moral anguish because they did not know which of the two rival candidates they ought to support. As they could not predict which would be victorious they were forced to wait; and to wait without being able to speak was a cruel punishment for this talkative people.

Towards three o'clock the rumour ran through the town that everything was settled, as San-Roman had recognised Orbegoso as the legitimate president and fraternised with his former comrades from Arequipa; and that his entry was deferred until the following Sunday so that he could, as an act of thanksgiving, attend high mass. The people were overcome with joy at the news, but alas! their joy was short-lived. At five o'clock an aide-de-camp came from Althaus to inform us that negotiations had broken down and that he himself would come that evening to give us an account of the whole affair. When the people heard what had happened they were too frightened to protest, but fell into a kind of stupor.

We were gathered in my uncle's study, not knowing, after so many contradictory reports, how things were going to turn out, when the unfortunate general happened to pass by, followed by the monk and several others. I went to the window and said to him: 'General, would you be good enough to tell us if there is really going to be a battle?'

'Yes, mademoiselle, tomorrow at daybreak, that is definite.' Struck by the tone of his voice, I began to pity him, and while he was talking to my uncle I examined him closely. Everything about him betrayed moral anguish pushed to its limits: his haggard eyes, the veins of his forehead stretched taut like cords, his distorted features, his tense muscles, all showed plainly enough that the poor distracted general had just been victim of a shameful deception. He could hardly stay in the saddle, great drops of sweat ran down his temples, his hands gripped the reins of his horse convulsively; I truly believed he was mad. . . . The monk was gloomy but impassive; I could not bear to meet his glance, it froze me. They stopped for only a few minutes; as they moved off, my uncle said to me: 'But Florita, the poor general is ill; he will never be able to command tomorrow.'

'Uncle, the battle is *lost*; that man is out of his mind, his limbs refuse to function. It is absolutely necessary to replace him, otherwise tomorrow he will commit every folly imaginable.'

Then, yielding to the impulse of my heart, I begged my uncle to go and find the prefect, the mayor, the military commanders, make them realise the critical position Nieto had put them in and compel them to take action to relieve Nieto of his command and appoint another general in his place.

My uncle looked at me in alarm and demanded whether I had gone mad in my turn, asking him to *compromise himself* by an act of this nature. And it is men like him who want to be in a republic! As we were talking, Althaus arrived.

'Florita is right,' he said. 'Your duty, Don Pio, is to assemble the chief citizens of the town immediately so that Nieto is relieved of his command this very evening. Nieto is not a wicked man, but his weakness and sentimentality have done more harm than downright wickedness could ever do. Today he sees the full extent of his blunders and his feeble mind is so appalled that he has lost his reason.'

My uncle did not dare say another word. Still haunted by the fear of being compromised, he feigned illness and went to bed.

Althaus told me that the whole army was disgusted with the general and there was talk in the camp of stripping him of his epaulettes.

'In a word, this is what happened: San-Roman had no provisions. He talked Nieto into giving him some by promising to recognise Orbegoso, and our general was simple enough to trust a promise dictated by sheer necessity. At last he came back; we were all exceedingly impatient after so long a wait. Morant asked him: "Are we definitely going to fight, General? And must we prepare for this evening?" "For tomorrow, monsieur, at sunrise." He brought with him three of San-Roman's officers; he has had them placed under arrest, and, just think of it, tonight he wants to have them shot. I tell you again, the man is mad. It is vital to replace him, but the choice of another leader is a very embarrassing matter; how are we to set about it? You see how it is: all these citizens who ought to be dying for the fatherland hide in the convents; your uncle goes off to bed; the Goyeneches, the Gamios, etc. are content just to weep and wail. Well, I ask you, what the devil can you do with such a bunch of

wet hens? I am quite certain we shall lose the battle, and
I'm thoroughly annoyed about it, because I detest that
Gamarra!'

Althaus clasped my hand and assured me he would
come to no harm: 'Don't worry about me,' he said, 'the
Peruvians know how to run away but not how to kill';
and he returned to the camp.

I was awakened before daybreak by an old *chacarero*
Althaus had sent to tell us that San-Roman, profiting
from the darkness of the night, had withdrawn towards
Cangallo and that Nieto had set off in pursuit with the
whole of the army, followed even by the *rabonas*.

When daylight appeared I climbed up to the roof and
saw no trace of either camp on the plain, so at last they
had gone to do battle.

Once again the domes of convents and churches were
thick with people, but they no longer formed the single
entity whose silence had so impressed me two days
before; now a confused and muffled murmur arose from
these huge masses and the continual movement which
agitated them was like the tumult of the waves in an
angry sea.

At nine o'clock there came the sound of artillery, and
firing continued with frightening rapidity. Then there was
deepest silence among the people, the silence of the
condemned man in the presence of the scaffold. At the
end of half an hour we noticed a cloud of smoke rising
behind the mountain; as the village of Cangallo lay at its
foot we assumed that this was where the fighting was
taking place. Towards eleven o'clock a number of soldiers
appeared on the flat summit: hardly another half-hour
had elapsed before they had disappeared behind the
mountain and only a handful remained, some on foot, the
others on horseback. With the help of old Hurtado's
excellent telescope I saw perfectly clearly that several of
them were wounded: one was sitting binding up his arm
with his handkerchief, another was bandaging his head,

yet another was lying across his horse; all were making their way down the difficult narrow mountain path.

At about half-past twelve the Arequipans finally realised the full extent of the disaster. We had before our eyes the spectacle of an army in flight, as magnificent in its way as a tempest and just as terrifying! I had witnessed the July Revolution of 1830, but then I was exalted by the heroism of the people and I had no thought of the danger; in Arequipa I saw only the misfortunes which threatened the town.

Suddenly Carillo's dragoons, well-mounted and carrying the flag of Peru on the tip of their lances, appeared on the summit and galloped at full tilt down the mountain in what must have been the greatest disorder ever inspired by fear; after them came the *chacareros* on their mules and donkeys, then the infantry, running among the horses and mules and throwing off their packs and rifles so as to be more agile; finally came the artillery bringing up the rear to cover the retreat. Behind them all came the wretched *rabonas* with one or two children on their backs, driving before them the loaded mules, and the oxen and sheep which Nieto had intended to accompany the army.

At this sight the whole town uttered a cry, a dreadful cry, a cry of terror that still reverberates in my soul! At the same instant the crowd disappeared; once again the domes and towers were no more than inert masses, and apart from the mournful sound of the tocsin from the cathedral, all was silence.

I was still there, alone on the housetop, when I felt my dress being pulled; I turned and saw my *samba* pointing towards the courtyards of my uncle and Senor Hurtado and motioning me to kneel. I did as she asked, and looking down I saw my aunt Joaquina, the three Cuello ladies (whose brother was in Carillo's dragoons) and seven or eight other women kneeling in prayer. The same scene was repeated in Hurtado's courtyard. I did not pray for those whom the battle had released from the sorrows of this life, but rather for the unhappy country where rapacious politicians continually provoke civil strife in order to plunder their fellow citizens.

Towards half-past one the wounded began to arrive. Ah! then there were harrowing scenes. More than a hundred women were waiting at the corner of our house, terrified of recognising a son, a husband or a brother among them. The sight of each wounded man provoked these women to such extreme despair that their wails of anguish were a torture to me. What I suffered that day was appalling!

We were all anxious about Althaus, Emmanuel, Cuello and many others; we could not understand why the general did not fall back and defend the town, according to plan. Over an hour had passed since the defeat and we were expecting the enemy to enter at any moment. Cuello arrived on the point of death; he had received a bullet in the side and had been bleeding for three hours; he was taken to hospital and I went with his sisters to help make him as comfortable as possible.

It was pitiful to see the courtyard of this hospital! The wounded were just set down anyhow upon the ground, and fear of the enemy only increased their sufferings, for in this country it is not the custom for the victor to give quarter to prisoners, and even the wounded in the hospitals are massacred. We managed to find a bed for poor Cuello in a dark little room already occupied by two other unfortunates whose cries were heart-rending.

As I returned to my uncle's I saw Emmanuel approaching at a gallop; we all surrounded him, eager for news; neither Althaus nor any of the other officers was wounded but both sides had suffered heavy losses. Emmanuel told us that the general intended to abandon the town because it was impossible to defend it; Nieto had sent him to spike the guns guarding the bridge and throw the rest of the munitions into the river. He told us all this in five minutes and asked me to get Althaus's things together quickly so that he would find everything ready for his flight. I hurried straightway to his house, and with the help of his negro slave, whom I was almost obliged to beat in order to make him obey me, I had a mule loaded with a bed, and a trunk packed with effects. My *samba*, together with another of my uncle Pio's slaves, went on ahead with the mule and the unwilling negro, to spare Althaus the embarrassment of his departure from the town. Having accomplished this first task, I set about preparing food and drink, guessing that my poor cousin would be in urgent need of refreshment. I heard a great sound of horses and ran to the gate; it was the general, followed by all his officers, passing through the town at a gallop. Then came the rest of the army, and my cousin entered the courtyard. I had had a fresh horse saddled for him; on seeing it, he dismounted, came up to me, took me by the hand, and said: 'Thanks, good Flora, thanks; has somebody taken my things?'

'The mule has already left, but it would be a good thing if your two aides were to join it, for the wretched negro refuses to follow you.'

'Have you anything to give these gentlemen to drink? They are quite exhausted.'

I gave them some good claret — they each took two bottles — and stuffed their pockets with sugar, chocolate, bread, and everything else I found in the house. They gave their horses some wine as well, and when both men and horses were a little refreshed, they set off.

Althaus could hardly speak, his voice was so hoarse from issuing orders, but as he hastily drank his tea he told me briefly that this time it was Carillo's dragoons who had lost them the battle; they had fired on Morant's artillery by mistake, thinking it was the enemy. 'I tell you, Florita, as long as these civilians refuse to learn military tactics, they will continue to make a mess of things. Now the general does not want to defend the town. I don't know why he is in such a panic; he thinks only of flight and has no fixed plan. When we got to Menao's house we had a lot of trouble to convince him that he should at least give the army time to regroup. It's his fault we have lost so many fugitives. When we got back to the *chicherias* we made a superhuman effort to get them together again, but in vain; these cowardly rascals, aided and abetted by the *rabonas*, go to ground like moles. What astonishes me, cousin, is that the enemy is so slow to arrive; I don't understand it at all.'

Emmanuel entered the courtyard. 'I've come to fetch you,' he said to Althaus. 'Everybody is leaving; the monk has loaded what little cash we have left onto his horse; the general has gone to embrace his wife, who has been brought to bed this very night; I am just off to say goodbye to my poor mother; come, cousin, we are only waiting for you now, let us be off.' Althaus hugged me tightly, commended his wife and children to my care, I kissed dear Emmanuel, and they left in great haste.

When I returned to the street of Santo-Domingo it was completely deserted; all the houses I passed on my way were carefully barricaded. The town appeared perfectly calm; but the bloodstained cobbles spoke eloquently of the calamity the town had just suffered and of the further calamities still in store.

Back at my uncle's I related all that Althaus and Emmanuel had told me. Everybody present condemned the general, but nobody was prepared to take any action whatsoever.

At five o'clock I climbed once more to the rooftop; all I saw was the great cloud of dust Carillo's dragoons had left behind them in their flight across the desert. They were making for Islay, where they knew they would find two ships to take them out of reach of San-Roman. I stayed for a long time sitting in the same place as in the morning. How changed the town was! Now it was shrouded in a deathly silence. All the inhabitants were at prayer, as if resigned to let themselves be massacred without offering the least resistance.

My uncle begged me to come down and go into the church of Santo-Domingo, where everybody in the house was making their way. Then it struck me that I had had nothing to eat all day; I drank a cup of chocolate, took my cloak and went to the church.

At every moment the watchers on the towers were asked if they could see anything on the mountainside; they always replied: absolutely nothing. Finally at seven o'clock three Indians presented themselves at the gate; they announced that the enemy had reached the *chicherias*, but that San-Roman did not wish to enter the town unless the authorities went to ask him. This news caused a great stir. The prefect and all the civic authorities had taken refuge in Santo-Domingo, and they declared that it was for the reverend fathers to make this concilia-tory gesture. The monks, who are not renowned for their courage, protested vigorously against this proposal, and a long discussion ensued. It was largely through my efforts that the monks were persuaded to undertake this mission. I knew they were all out-and-out Gamarrists. I spoke to the Prior and to Don Jose, my aunt's chaplain; in short, I did so well that they decided to go. Four or five officials from the town hall went with them, and an hour later we saw them return at the head of two regiments, one of cavalry, the other of infantry: so the Gamarrists won the day. On Saturday 5 April, at eight in the evening, they took possession of the city of Arequipa.

When the Prior and his monks returned to the monas-tery, they reported to us all they had learned.

'My brothers,' said the worthy Prior, 'I confess that I am ill at ease; everything I heard those Indians say con-vinces me that they intend us harm. I will not mince matters, your presence here increases my fears. Every-body knows that you have brought all your valuables to our convents and monasteries, so it stands to reason that if these soldiers start looting, they will make straight for the churches.'

At these words everybody uttered a cry of alarm; Father Diego Cabero, the most authoritative figure in the community, began to upbraid the poor prior, my uncle defended him, and the discussion soon became a dispute. I profited from the altercation to slip away, as I was alarmed to see myself condemned to spend the night in such a place. There were nearly as many fleas here as in Islay, and it was too disgusting to have to stay with people who came up to speak to you clutching their chamber-pots under their arms! I approached Father Cabero's brother, the monk Mariano, and suggested that after the argument that had just taken place, it would be better if he and his brother went back home, and that if their sisters would consent to accompany them, I would ask them to give me shelter. After some hesitation the two monks agreed and helped me to persuade their sisters as well. I went out first with them to make sure that the street was empty and to open the gate of their house, then they went back to fetch their ladies, and the moment they were inside, the gate was barred. We all gathered in a room at the back of the house. Several times soldiers rapped on the gate with their rifles; the poor ladies shook with fear, and it was all the monks could do to calm them.

Towards midnight I felt an irresistible need for sleep; there was no bed, so I threw myself down upon a lumpy straw mattress and slept profoundly until eight o'clock the next morning.

XIII

A temptation

When I awoke I found everyone around me in a state of agitation: they said soldiers had been through the town during the night robbing everybody they encountered, and two people had been killed.

It was Sunday, and as the Cabero ladies did not want to miss mass, we were escorted there by the two monks. What a disgusting spectacle the church presented! A confused mass of men, women, children, even dogs, a clutter of beds, stoves, *chamber-pots*, a thick haze of smoke: it was truly scandalous! Mass was being sung in one corner, people were eating and smoking in another. I went to see my uncle and aunt who were installed in the prior's cell with seven or eight other people. I was quite unable to persuade my uncle to return home; fear of pillage still held him back. As I was not at all afraid, I went back alone to write up the three days which had just elapsed, and as that evening my uncle still insisted on staying in the monastery, I spent the night in the house with nobody except my *samba*. This girl said to me: 'Don't be afraid, mademoiselle, if the soldiers or the *rabonas* come looking for loot, I am Indian like them, their language is the same as mine, I shall tell them "My mistress is not Spanish, she is French, so don't hurt her." I am quite sure they won't, as they only hurt their enemies.' Thus spoke my aunt's slave, a girl of fifteen; but whatever age he is, the slave has never loved his masters, no matter how kind they are.

On the second day I was still alone when two officers came asking to speak to Don Pio. I did not like to tell them my uncle was in hiding, so I invited them in, told them Don Pio happened to be away, and asked them what they wanted with him.

'Mademoiselle, we would like your uncle, as one of the important people in the country, to come and talk to Colonel Escudero, who has taken command now that San-Roman has been killed in battle. We are the victors, and the people of Arequipa are abusing our moderation by continuing to treat us as enemies. Ever since we entered the town all the houses have been barricaded. Our troops are without bread, our wounded are left dying on the battlefield, while the townsfolk insist on staying in the convents as if we came here to massacre them. You are the first person to whom we have been able to communicate our needs; but you realise, mademoiselle, this state of affairs cannot last any longer.'

I spoke for a long time with these gentlemen and found them very courteous. When they had left I ran to Santo-Domingo to warn my uncle and the others who had taken refuge there. As soon as they knew that San-Roman was dead and Colonel Escudero commander in his place, their minds were easier, for Escudero was known and liked in Arequipa. Nearly everyone left the monastery to return home, and my uncle went off straightway to see Escudero.

When he returned he told me: 'We are saved; as for me, I have nothing more to fear; Escudero owes me much and is devoted to me. As the death of San-Roman has left the army without a leader, would you imagine it, he proposed to appoint me!'

'Would you accept?'

'Oh no! I'd take good care not to; in such situations it is necessary to hold aloof. Later on, when things are quieter, I shall see if I can find something to suit me, but I don't want any more military commands, I'm too old.'

'But, uncle, it seems to me that this is just the time when men like you should offer the benefit of their talents and experience.'

'Florita, it is very lucky for you that you are not a politician, your devotion would be your ruin; far from offering my services to these amateurs, I want to let them be overwhelmed by troubles and difficulties; the more they have, the more they will need me; they will come begging, and then I shall be able to make my own terms.'

I looked at my uncle and all I could say was: poor Peruvians!

In the event Don Pio offered Escudero a loan of two thousand piastres; he advised the Goyeneches, Ugarte and others to follow his example. The bishop offered four thousand piastres, his brother and sister two thousand each; the rest gave similar sums.

During all these troubles foreigners and their property were respected. When Escudero arrived, M Le Bris and the heads of two English companies made him a small loan to provide for the needs of his army, which had gone three days without an issue of bread; but this loan was voluntary.

On the third day, Tuesday, Escudero issued a proclamation ordering that the gates of every house were to be opened within three hours and left open, as was customary, warning that any left closed would be broken open by the soldiers. This forced people who had stayed in the convents to return home. As a further encouragement to these poor townsfolk Escudero ordered his soldiers to show themselves in the town, with strict instructions not to insult anybody.

We knew through Althaus that Nieto and all his army had reached Islay on Sunday 6 April, that they had spiked the guns there, burned the customs records and forced the administrator, Don Basilio de la Fuente, to leave for Lima; and that they themselves, after laying waste the countryside, had embarked on three Peruvian ships for Tacna.

Escudero had entered Arequipa on Sunday during the night, so nobody knew exactly how many soldiers he had with him. At first it was announced that San-Roman was dead; four days later the rumour spread that he was only wounded; finally, at the end of a week, he came to Arequipa, and he too entered during the night.

Here is the explanation of this affair as Escudero himself told it to me:

After he had managed to deceive Nieto three days in succession just so that he could obtain victuals for his troops, San-Roman withdrew to Cangallo, never dreaming that Nieto would follow. Before giving battle he wanted to consult Gamarra and ask him for reinforcements, but at Cangallo he found Escudero with four hundred men sent by Gamarra. While they were entertaining the new arrivals Nieto's army suddenly appeared on the summit of the mountain: then there was great confusion. San-Roman had given his soldiers permission to bathe; some of them were naked. When they saw the Arequipans they thought all was lost; without Escudero, who restored order, they would all have taken flight. The battle was joined and they fought bravely, but soon they began to run out of ammunition, and then there was panic. When San-Roman saw his soldiers in confusion he thought the battle was lost and that the best thing for him was to flee as well, so together with some of his suite he went off as fast as his horse could carry him. So these two valorous champions, each afraid of the other, each fled the field in his turn; they went without stopping for a day and a night, putting a distance of *two hundred miles* between them! Nieto's terror took him as far as Islay, one hundred miles to the south, San-Roman's to Vilque, over one hundred miles to the north. By a miracle, part of San-Roman's army rallied and turned back towards Arequipa: one of San-Roman's officers whom Nieto was holding prisoner in the town hall saw Nieto's army in flight and profited from the confusion to escape on the first horse he found. As he knew the region well he cut across country and reached Cangallo in an hour, where he called upon the fugitives to stop, and told them that Nieto, thinking himself beaten, had abandoned the town and was fleeing towards the port. Escudero and a few others spent the whole night and part of the next day reassembling the soldiers; they succeeded in mustering nearly a third of their force, then, confident they would not encounter any opposition, they advanced on Arequipa. But had it not been for this officer who escaped, the two armies would have continued to flee in opposite directions and the town would have been spared the sight of both defenders and attackers. Somebody had to go all the way to Vilque to inform San-Roman that he had won the battle, and he did not enter Arequipa until a week later. The reason given for this delay was that he had been wounded in the thigh, but this was quite untrue.

My uncle, who has the gift of getting on well with all parties, was, if not in the confidence of the Gamarrists, at least on very good terms with them. Every day we had these gentlemen to dinner and our house was never empty from morning to night. In the course of my conversations with the officers of this army I was surprised to see how superior they were to Nieto's; Messrs Montoya, Torres, Quiroga and above all Escudero, are all very distinguished men.

Escudero is one of those adventurous Spaniards who left the beauties of their native Spain to seek their fortune in the New World; a man of great learning, he is, as occasion demands, soldier, writer, or trader. He has a lively mind, an inexhaustible imagination, a cheerful nature, and a persuasive eloquence. He writes with burning conviction, yet he is popular with all parties.

This extraordinary man was the devoted friend, trusted adviser and tireless secretary of Senora Gamarra; for three years he had fought under her command, accompanied her on all her campaigns and never recoiled from any of the audacious enterprises that this woman of truly Napoleonic ambition conceived.

Colonel Escudero and I were friends from the start, for our natures were in harmony. He confided in me a great deal and kept me informed of all that passed in the Gamarra camp; from what he told me I understood that San-Roman had committed just as many blunders as Nieto.

'What an unhappy country this is!' Escudero said to me. 'The men of blood and destruction have put the Peruvians in a lamentable position and I really do not know who will be able to get them out of it.'

'But how is it, colonel, that when you perceive better than anybody else the cause of the trouble, you have not sought to remedy it?'

'On the contrary, mademoiselle, I think of nothing else, but I can only point out ways of doing good, I lack the authority necessary to carry them out. Senora Gamarra is an exceptional woman, but all her efforts are directed towards consolidating power in her hands; my plans for the public good are always thwarted by her ambition; and devoted though I am to her service, I see myself constantly forced to act in ways that go against my will.'

As I listened to Escudero it was plain to me that he was weary of the yoke imposed on him by his all-powerful mistress and that he was only looking for a pretext to escape. He came to see me every day and we had long conversations together. I had plenty of time to get to know him and I realised that he was perhaps the only man in Peru capable of seconding my ambitious plans. I suffered at the misfortunes of the country I had come to look upon as my own; I had always had a passionate desire to contribute to the good of the world, and I had always wanted an active and adventurous life. I imagined that if I could inspire Escudero with love for me, I would gain a great influence over him. Then once again my inner conflict revived and I was in mental torment; the idea of an association with this witty, daring, carefree man appealed to my imagination. If I take a chance with him,

I thought, what does it matter if I do not succeed, when I have nothing to lose? The voice of duty would probably have been powerless to make me resist this, the strongest temptation I have ever felt in my life, had not another consideration come to my aid. I feared the moral depravity which invariably accompanies the enjoyment of power. I feared to become hard, despotic — a criminal, even — like those who were now in power. I trembled to think of participating in the government of a country where my uncle lived . . . my uncle whom I had loved so tenderly, and whom I loved still, but who had done me so much harm! I did not want to risk giving way to a moment of resentment, and I can say here, before God, that I sacrificed the position I knew I could easily make for myself to the fear of having to treat my uncle as an enemy. The sacrifice was all the greater for the fact that Escudero pleased me. Many thought him ugly, but not I. He would have been between thirty and thirty-three, of medium height and very slim, with a dark skin, very black hair, sparkling yet soulful eyes and pearly teeth. His tender glance and melancholy smile lent his face a lofty and poetic air which quite carried me away. With such a man it seemed to me that nothing would have been impossible. I have the deep-seated conviction that had I become his wife I would have been very happy. In the midst of political turmoil he would have sung me ballads or played his guitar as unconcernedly as when he was a student in Salamanca. Once again it took me all my moral strength not to succumb to the tempting prospect. . . . I was *afraid of myself*, and I judged it prudent to escape this new danger by flight, so I resolved to leave immediately for Lima.

Nobody could understand why I was in such a hurry to depart. In vain did they warn that the road to Islay was infested with deserters, in vain did they paint an exaggerated picture of the perils I would run, I was deaf to all warnings. In my eyes no danger could equal that to which staying in Arequipa exposed me; to escape from it I would have crossed all the deserts on earth. I made it my excuse that it was essential for me to leave if I wished to get back to Europe before the bad season; and as in their hearts all at my uncle's were glad to see me go, there were no further objections.

An Englishman of my acquaintance, Mr Valentine Smith, was going to Lima, and I asked him if he would mind having me as a travelling companion. He accepted my proposal; we struck a bargain with an Italian captain whose ship was at Islay, and it was settled that we should leave on 25 April.

Before I left I had the dreary round of visits to carry out. According to etiquette I ought to have gone to everybody I had visited when I arrived, but I limited myself to a few principal families with whom I was on good terms and sent cards to the others.

These visits enabled me to judge the extent of the evils the war had inflicted on this unhappy town. In each house I saw mourning and tears. But it seemed to me that even worse than the losses occasioned by death were the discord and hatred which civil strife had sown in the bosom of so many families. There was deep enmity between relations, between brothers; the name of freedom was never mentioned in their political disputes: each had supported the leader from whom he hoped to gain the most.

These poor Arequipans envied me my lot. In every house they said: 'Ah! mademoiselle, how lucky you are to be leaving a country where brother cuts the throat of brother, where the extortions of our *friends* prevent us from satisfying the demands of our *enemies*!'

When I went to bid farewell to the bishop and his family I had a striking example of the disasters liable to afflict the fools who seek happiness in material things outside themselves. The Goyeneches had never been happy unless they were sitting on piles of gold, and the loss of part of their wealth had upset the balance of their minds. Mademoiselle de Goyeneche was particularly affected: her eyes were fixed and staring, her gestures jerky, her expression very strange: she spoke so volubly that it was almost impossible to understand what she said. I noticed that she kept calling me Don Pio and my uncle Florita. Her unnatural animation was quite frightening; I whispered to my uncle: 'The poor girl is mad.'

The bishop resembled a skeleton, his face was so shrunken and gaunt; clothed all in silk and gold, sunk in the depths of a large armchair, betraying hardly a sign of life, he seemed to be officiating at his own funeral. I was touched at the sight, even if on reflection I found something absurd in the suffering which was taking him to the tomb. I asked myself how he could be so keenly affected by the loss of his gold, when he spent so little on himself and did nothing to alleviate the plight of others? But I sought in vain; for me, avarice has always posed a moral problem to which I have never been able to find an answer. If this prelate had distributed his riches to the poor, his enemies would have been powerless to harm him.

I also wanted to pay a visit to San-Roman; I had not yet seen him. He had not been out because it was necessary to make people believe the story about his broken leg. My uncle, fearing my outspokenness, did all he could to dissuade me and only agreed to accompany me when Escudero offered to be my escort. As we entered we saw a group of officers standing in the drawing-room engaged in animated conversation; the moment they saw us they hurried into the neighbouring room. I wanted to follow them in order to surprise the victorious general standing all unaided on his own two legs, but my uncle guessed my malicious intention and held me back, saying, 'Wait until they announce us.'

Two or three of those gentlemen came up to me and said:'Senorita, the general is very flattered by your visit

Fortunately he is a little better; you will find him lying on a couch.' I entered the bedchamber, and San-Roman apologised for not getting up to receive me. He was not lying down but sitting up with his leg resting on a stool. This San-Roman, so feared by the Arequipans, had nothing at all intimidating about him; he was about thirty, his face was frank and cheerful, but his hair, his beard and the colour of his skin showed that he had Indian blood in his veins, a fact which made him ugly in the eyes of Peruvians of Spanish descent.

Our conversation was somewhat unusual, being at the same time both light-hearted and serious. San-Roman spoke well, but he had a failing which played havoc with the reserve my uncle had advised me to adopt: he went off into peals of laughter at the slightest provocation. This excessive hilarity was very much at odds with the grave demeanour of everyone around him, but it put me at my ease, and I managed to laugh a fair amount myself.

'Is it really true, mademoiselle,' he asked, drawing himself up proudly, 'that the people of Arequipa were afraid of me?'

'They were so afraid of you, colonel, that I had begun to call you *Croquemitaine*.'

'And what does that mean?'

'It's the bogeyman that nursemaids in France use to frighten little children. If you're not good, if you don't do as you are told, they say, I'll call *Croquemitaine* and he'll come and eat you. So the child is terrified and obeys immediately.'

'Ah! the comparison is charming! Nieto is the nursemaid, the Arequipans are the little children, and I am the bogeyman who eats them up.'

'Poor Arequipans! Are you really going to eat them up?'

'May God keep me from such a thing! No, on the contrary, I come to restore peace and encourage work and trade so that they will have something to eat themselves.'

'A noble aim, colonel; I am curious to know how you propose to achieve it.'

'By Senora Gamarra's methods, mademoiselle; that is, we shall close our ports to all those foreign vessels which compete to infest our country with goods so cheap that even the black slaves strut about in their cloth. You know that Peruvian industry can never flourish in the face of such competition, and as long as people here can obtain things they need from the foreigner for next to nothing they will never buckle down to producing them themselves.'

'Colonel, you cannot train manufacturers as you train soldiers, nor can you raise factories as you raise armies, by force.'

'This system is not as difficult to put into effect as you seem to think; our country furnishes all the raw materials — flax, cotton, silk, wool of incomparable fineness, gold, silver, lead, and so on; as for machinery, we shall import it from England, together with workers from every corner of the earth.'

'A bad system, colonel! Believe me, you will never encourage competition and love of work by isolating yourselves.'

'And I believe, mademoiselle, that *necessity* is the only spur which will compel our people to work; besides, our country is in a better position than any country in Europe, for we have no large army or navy to maintain, no huge debt to support. We are therefore in a favourable position to develop our industry, and when peace is restored and we have prohibited the consumption of foreign goods, there will be nothing to prevent the factories we set up from prospering.'

'But you forget that for a long time to come the cost of labour will be higher here than it is in Europe. You have only a small population; would you have it employed in producing cloth, watches, furniture, and so on? If so, what will become of agriculture, which is already backward enough, and the exploitation of the mines, which you have been forced to abandon for want of labour?'

'As long as we have no factories, the foreigners will continue to carry off our gold and silver.'

'But, colonel, gold and silver are what this country produces, and more than anything else, they would lose their value if you could not exchange them for products from outside. I repeat, the time for setting up factories has not yet arrived; before you even think of such a thing you should instil in your people the taste for luxury and the comforts of life, create needs for them in order to make them work; and it is only through the free importation of foreign merchandise that you will succeed. As long as the Indian goes barefoot and is content with just a sheepskin for his only clothing and a little maize and a few bananas for food, he will never work!'

'Well done, mademoiselle! I see you are a fervent champion of your country's interests.'

'At a time like this I am not likely to forget that I come from a Peruvian family. I ardently desire to see this nation prosper. Educate the people, improve communications, encourage free trade, and you will see public prosperity advance with giant strides. It is precisely through the use of such simple means as I propose that your brothers in North America have been able to astonish the world with the rapidity of their progress.'

Our conversation was long: my gaiety and gravity so charmed the conqueror that when I rose to take my leave, he stood up at the same time, quite forgetting his *broken leg*. I was malicious enough to let him take several steps, in spite of the alarmed faces of the officers present, before I said: '*General*, I do not want you to go any further; you are ill, your wound is very dangerous. Stay well wrapped up in your cloak, don't talk political economy, smoke good cigars, and if you follow this routine, I hope you will recover in time.' San-Roman thanked me for taking such a sincere interest in him, and began to limp as he returned to his couch.

Escudero came to see me in the evening, and the moment I saw him I burst out laughing so heartily that he could not help laughing with me. We had understood each other.

'Dear Florita, the world is like that: a perpetual comedy in which we are by turn actors and spectators. Perhaps at this very moment General Nieto is going around Tacna with his arm in a sling. Well, God save us, these little deceptions are very harmless.'

'No doubt, colonel; but you must admit that when somebody has it announced in public that he has a broken leg, he ought to remember and not get up on his own two legs to escort young ladies to the door.'

'And it is you, who know so well the power of those eyes like a gazelle's, who reproach San-Roman for having forgotten in your presence that he was supposed to have a broken leg! Ah! mademoiselle Flora, that is ungenerous of you!'

'Colonel, generosity has nothing to do with it; San-Roman's position was bound to seem ridiculous to me, and in any case, you have just been laughing at it yourself!'

'Ah! it's different for me; I am like our dear friend Althaus, I laugh at everything; besides, I haven't made a conquest of the conqueror like our lovely Florita.'

'Really? Ah! that reconciles me with him; I did not think he was very pleased with me after the home truths I told him about his absurd policies.'

'On the contrary, he was so pleased with you that he told me: "If I were free, I would ask for that young lady's hand in marriage. I cannot understand how the rest of you can let her go." '

'Well, he certainly seems very sure of himself, our Monsieur Croquemitaine. Do you know, Escudero, the men of this country are quite extraordinary; when I tell people in Europe the sort of things they do, nobody will believe me.'

'You must not let that stop you from writing about your travels, though, and if the French do not believe you, perhaps the Peruvians will profit from your courage in telling them the truth about themselves.'

Before leaving Peru I wanted also to say goodbye to my cousin the nun of Santa-Rosa. I paid this visit alone. Everybody admires Dominga's courage and determination, but she lives in isolation, and although she is related to the wealthiest and most influential families in the country, *nobody dares to see her*, so great a hold do prejudice and superstition continue to exert on this ignorant and credulous people. Dominga's mother has callously rejected her, and only her brother and one of her aunts take her part. People criticise her love of luxury as if it were a crime, as if after returning to the world she ought still to observe the absurd austerities of the convent. I understand that her pleasures may well seem childish to those whose minds are preoccupied with lofty and serious thoughts. I have very simple tastes myself, but I find it quite natural that the poor recluse should want to make up for the eleven years of captivity, the torments and privations she had to suffer in Santa-Rosa.

That evening I found her busy learning French. She looked enchanting in her pretty pink and black check silk dress, little black lace apron and black tulle mittens. Her shoulders were bare and a pearl necklace graced her neck; her ebony hair, shining like the finest silk, fell upon her breast in several ringlets artistically entwined with pink satin ribbons; her lovely face was tinged with melancholy and suffering which lent her whole person an indefinable charm.

When she saw me she ran up to me and said in accents which filled me with sadness: 'Dear Florita, is it really true that you are returning to France?'

'Yes, cousin, I am leaving and I have come to say goodbye.'

'Ah! Florita, how lucky you are and how I envy you!'

'Dear Dominga, are you so unhappy here, then?'

'More than you can imagine . . . much more than I ever was in Santa-Rosa. . . .'

As she uttered these words she wrung her hands in despair, and raised her big sad eyes to heaven as if to reproach God for having given her so cruel a fate.

'What, Dominga, when you are *free*: when you are so beautiful, so charmingly dressed, you are more unhappy now than when you were a prisoner in that gloomy convent, shrouded in your nun's veil? I confess I do not understand you.'

The young woman threw back her proud head, and looking at me with a sardonic smile she said: 'You call me *free*? In what country can a frail creature oppressed by a wicked prejudice be called *free*? Here, Florita, in this room, in her pretty silk dress, Dominga is still the nun of Santa-Rosa! Through courage and perseverance I managed to escape from my *tomb*, but the woollen veil I took is still here on my head, it separates me for ever from the world; in vain did I fly from the cloister, the indignation of the people is driving me back. . . .'

I was dumbfounded. . . . So, I thought, this is the sort of society produced by the cult of Rome! I gazed sadly at my poor cousin as she paced the room. So many charms, so much capacity for happiness, lost because fanaticism held this graceful creature in its clutches.

'Dear Dominga,' I said, 'Come, bid me farewell; I see that my presence here distresses you. I certainly did not come with that intention, for I love you out of sympathy; my misfortune is even greater than your own. . . .'

'Oh! impossible!' she cried in ringing tones, flinging herself into my arms. 'Impossible, for mine is more than human strength can endure!'

She held me tightly embraced and I felt her heart

beating as if it would burst its bonds, yet she did not weep. There was a long silence: each of us felt that we were in a situation when a single word suffices to release a flock of painful thoughts. . . .

At last Dominga broke away from me in a sudden movement and said in a terrible voice: 'Ah! Flora, you blaspheme when you say you are more unfortunate than I! You, unfortunate, when you are welcome wherever you go, when you are free to come and go as you please, when you can marry the man you love. . . . No, no, Florita, I alone have the right to complain! If people see me in the street, they point me out and curse me; if I want to share in the happiness of some special occasion, people repulse me and say: "This is no place for a bride of Christ; go back to your cloister!" When I apply for a passport, I am told: "You are a nun; you must stay at Santa-Rosa!" If I want to marry the man I love, they say: "You are a nun, the bride of Christ; you must live at Santa-Rosa!" Oh! damnation! damnation! I shall always be a nun!'

And I, I muttered under my breath, I shall always be *married*!

I did not try to console Dominga; there is no consolation for such bitter grief. I stroked her hair; I cut off a tress which I still treasure.

Towards ten o'clock there was a knock at the door; it was the young doctor who had helped her to obtain the corpse. She stretched out her hand to him and said in a broken voice: 'Florita is leaving . . . and I. . . .'

'And you too,' interrupted the young man, 'you too will leave soon! Be patient, and it will not be long before you see my beautiful Spain and my dear mother, who will love you like her own daughter.'

At these words poor Dominga sighed with renewed hope; the smile returned to her lips and she said in a tone of mingled love and doubt: 'May God hear you, Alfonso, but alas! I fear I shall never enjoy such happiness!'

This last scene gave me an insight into my cousin's

sorrows and made me understand how much she had to suffer. . . .

The moment of my departure was drawing near. At my uncle's everybody went about with long faces, but I had read their thoughts, and their regrets were like the tears shed by the principal beneficiaries of a will. Whatever respect they may have shown me, my lack of standing in the household was plain for all to see. The extreme simplicity of my dress was proof enough that my wealthy family made no attempt to compensate me for my poverty by giving me presents; and in the house of Don Pío people saw the only daughter of his brother Mariano treated like a stranger. However, I was calm and resigned: neither by word nor look did I show the least sign of discontent. Never since the scene I had had with my uncle had I permitted myself the slightest allusion to the way I had been treated. But my dignified demeanour made them as uncomfortable among themselves as they were with others. My presence was a constant reproach to them all, and my uncle, who was really fond of me, was smitten with remorse.

I took the opportunity to ask my aunt whether she would entrust her son Florentino and her second daughter Penchita to my care, so that they could be brought up in France in a manner appropriate to their position in society. My aunt replied that while she would consent to her son going, nothing in the world would induce her to let Penchita go. 'Oh! never would I consent to let her set foot in a country where our holy religion is held up to ridicule!'

As my aunt refused me, I addressed myself to my uncle, but all my persuasion could not move him. He objected that Florentino was too young and his character had been ruined by his mother. The poor man went to great lengths to conceal the real reason for his refusal. My uncle has always been the sole master in his household, and he would rather die than see his influence weakened.

So he did not want his son to acquire new ideas and develop his intellect. In his view the immense wealth he would leave his children was sufficient compensation for their lack of education. But wealth is so unreliable an asset that it is the height of folly to stake one's future on it. After all, my birth entitled me to as large a share of my grandmother's fortune as Don Pio himself. My father certainly thought so: his daughter, he said, would have an income of forty thousand francs one day. Yet I have to work in order to live and bring up my children. I would have liked my uncle's children to acquire the sort of knowledge which would make them useful to society, protect them from temptation in prosperity and provide them with subsistence in adversity, but it was not in my power; God did not permit my uncle to give his consent.

However, on the eve of my departure, Don Pio repeated the promise he had made me in front of the whole family: as soon as peace was restored he would take steps to make sure I received the allowance of two thousand five hundred francs he was making me, and he gave me a letter for M Bertera authorising him to pay me the full sum in advance.

XIV

My departure from Arequipa

On Friday 25 April Mr Smith came for me at seven in the morning; I was ready to mount my horse and showed no sign of agitation, yet I felt a keen emotion at leaving the house where my father was born, for where was I going now? I did not know. Weary of disappointments, I no longer made plans; rejected everywhere, without family, fortune or profession, without even a name I could call my own, I was abandoning myself to chance, like a balloon which falls where the wind takes it. I bade farewell to those walls, invoking my father's spirit to give me strength; I embraced my aunt and pitied her in my heart for her coldness towards me; I embraced her children and pitied them too, for they will have sorrow in their turn. I said goodbye to the crowd of servants gathered in the courtyard, then I mounted my horse and left that temporary refuge for ever, to commit myself to the grace of God. My uncle, my cousin Florentino and a few friends accompanied me. We rode along in silence; at Tiavaya we paused, and I looked back towards Arequipa and its charming valley, then I looked at my uncle. At this point, as the road became narrower, I went first and passed through the village. When we were once again in open country I stopped to wait for my uncle, but I could no longer see him. . . . M Le Bris told me that to spare me the distress of a final farewell he had taken advantage of the bend in the road to turn back to Arequipa without my noticing. It was all over. . . . I would never see my uncle again. . . . I cannot express how painful the thought was to me. I felt such bitter grief that for a moment I considered returning to Arequipa just to see him once more. If I had not been forced to quarrel with him over my inheritance, we would have loved each other sincerely. I had no sympathy with the politician in him, but everything else about him pleased me; never have I met a man whose conversation was more instructive, whose manners were more agreeable, and whose wit was more entertaining.

At Congata we found a good meal waiting for us, thanks to the consideration of Mr Smith. There we met old acquaintances and stayed at M Najarra's until the heat had somewhat abated. Towards midday the sea wind began to blow and we set off once more. I felt a pang of regret at separating from my two best friends M Le Bris and M Viollier; for seven months they had shown me much kindness and I felt sincere friendship for them both.

Mr Smith had a very intelligent Chilean manservant, and my uncle had sent along one of his most reliable clerks to look after me until I embarked. In addition the gallant Colonel Escudero had provided me with an armed escort, Lieutenant Monsilla and two lancers.

This journey was much less arduous than the previous one as I was provided with everything necessary to protect me from sun, wind, cold and thirst. I had two good mules, so that I could change mounts, and Mr Smith was good enough to place his second horse at my disposal. My aunt Joaquina had lent me two saddles, an English one for the horse and another for the mule. Finally, the attentions Mr Smith showered upon me made him seem a second Don Balthazar, for with his ten years' experience of such journeys my present companion was a match for the other.

When we reached the summit of the first mountain we made a halt. I dismounted and went to sit on the self-same spot where seven months earlier I had been set down almost at death's door. I stayed there a long time admiring the lovely valley of Arequipa and bidding it my last farewells, then as one thought led to another I reflected that had I been free and able to live with a man of my own choice, I could have been as happy there as in most of the countries of Europe. These reflections moved me to sadness. 'Mademoiselle,' said Mr Smith, who had roamed the world since he was sixteen and could not understand how one could become attached to any country, 'don't grieve for Arequipa; no doubt it is a pretty town, but the one I am taking you to is a veritable paradise. Here's to Lima, I say! If you cannot be a Member of Parliament with an income of ten thousand a year, better come and live in Lima!' Thus the natural gaiety and wit of Mr Smith helped change the course of my thoughts.

When you go from Arequipa to Islay you have the sun behind you and the wind in front, so you suffer far less from the heat than you do when going from Islay to Arequipa. I stood up to the journey very well; besides, my health had improved and I felt better able to endure its rigours this time. At midnight we arrived at the inn and I threw myself fully dressed upon my bed while supper was being prepared. Mr Smith had a miraculous talent for making light of difficulties, and now he saw to everything — food, muleteers, animals — with remarkable speed and tact. Thanks to him we had a very good supper, after which we all stayed up talking, for none of us could sleep. At three in the morning we set out once more: the cold was so bitter that I wore three ponchos. When dawn appeared I was overcome with an irresistible desire for sleep and begged Mr Smith to let me rest for just half an hour; I threw myself upon the ground and without giving the servant time to put down a mat for me I fell into so deep a sleep that nobody dared attempt to make me more comfortable. They let me sleep for an hour and I felt all the better for it; we were by then in the open pampa, so I mounted the horse and crossed the vast expanse at a gallop, in fact I managed the horse so well that Lieutenant Monsilla could not keep up with me, much less the two lancers. In the end Mr Smith himself had to beg me to have mercy on his fine Chilean mare as he was afraid I would wear her out.

At midday we reached Guerrera, where we made a halt; we ate beneath the fresh shade of the trees, then arranged our beds on the ground and slept until five. We climbed the mountain at an easy pace and reached Islay at seven. Great was the surprise of Don Justo when he saw me. He is extremely kind and hospitable to all travellers and showed me particular attention. Islay was greatly changed since my previous stay. This time I was not invited to any balls. Nieto and his brave soldiers had laid the town waste in the twenty-four hours they had spent there; as well as requisitioning food they had practised every kind of extortion to obtain money from the unfortunate inhabitants. The good Don Justo never stopped repeating: 'Ah! mademoiselle, if I were younger I would leave with you; these endless wars have made it impossible to live here. I have already lost two of my sons, and I expect any day to hear of the death of the third, who is in Gamarra's army.'

I stayed three days in Islay waiting for our ship to leave, and I would have been very dull without the company of Mr Smith, who also introduced me to the officers of an English frigate moored in the bay. I am happy to say that I have never met officers as distinguished for their manners and their intelligence as those of the *Challenger*; they all spoke French and had spent several years in Paris. They were in town clothes and their dress was remarkable for its immaculate cleanliness and elegant simplicity. The commander was a superb man, the ideal of masculine beauty. He was only thirty-two, yet a profound melancholy weighed upon him; all his words and deeds were tinged with a sadness which was painful to behold. I asked one of his officers the reason for this, and he said: 'Ah! yes, mademoiselle, he has good cause for sadness; for seven years he has been married to the loveliest woman in England; he loves her to distraction, just as she loves him, yet he must live apart from her.'

'What is the reason for this separation?'

'His profession; as he is one of our youngest captains he is always being sent on remote postings of three or four years' duration. We have been in these latitudes for three years, and we shall not be in England for another fifteen months. Judge for yourself what cruel suffering so long an absence causes him!'

'To say nothing of his wife! . . . But has he no fortune, then, to remain in a career which causes him and the woman he loves such torture?'

'No fortune! He has five thousand pounds a year of his own, and his wife, the richest heiress in England, brought him two hundred thousand; she is an only child and will have twice as much again on the death of her father.'

I was astonished. 'Then tell me, monsieur, what power is it that obliges your commander to live apart from his wife for four years, to languish on board his frigate and condemn so beautiful a woman to tears and grief?'

'It is necessary for him to attain a high position; our commander obtained this rich heiress from her father only on condition that he became an admiral. The young couple agreed, and to fulfil their promise he will have to stay at sea for at least another ten years, for with us, promotion depends on seniority.'

'So he accepts that he must live another ten years separated from his wife?'

'Yes, he must, in order to keep his promise; but when that time is up, he will be an admiral, he will enter the House of Lords, perhaps become a government Minister and end up one of the most powerful figures in the state. It seems to me, mademoiselle, that to attain such a position it is worth suffering for a few years!'

Ah! I thought, for the sake of such paltry tokens of grandeur men will trample underfoot everything that is most sacred! God himself was pleased to endow these two beings with every gift, beauty, brains and wealth; and the love they bear each other should have ensured for them a happiness as great as our nature is capable of enjoying; but the arrogance of a crazy old man has destroyed this prospect of earthly felicity: he insists that the best twenty years should be struck out of his children's lives. When they are reunited the wife will have lost her beauty, the husband his illusions; but he will be an admiral, a peer of the realm, a Minister, etc. What ridiculous vanity!

I cannot describe the bitter reflections this story caused me. Everywhere I encountered moral anguish; everywhere I saw that it proceeded from the evil prejudice that sets man against Providence, and I raged at the slow progress of human reason. I asked the handsome commander if he had any children. 'Yes,' he replied, 'a daughter as beautiful as her mother, and a son who is said to look very much like me; I have not seen him, he will be four years old when I do, if God permits it.' And the unhappy man repressed a sigh. He was still sensitive, because he was still young, but by the time he is fifty he will probably be as unfeeling as his father-in-law; and perhaps he will exact from his own son and daughter sacrifices as cruel as those imposed on him. This is how the prejudices which deprave our nature are transmitted; and the sequence will not be broken until there arise beings endowed by God with a firm will and resolute courage, who are prepared to suffer martyrdom rather than endure servitude.

On 30 April at eleven in the morning we sailed out of the Bay of Islay, and on 4 May at two in the afternoon we dropped anchor in the roads of Callao. This port did not seem to be as busy as Valparaiso. Recent political events had had a disastrous effect on trade and there were fewer ships than usual.

From the sea Lima is clearly visible on a hill surrounded by the mighty Andes. The size of the city, together with the imposing height of its many bell-towers, lend it an air of grandeur and enchantment.

We stayed at Callao until four o'clock waiting for the coach for Lima, which gave me ample time to examine the town. Like Valparaiso and Islay, Callao has grown so rapidly in the past ten years that after an absence of two or three years captains hardly recognise the place. The finest houses are owned by English or American merchants; they have large warehouses there, and their commercial activities give rise to continual movement between the port and the city some five miles away. Mr Smith took me to the house of his correspondents, and here once more I found all the luxury and comfort characteristic of the English. The servants were English, and like their masters they were dressed just as they would have been in England. The house had a verandah, as do all the houses in Lima, and this is very convenient in hot countries, as it gives shelter from the sun and enables one to walk all round the house to take the air. This particular verandah was embellished with pretty English blinds. I stayed there for some time and could survey in comfort the one long wide street which constitutes the whole of Callao. It was a Sunday, and sailors in holiday attire were strolling about: I saw groups of Englishmen, Americans, Frenchmen, Dutchmen, Germans – in short, a mixture from nearly every nation – and I heard snatches of every tongue. As I listened to these sailors I began to understand the charm they find in their adventurous life and the enthusiasm it inspired in that *true sailor* Leborgne. When I tired of looking at the street I cast a glance into the large drawing-room whose windows overlooked the verandah, where five or six immaculately dressed Englishmen, their handsome faces calm and impassive, were drinking grog and smoking excellent Havana cigars as they swung gently to and fro in hammocks from Guayaquil suspended from the ceiling.

At last it was four o'clock and we climbed into the

coach. The driver was French and all the people I found there spoke French or English. I met two Germans, great friends of Althaus, and immediately I felt at home. It was the first time I had been in a coach since I left Bordeaux, and the pleasure this gave me kept me happy all through the two-hour journey; I really thought I was back in civilisation.

The road out of Callao is bad, but after a mile or so it becomes tolerably good: very wide, smooth, and not too dusty. Just over a mile from Callao, on the right, lie the extensive ruins of some Indian city which had already ceased to exist when the Spaniards conquered the country. It would probably be possible to discover from Indian chronicles what this place was and how it came to be destroyed; but up to now the history of the Indians has not inspired sufficient interest in their conquerors for them to devote themselves to such research. A little further, on the left, is the village of Bella-Vista, where there is a hospital for sailors. Half-way to Lima, our driver stopped at an inn kept by a Frenchman, and after that, the city spread before us in all its magnificence, while the surrounding countryside provided a wealth of luxuriant vegetation in every shade of green: there were giant orange trees, clumps of bananas, lofty palms and many other species native to these regions, each with its distinctive foliage.

A mile or so before one enters the city the road is lined with great trees, and the effect of this avenue is truly majestic. There were quite a few people strolling on either side and several young men on horseback passed by our coach. I was told that this avenue is one of the principal promenades in Lima; among the women many were wearing the *saya*, and this costume struck me as so bizarre that it captured all my attention. Lima is a closed city, and at the end of the avenue we arrived at one of the gates. Its pillars are made of brick, and the façade, engraved with the arms of Spain, had been defaced. Officials searched the coach, just as they do at the gates of Paris. We went through much of the city; I thought the streets looked spacious and the houses quite different from the houses in Arequipa. Lima, so splendid from a distance, does not live up to its promise when you are inside; the houses are shabby, the windows are unglazed, and their iron grilles create an impression of suspicion and constraint; at the same time it is depressing to see so little sign of life in the streets. The coach stopped at a pleasant-looking house from which emerged a large stout lady whom I recognised immediately from the description the gentlemen of the *Mexicain* had given me as Madame Denuelle. This lady opened the door of the coach herself, helped me to alight, and said in the most affable manner: 'Mademoiselle Tristan, we have been impatiently awaiting your arrival for a long time. M Chabrié and M David have told us so much about you that we are very happy to have you with us.'

XV

A French hotel in Lima

— ❧ —

Madame Denuelle conducted me to a drawing-room furnished in the French style. I had hardly been seated for five minutes when more than a dozen Frenchmen came in, all eager to see me. I appreciated their interest, chatted a few moments with each one, and did my best to thank them for their warm welcome; then Madame Denuelle took me to the accommodation she had set apart for me, a small sitting-room and a bedroom.

I had left Arequipa with letters for a number of people in Lima, and Mr Smith, obliging as ever, had offered to deliver them for me, so that an hour after my arrival these people flocked to the hotel to hear the latest news. So eager were they that I was asked twenty questions at once. Don Basilio de la Fuente, who like me was staying at Madame Denuelle's, wanted to know what had happened to his wife and his eleven children; one lady wept for her brother who had been killed, another worried about her sister, Nieto's wife, who was virtually a prisoner in Santa-Rosa; and everybody was apprehensive, not without cause, lest Madame Senora should return to Lima, where she had so many old scores to settle.

On this first meeting the inhabitants of Lima struck me as being even more boastful and timid than the Arequipans. Towards eleven in the evening Madame Denuelle intimated to them that I must be in need of rest, and to my great relief they withdrew, for I could hold out no longer, I thought my head would burst. Mr Smith told me that he had gone in person to deliver the letter for my aunt, the beautiful Manuela de Tristan, wife of my uncle

Don Domingo, then Governor of Ayacucho; and she had asked him to call for her, as she wanted to come and see me that very evening. So she came the moment my other visitors had left: I felt this was very considerate of her.

From all I had heard about the extraordinary beauty of my aunt from Lima I was naturally expecting to see a superb woman; nevertheless the reality surpassed everything I had imagined. I did not dare to touch her, but she took my hand and held it while she greeted me in words so affectionate that they had me spellbound. I am not competent to describe such beauty: Raphael never gave his Virgins so noble a brow, so perfect a nose, so sweet and fresh a mouth. Her skin has the delicate bloom of a peach, her light brown hair, shining and soft as silk, falls in long rippling waves upon her rounded shoulders. She is a little too plump, perhaps, but as she is tall this does not impair her elegance. Her short-sleeved dress of white muslin embroidered all over with tiny rosebuds was cut very low with the waist tapering to a point in front, a style which set off all her best features, her neck, shoulders, arms and bosom. She wore long ear-rings, a string of pearls adorned her swan-like neck, and a variety of bracelets enhanced the whiteness of her arms. A long velvet cloak of midnight blue lined with white satin draped her lovely form, and a black lace veil thrown negligently over her head hid her face from the curious gaze of passers-by. She had stopped speaking but I was still looking at her, I could still hear her, and all I could say in reply to her kind offers of help was to cry: 'Oh! my dear aunt, how beautiful you are!' Who can explain the magical power of beauty? In whatever form it manifests itself, ethereal, visible, palpable, its gentle influence pervades my whole being: and in its presence my soul, palpitating with pleasure and admiration, is raised up to heaven.

My beautiful aunt was very insistent that I should stay

with her; I thanked her, while demurring at the inconvenience this might cause her, and as it was so late we put off any decision until the next day. When she had gone, Madame Denuelle stayed talking, so it was after one o'clock when I found myself alone.

As early as eight next morning Madame Denuelle entered my room, and quickly directing the conversation towards the subject of my aunt, told me with an embarrassed air that out of concern for me she felt she ought to let me know one or two things about Senora Manuela de Tristan. She informed me that for many years Manuela had been on intimate terms with an American whom she loved very much and of whom she was exceedingly jealous. If I had not already decided to decline my aunt's offer, what I had just learned would have been sufficient to prevent me from accepting it. I had come to know enough of the human heart to understand that I must not go and live with a woman if I did not want to risk becoming the object of her jealous suspicions and provoking her enmity, which I was certainly anxious to avoid. When I left my uncle's house I made a solemn vow never to accept the hospitality of any relation. I mentioned this once to Carmen, and she said: 'You are right, Florita, it is better to eat bread at home than to eat cake with relations.' So I reassured Madame Denuelle, settled terms with her at the rate of two piastres a day, and when my aunt returned at eleven, to collect me, she said, I gave her to understand that her offer would be an embarrassment to us both, and it was agreed that I should remain at the hotel. I had the impression that my tact was much appreciated.

However, my financial situation could hardly fail to give me cause for concern. I had left Arequipa with only a few hundred francs. It is true that my uncle had given me a letter of credit for four hundred piastres, but this was intended solely to pay for my passage; he had stipulated that I could not draw the money until the moment of departure, thus making it clearly understood that he was giving it me only on condition that I left the country. There were no ships about to sail, and I knew from Mr Smith that there would be none for two months. A stay of that length at the hotel would cost one hundred and twenty piastres, and I would also have to spend a little on my toilet, so I estimated that I would need at least two hundred. I can safely say that I have experienced every misfortune except one, I have never been in debt. Fear of falling into debt has always dominated my actions, and by carefully calculating my expenditure in advance, I have managed never to owe anybody a sou. When I arrived at the figure of two hundred piastres and found I had only twenty in my purse, I confess I was very alarmed. I have already said how shabby my wardrobe was, but now I sat down to examine it piece by piece, and taking my pen I worked out what I could get for all these rags if I were to sell them just before I left: the grand total came to exactly two hundred piastres. When I realised this, I was happy, oh so happy! On leaving Escudero I had renounced all my grand ambitious plans and now I never wanted to hear another word about politics. I became young and light-hearted again, and for the first time in my life I had not a care in the world. I have never enjoyed better health: I grew visibly fatter, my complexion was clear and fresh, I had a good appetite, I slept well — in short, I can say that these two months were the only period in my life when I did not suffer.

The day after my arrival, though, I had a slight disagreement with the French consul, M Barrère: this is what happened. When I left Arequipa the French residents there took advantage of the opportunity to address a petition to M Barrère asking him to invest M Le Bris with special powers so that he could protect their interests, which were seriously affected by recent political events. I understood their predicament very well and promised to fulfil my mission. First thing in the morning

I sent the consul my compatriots' letter and wrote him a few words myself to inform him that I had been asked to give him a verbal account of the plight of the French in Arequipa, adding that the matter was urgent but that I was indisposed, so if he cared to honour me with a visit I would be able to tell him immediately all that it was important for him to know. These are the exact words of my letter. My readers will perhaps find it hard to believe, but M Barrère found it *an insult to his dignity as consul.* He asked who I was and where I had been brought up, that I should be so ignorant of the proprieties as to think it was for him, the consul, to pay me a visit. Two or three friends came and told me that the whole town was talking about the *haughty* letter I had sent the consul and how shocked he was. I was amazed; fortunately I had kept a copy of my letter and read it to everybody, so they could not understand why it had made M Barrère so angry. I imagine he must have realised how discourteous his conduct had been, especially towards a woman, for the following evening he sent his nephew to apologise for not having come to see me himself as his health prevented it; this young man introduced himself as his uncle's secretary, in which capacity he asked me to communicate my business to him; but he seemed so incapable of understanding the simplest thing that I did not care to enter into details with him, but dismissed him, saying that I would convey to his esteemed uncle the consul by letter what I would have preferred to tell him by word of mouth. And these are the men responsible for looking after French interests abroad!

As for me, during my stay in Lima I did not have to fight over my inheritance, nor were there any great upheavals similar to those I had witnessed in Arequipa, so my observations were entirely confined to the people I met and the places I visited. Within a week Madame Denuelle had acquainted me with everything that was happening in the city. Never have I led so varied or entertaining an existence; all the same, I would not have wished it to continue indefinitely. I had hardly a moment in which to write my journal, for as soon as I was alone, Madame Denuelle would come up to my room, and her unceasing flow of conversation was as instructive as it was diverting. What put me in her good graces was the fact that I was a good listener. However, I had little time to spare for her. In the mornings I explored the city; in the afternoons I was often invited out to dine, and all my evenings were taken up with visits, outings, plays, meetings and intimate conversations with my new friends.

XVI

Lima: its manners and morals

My aunt Manuela was a great help to me: she took me all over the city and introduced me into high society. She showed me much friendship, but it was not of the kind to establish a bond of sympathy between us. Beautiful though she is, her expression lacks frankness and she never looks one in the face. She cultivated me out of the interest it is natural to feel when a hitherto unknown relation, born six thousand miles away, suddenly appears upon the scene. I spent whole days in her company, charmed by her wit but pained by the insensitivity of her heart.

Lima is a city still entirely devoted to sensual pleasures, a place where wit and beauty contend for supremacy, like Paris under Louis XV. Generous sentiments and private virtues cannot exist when they have no opportunity for expression, and so few of the people are literate that the upper classes have little to fear from the freedom of the press.

All the most distinguished men in the country gathered at my aunt's house: President Orbegoso, the English General Miller and the French Colonel Soigne, both in the service of the republic, Salaverry, de la Fuente, and many more. I met only two women there: the rest shunned my aunt's society because they considered her conduct so improper. Evenings at her house passed in a most agreeable manner: she would sing to us, in Italian, the finest arias from Rossini's operas, and when she was tired everybody would talk politics. Like all the women in Lima, my aunt is very interested in politics, and in her society I was able to form an opinion of the men at the head of the government. Orbegoso and the officers around him seemed complete nonentities to me. I also saw the famous priest Luna Pizarro again. In my view he does not live up to his reputation and is not nearly as able as Valdivia. In discussion he displayed a passion for demolition but no interest in reconstruction. Personal ambition is the driving force behind all these men. The old priest aimed to supplant the Bishop of Arequipa, and it was to achieve this end that he had turned politician. Had it served his purpose any better no doubt he would have become a courtier. Unfortunately the masses are still too backward for any true leaders to arise from their ranks, or for them to form any judgment of the men who control their lives.

Lima, which has a population of nearly eighty thousand today, was founded by Pizarro in 1535. The city contains some very fine monuments, a great number of churches, and many convents and monasteries. The houses are built in a uniform style; the streets are long, wide and well laid out. Nearly all have drainage channels on either side, though some have only one running down the middle. The houses are built of brick, wood and clay and painted in various light colours: blue, grey, pink, yellow, etc. They have only two storeys and their roofs are flat; the walls rise higher than the ceilings, which gives the houses an unfinished look. Some of these roofs serve as gardens and have pots of flowers on them, but few are strong enough for such a use. It never rains; if it did the houses would soon be nothing but heaps of mud. The interiors are well planned: the drawing-room and dining-room form the first courtyard, the kitchen and slaves' quarters the second. The bedrooms are on the upper floor, all furnished with great luxury, depending on the wealth and rank of their owners.

The cathedral is magnificent; the woodwork of the choir is of exquisite workmanship, the altar-rails are of silver and the altar itself is extremely ornate. The little side chapels are charming; each canon has his own. This church is of stone and so solidly built that it has withstood the strongest earthquakes without showing the least sign of damage. The two towers, the façade and the flight of steps leading up to it are of a grandeur rare in our old Europe and certainly unexpected in a city of the New World. The cathedral occupies the whole eastern side of the main square, with the town hall facing it. This square is the Palais-Royal of Lima, with arcades containing fine shops on two sides and a superb fountain in the middle. At every hour of the day it is a scene of bustling activity: in the morning there are the water-carriers, soldiers, processions, etc., and in the evening many people come there to stroll, and you see hawkers selling ices, fruit and cakes, and street entertainers amusing the public with their dances and other antics.

Among the religious houses for men, the most remarkable is the monastery of St. Francis. Its church is the richest and the most unusual of all those I saw. When women wish to visit a monastery they go about it in a very odd way: they say they are *pregnant*, whereupon the good fathers, professing a holy respect for the wishes of women in that condition, throw open every door to them. When we went to the monastery the monks teased us in the most indecent fashion. We went up the towers, and as I was energetically climbing the steps, the prior, seeing that I was slim and agile, demanded to know *if I too were pregnant*! I was dumbfounded at such an unexpected question and my embarrassment provoked much laughter together with such suggestive remarks that even Manuela, who is not shy, did not know where to look. I emerged from the monastery quite scandalised, but when I complained, people said, 'Oh, that is just their way, they love to joke. Everybody thinks they are the nicest monks of all.' And people here still put their faith in men like these!

I also went to visit a nunnery, the Convent of the

Incarnation, but there is nothing religious about it as
nobody observes any rules. It is just a house like any
other: there are twenty-nine nuns, each with her own
lodging where she cooks, works, looks after children,
talks, sings and behaves just as she likes. We even saw
some who were not wearing the habit of their order. They
take in lodgers who come and go and the door of the
convent is always open. It is hard to see the point of this
way of life; one is almost tempted to think that the
women here have only taken refuge within these walls in
order to be more independent than they could be outside.
I met there a pretty young Frenchwoman of twenty-six
with her little daughter of five; she was living in the
convent to save money while her husband was away on
business in Central America. I did not see the Prioress;
they told us she was ill. These nuns, of a kind new to me,
struck me as little more than idle gossips; their convent
was dirty and neglected, different in every respect from
Santa-Rosa and Santa-Catalina. As I could find nothing
worthy of my attention I climbed the tower to get a
bird's-eye view of the city. This superb city is the most
wretched sight when seen from above; the mass of roof-
less houses look more like ruins, in shocking contrast
with the monasteries and the many majestic stone
churches whose lofty height and solidity seem to defy
time. You feel instinctively that there must be a similar
lack of harmony in the way society is organised here, and
that the time will come when the people's houses will be
more beautiful and the churches less sumptuous. My view
could not have been more varied: the surrounding
countryside is very picturesque. In the distance was
Callao, its two forts and the island of San Lorenzo framed
by the snow-capped Andes and the Pacific Ocean. What a
magnificent panorama!

My visit to the convent had fallen so far short of my
expectations that I was not tempted to see any more. I
had gone there in the hope of experiencing the exaltation

which a life of abnegation and devotion ought always to inspire, no matter what the religion, but all I found was yet further evidence of the decline of faith and the decay of the religious life.

The Mint is a handsome building and seemed to be efficiently run. In the past few years it has undergone notable improvements: they have imported from London immense rolling-mills which work by water power, as do the scales for weighing the coins. The coins themselves cannot compare with ours in Europe because of the lack of skilled engravers. In the year 1833 three million piastres were struck in silver and one million in gold.

I could not repress a feeling of terror when I entered the prisons of the Holy Inquisition. A great deal of care went into the construction of this edifice, like everything the Spanish clergy did at a time when it was the supreme authority in the state and there was no lack of money to proclaim its magnificence. There are twenty-four cells, each about ten feet square, with one small window which admits air but little light. One can also see the secret vaults and dungeons reserved for the harsher forms of punishment and for the disposal of the unfortunate victims. The Hall of Judgment has a beauty in keeping with its terrible function. It is extremely lofty, and the walls are panelled for much of their height with admirably carved woodwork. The two small barred windows admit only a pale and watery light. The Grand Inquisitor sat upon a throne and the judges were placed in the sort of alcoves usually reserved for statues. Their impassive demeanour, the sombre aspect of the chamber, and its remoteness from all human habitation, must have been enough to paralyse their unfortunate victim with terror the moment he entered. Since the independence of Peru in 1821 the Holy Inquisition has been suppressed and the building now houses a natural history collection and a museum. The collection comprises four Inca mummies still apparently in their original condition, though less carefully prepared than their counterparts in Egypt, a few stuffed birds, and a small number of shells and mineral samples. What I found most interesting was a large assortment of ancient vases used by the Incas. These people gave their vessels grotesque shapes and engraved them with symbolic figures. As for pictures, there are only three or four miserable daubs, and those not even framed. There is not a single statue. M Rivero, a learned man who has spent some time in France, is the founder of this museum. He does all he can to enrich it, but he has no support; the republic does not provide funds for such a purpose, so his efforts are unavailing. A taste for the fine arts does not develop until nations come of age; it is when people are weary of wars and political upheavals that they turn to the arts and bring new life to their jaded existence.

During my stay in Lima I went several times to attend debates in Congress. The Chamber is very pretty, though too small for its new use; it is oblong in shape and was formerly used for academic meetings and the delivery of formal speeches by important officials. For the past ten years there has been talk of building a new Chamber, but the republic's finances are all absorbed by the Ministry of War, and not one piastre is spent on essential works. The senators, as they style themselves, sit in four rows in the shape of a horseshoe, with the president at its centre. In the middle of the chamber are two large tables where the secretaries sit. The senators have no special costume; each attends in the dress belonging to his profession − soldier, priest or ordinary citizen. Above the assembly there are two tiers of boxes for the use of officials, foreign representatives and the general public. The back is arranged as an amphitheatre and reserved solely for ladies. Each time I went there was a large number of ladies present, all wearing the *saya* and reading newspapers or talking politics. The members of the assembly habitually speak from their seats; there is a rostrum, but only rarely did I see it in use. This Assembly is far more serious than ours.

Nobody ever interrupts a speaker but listens in religious silence to every word. The Spanish language is so beautiful and the Spanish-speaking peoples have as a rule so rich an imagination that all the orators I heard seemed to be very eloquent, particularly the priests. But as I listened to their flowery phrases I thought of Valdivia's newspaper, Nieto's harangues, the prefect's proclamations; I compared the actions of Arequipa's leaders with their words, and I knew how to interpret the speeches of the orators in Congress and how to judge the courage, disinterestedness and patriotism they displayed.

The presidential palace is vast, but badly built and badly situated. The interior is most inconvenient; the long and narrow drawing-room is more like a gallery, and all the furniture is very shabby. As I entered I thought of Bolivar and what my mother had told me about him: he who loved luxury, pomp and ceremony so much, how could he bring himself to live in this palace which was less imposing than the foyer of the hotel he had occupied in Paris? But in Lima he was supreme leader, whereas in Paris he was nobody; and love of power makes one overlook such disadvantages. While I was in Lima there were no balls or grand receptions at the palace, much to my annoyance, as I was curious to see one of their ceremonial occasions.

The Town Hall is very large but contains nothing worthy of mention. I found the library more interesting: it has a fine situation, the rooms are huge and well maintained, the books are nicely arranged on shelves, there are tables covered with green baize and surrounded with chairs, and one can find all the newspapers of the country there. The library has a total of twelve thousand volumes, most of them French: Voltaire, Rousseau, the bulk of our classics, all the histories of the revolution, the works of Madame de Staël, books of travel, memoirs, Madame Roland, and so on. It gave me great satisfaction to see our best authors in this library. Unfortunately the taste for reading is still insufficiently widespread for many people to profit from it. I also saw French translations of Walter Scott, Lord Byron, Fenimore Cooper and many others, besides several works in English and German, in addition to all the best that Spain has produced; to sum up, this library is very fine, considering how backward the country is.

Lima has a very pretty theatre, though small; it is tastefully decorated and extremely well lit, making the women and their toilettes look ravishing. At the time there was only a poor Spanish company performing the plays of Lope da Vega and mutilated versions of French farces. I saw *Le Mariage de raison*, *La Jeune Fille à marier*, *Le Baron de Felsheim*, etc. The company was so wretched that it did not even possess any costumes. For three or four years there had been a very good Italian company which, according to Madame Denuelle, gave good and successful performances of the best operas. But the prima donna became pregnant and wanted to leave, her distracted lover followed her, and the rest were forced to seek their fortune elsewhere. They perform only twice a week, on Sundays and Thursdays; each time I went I saw few people there. In the intervals everybody smokes, even the women. The theatre would be far too small if the population had as much enthusiasm for the drama as they have for bullfighting.

The size of the arena built for this sort of spectacle shows plainly enough what is the Peruvians' ruling passion. For a long time I managed to resist the persuasion of the ladies among my acquaintance, who all offered me their boxes, I had so much trouble to overcome my revulsion for this kind of butchery; however, as I wished to study the customs of the country I could not confine myself to the drawing-room, I had to observe the people wherever their tastes might take them. So one Sunday I went to the bullfight, together with my aunt, another lady and Mr Smith. There I found a huge crowd of people, five or six thousand, perhaps more, all very well dressed in accordance with their station, and all in a state of joyous expectancy. Twenty tiers of benches surround the arena, and above them is a gallery divided into boxes for the use of the aristocracy. The sight of suffering distresses me so much that it genuinely pains me to describe the barbarous and disgusting spectacle of which I was a witness.

In the arena there are four or five men on horseback, each holding a little red flag and a short sharp-pointed lance. In the middle of this arena there is a sort of circular cage made of stakes fastened close together so that the bull cannot thrust his head between them. Three or four men stand inside this cage; they emerge to open the door by which the animal enters the arena, and then they proceed to provoke it by throwing fire-crackers on to its back, into its ears, and tormenting it in every way imaginable. The moment there is any danger of their being gored, they quickly retreat into their cage. I do not think anybody could repress a strong feeling of terror at the sight of the bull as it bounds into the arena and charges furiously at the horses; it bellows with rage, its hair bristling, its tail lashing its sides, its nostrils distended. Its convulsive fury is terrifying; in leaps and bounds it pursues both horses and men, who nimbly evade it.

I can understand the powerful attraction these spectacles can have in Andalusia, for there the bulls are superb and need no goading, the horses are fiery and eager for the fight, the toreadors of the region, dressed like pages and sparkling with sequins, have an almost magical grace and courage as first they play with the furious animal, and then dispatch it with a single blow. All this lends these bloody spectacles a certain grandeur, but in Lima there is no poetry, only butchery. In this country with its mild and enervating climate the animals lack vigour and the men lack spirit. Ten minutes after the bull is loosed it begins to tire; and to prevent the spectators from becoming bored, the men emerge from their cage carrying a long-handled sickle and hamstring the poor animal from behind. Now it can use only its two front legs, and it is pitiful to see it dragging itself along. At this point the brave toreadors of Lima throw yet more fire-crackers at it, stab it repeatedly with their lances and, in short, kill it on the spot, for all the world like clumsy apprentice butchers. The wretched animal struggles and utters muffled groans, while big tears fall from its eyes; finally its head sinks into the pool of blood all around it. Then they sound fanfares, as the dead animal is placed on a cart and carried off at a gallop by a team of four horses. Meanwhile the people clap their hands, shout, and dance up and down in a frenzy of excitement which seems to turn every head; eight armed men have just killed a bull – what a fine subject for enthusiasm! I was revolted at the sight and wanted to leave immediately after the first bull was killed, but the ladies told me: 'You should stay; the last bulls are always the fiercest; you might see some horses killed and some men hurt.' And they stressed the word *men* as if to say: Then it would be more interesting. We were in luck, as it happened: the third bull disembowelled a horse and nearly killed its rider, whereupon the men with sickles took fright and hacked at all four of its legs. The animal, panting with rage, fell bathed in its blood; as for the horse, its bowels were hanging out of its stomach. At this sight I left in a great hurry, feeling that I was going to faint. Mr Smith was pale and all he could say was: 'This is a disgusting and inhuman spectacle.'

Leaning on his arm I walked for some time along the promenade on the bank of the river. The pure air revived me, but I was still upset; the attraction which the spectacle of suffering holds for an entire nation seemed to me a sign of the deepest corruption. I was preoccupied with these reflections when we saw my beautiful aunt approaching in her carriage; as soon as she was within hailing distance she cried: 'How sensitive you are, Florita!

Why run away like that at the best moment? Oh, if only you had seen the last one! What a magnificent animal! It was really frightening! There was such excitement in the arena, it was marvellous!' Wretched people, I thought; are you so utterly devoid of pity that you can find pleasure in such scenes!

The river Rimac much resembles the river at Arequipa, for it too flows over a bed of stones between rocks. The bridge is quite handsome, and it is here that men congregate to watch the women pass on their way to the Paseo del Agua. But before I continue I must tell the reader about the costume peculiar to the women of Lima, the advantage it gives them and the influence it has on their morals, customs and character.

There is no place on earth where women are so *free* and exercise so much power as in Lima. They seem to have absorbed for their use alone what little energy the warm, heady climate allows the fortunate inhabitants. In Lima the women are as a rule taller and better built than the men. At eleven or twelve they are fully developed; nearly all of them marry at about this age and are very fertile, commonly producing from six to seven children. They have healthy pregnancies, give birth easily, and are quick to recover. Nearly all of them nurse their babies, but they are always helped by a wetnurse, a custom which comes to them from Spain, where the children in well-to-do families always have two women to feed them.

The women of Lima are not as a rule beautiful, but there is something irresistibly attractive about their faces; there is no man whose heart does not beat faster at the sight. They are not dark-skinned, as many Europeans believe; on the contrary, the majority are very white, while the rest are different shades of brown according to their diverse origins, but their skin is always smooth as velvet and their complexion glowing with vitality. Their colouring is rich: bright red lips, lovely black hair which curls naturally, admirably shaped black eyes, and an expression of mingled wit, pride and languor hard to define, but in which lies all their charm. They express themselves with great facility and their gestures are no less eloquent than their words.

Their costume is *unique*. Lima is the only city in the world where it has ever appeared. People have consulted the most ancient chronicles, but in vain; nobody has yet discovered its origin. It has nothing in common with the various Spanish costumes, and it is quite certain that it was not brought from Spain. It was found on this spot at the time Peru was discovered, and it is at the same time common knowledge that it has never existed in any other South American city. This costume, called the *saya*, is a skirt, worn with a sort of sack called a *manto*, which envelops the shoulders, arms and head. I can hear our elegant Parisiennes protesting at the simplicity of this style of dress; little can they imagine the advantage it gives to the coquette. It is only in Lima that you can have it made; the women there claim that only a woman born in Lima is capable of making it, and that a woman from Chile, or even from Arequipa or Cuzco could never acquire the art of *pleating the saya*.

To make an ordinary *saya* it takes between sixteen and eighteen yards of satin and some lightweight silk or cotton fabric for the lining. In exchange the seamstress brings you a narrow skirt which reaches from waist to ankles and is so tight that it allows just enough room to put one foot in front of the other and to take very little steps. Thus you are encased in this skirt like a sword in a sheath. It is entirely pleated from top to bottom with very narrow pleats so finely worked that it is impossible to see the stitches. However, these pleats are so firmly made and give the skirt such elasticity that I have seen fifteen-year-old *sayas* which were still flexible enough to reveal the whole shape of the body and to give with every movement of the wearer.

The *manto* is pleated in the same way, but as it is made in a very light material it is not as durable as the skirt, and the pleats cannot stand up to the constant movements of the wearer and the humidity of her breath. Women in good society have their *sayas* made in black satin, while fashionable ladies also have them in less common colours such as violet, maroon, bright green or deep blue, but never in light shades, as these are favoured by prostitutes. The *manto* is always black. It completely covers the bust and most of the head, leaving only one eye uncovered. The women of Lima always wear a little bodice, of which only the sleeves are ever seen, and whether they are short or long, this bodice is made of some rich fabric such as velvet, coloured satin or tulle; although in fact most women have their arms bare in all seasons. Their footwear is elegant enough to catch every eye: they wear pretty embroidered satin slippers in every colour, with ribbons in some contrasting shade, and fine silk stockings in various colours with richly embroidered clocks.

The women of Lima wear their hair parted in the middle and falling in two immaculate tresses tied in a big bunch of ribbons. However, this is not the only style, as some women wear their hair like Ninon de Lenclos, in long clusters of ringlets right down to their bosom, which in accordance with the custom of the country they nearly always leave bare. A few years ago the fashion for wearing big embroidered crêpe-de-Chine shawls was introduced. This has made their costume more decent by hiding their nakedness and any part of their bodies which was a little too prominently outlined. A further luxury they affect is to carry an exquisite embroidered handkerchief trimmed with lace. Oh! how enchanting they are, with their beautiful black *saya* shining in the sun; how graceful the movements of their shoulders are, as first they draw their *manto* right over their face, then slyly draw it aside! What fine supple figures they have, and how sinuously they sway as they walk! How pretty their tiny feet are, and what a pity they are just a little too plump!

Put such a woman in a Paris gown, and she is no longer the same person: one looks in vain for the seductive woman one encountered that morning in the church of St Mary. For in Lima foreigners go to church not to hear the monks sing mass but to admire these unique women in their national costume. A number of foreigners have told me what a magical effect the sight of these women produced on their imagination. They fancied they had landed in Paradise, and that it was to compensate them for the hardship of a long voyage that God had set them down in this enchanted land. These flights of fancy are not implausible when one sees the follies and extravagances that these beautiful women lead foreigners to commit. Men follow them out of a burning desire to see their features, which they so carefully hide from view; but it takes an expert to follow a woman in a *saya*, as the costume tends to make all women look alike. I can say without fear of contradiction that if a lovely form and a magnetic glance were sufficient to ensure women the supremacy they are destined to possess, the women of Lima in their *sayas* would be proclaimed queens of the earth; but while this kind of beauty may excite the senses, only spiritual, moral and mental qualities can prolong its reign.

For God has endowed woman with a heart more loving and devoted than that of man; and if, as there can be no doubt, it is through love and devotion that we honour the Creator, then woman has an incontestable superiority over man, but she must cultivate her intelligence and exercise her self-control in order to retain it. Only on those conditions can she acquire the influence which comes from the power God has given her. But when she fails to recognise her mission, when, instead of being the inspiration of man and improving his character, she seeks only to seduce him, her authority disappears together with the desire she has aroused. Thus, when

these enchanting women of Lima, who have never directed their lives towards any noble purpose, first electrify
the imagination of young foreigners and then proceed to
show themselves as they really are, heartless, uncultivated,
shallow, and above all, mercenary, the powerful fascin-
ation produced by their charms is immediately destroyed.

For all that, the women of Lima dominate the men
because they are so far above them in intelligence and
will-power. But the stage of civilisation the Peruvians
have reached is still far behind ours in Europe. Nowhere
in Peru is there any institution for the education of either
sex: the intelligence can develop only through its native
resources. Thus the pre-eminence of Lima's women,
however inferior they may be to European women from a
moral aspect, must be attributed to the superior intelligence with which God has endowed them.

However, I must point out how much their style of
dress has contributed to the great freedom and powerful
influence they enjoy. If they should ever abandon it, they
would have to adopt an entirely different set of values. To
prove my point I will touch briefly upon one or two
customs of Lima society so that the reader will be able to
appreciate the justice of my observation.

The *saya*, as I have said, is the national costume; all
women wear it whatever their rank, and it is respected as
part of the culture of the country just as the Muslim
woman's veil is in the Orient. At all times of the year the
women of Lima go out in this disguise, and if anybody
ever dared to lift the *manto* which covers the whole of her
face except one eye, public indignation would be aroused
and that person would be severely punished. It is accepted
that *every woman may go out alone*; the majority have a
negress following behind, but they are not obliged to do
so. This costume so alters a woman – even her voice,
since her mouth is covered – that unless she is very tall
or very short, lame, hunchbacked or otherwise conspicuous, it is impossible to recognise her. I am sure it needs

little imagination to appreciate the consequences of this time-honoured practice which is sanctioned or at least tolerated by law. A woman breakfasts with her husband in her little French *peignoir*, her hair pinned up exactly like a Parisienne's; and later on, if she wants to go out, she slips on her *saya* — without a corset, as the underskirt is quite tight — lets down her hair, puts on her *manto* and goes wherever her fancy takes her; she meets her husband in the street, and he does not recognise her; she flirts with him, leads him on, lets him offer her ices, fruit, cakes, gives him a rendezvous, leaves him, and immediately starts a new conversation with an officer passing by. She can let this new adventure go as far as she pleases without ever taking off her *manto*; then she goes to visit friends, takes a walk, and is back in time for dinner. Her husband does not ask where she has been, for he knows perfectly well that if it suits her better to hide the truth from him, she will lie, and as he has no means of restraining her, he takes the wisest course, which is not to worry. So these ladies go out alone to the theatre, to bullfights, to public gatherings, to balls, to churches and to pay visits; and they are accepted everywhere they go. If they wish to speak to anybody they do so, then take their leave, so that they remain free and independent in the midst of the crowd, far more so than the men. This costume has the enormous advantage of being at the same time economical, very clean, comfortable, ready to put on immediately, and never in need of the slightest attention.

There is one further custom I must not omit to mention: when the women of Lima want to make their disguise even more complete, they put on an old bodice, an old *manto*, and an old *saya* which is falling into rags and losing its pleats; but to show that they come from good society they wear immaculate shoes and stockings and carry one of their finest handkerchiefs. This is a recognised form of disguise and is known as *disfrazar*. A *disfrazada* is looked upon as eminently respectable, so nobody ever accosts her; indeed, people are very timid about approaching her, and it would be improper and even *dishonourable* to follow her. It is supposed, and rightly, that if she has disguised herself it is because she has important reasons for doing so, and consequently nobody should claim the right to investigate her movements.

From what I have just written about the costume and customs of the women of Lima it is easy to understand that they must have a completely different outlook from European women, who from their earliest childhood are the slaves of laws, morals, customs, prejudices, fashions and everything else whereas beneath their *sayas* the women of Lima are *free*, enjoying their independence and confident in that genuine strength which all people feel within them when they are able to act in accordance with their needs. In every situation the woman of Lima is always *herself*; never does she submit to any constraint. When she is young she escapes the domination of her parents through the freedom her costume allows her; when she marries she does not take her husband's name but keeps her own; when she is tired of staying in, she puts on her *saya* and goes out, in the same way as a man does when he takes up his hat. Freedom of action characterises everything she does.

In their more intimate relationships, whether these are casual or serious, the women of Lima always preserve their dignity, although their conduct in this regard is certainly very different from ours. Like all women they measure the strength of the love they inspire by the scale of the sacrifice their lovers are prepared to make; but just as ever since their country was discovered, only its gold has had the power to lure Europeans so far from home, gold alone, to the exclusion of talent and virtue, has always been the sole object of consideration, the sole motive for every action; and the women of Lima, consistent in their conduct and acting on the same principle, recognise no proof of love except the masses of gold they are offered, and their vanity is satisfied in proportion to the size of the sum or the cost of the gift. When anybody wants to give some idea of the violent love a gentleman feels for a lady, the expression used is always: 'He gave her gold by the sackful!' just as we would say: 'He killed himself for love of her!' So the wealthy woman always accepts money from her lover, even if she ends up giving it to her servants, for to her it is a *proof of love*, the only thing which can convince her that she is loved. The vanity of foreign travellers blinds them to this truth, and when anyone told us about the success he had had with the women of Lima he did not mention that it had cost him a small fortune, right down to the valuable keepsake he gave his beloved when he left. These customs are very strange, but they are real enough: I saw several ladies in high society wearing men's rings, watches and chains. . . .

The women of Lima spend little time on their households, but as they are very energetic, this is sufficient to keep everything in order. They have a marked inclination for politics and intrigue; it is they who find posts for their husbands, sons and all the men who take their fancy, and there is no obstacle they cannot overcome to achieve their ends. Men do not meddle in this sort of business, and they are right: they would not acquit themselves nearly as well. The women are very fond of pleasure and festivities, and love social gatherings, where they gamble for high stakes and smoke cigars. They go riding, not side-saddle like English women, but in breeches like the men. They have a passion for sea-bathing and swim extremely well. As for their accomplishments, they play the guitar, sing rather badly (though a few are good musicians) and dance their native dances with a charm it is impossible to describe. These women have no education as a rule, they do not read at all, and they are ignorant of everything that is happening in the world. They have much natural wit, a quick understanding, a good memory and a surprising amount of intelligence.

I have described the women of Lima exactly as they are and not as certain travellers depict them; it has hurt me to do so, as I was deeply grateful for their generous hospitality, but my rôle of conscientious traveller made it my duty to tell the whole truth.

I have spoken of the theatre and the bullfights but I have omitted the spectacle the churches provide for the population of Lima; this has a large following, as the perpetual need for distraction takes people there each day. In Lima everybody goes to mass two or three times: once at the cathedral, because its beauty attracts a large number of pretty women and foreigners; once at the church of St Francis, because the holy fathers distribute excellent consecrated bread, the organ is magnificent and the priests richly dressed; and once at the church of the Infant Jesus, because there one can enjoy the singing of its innumerable caged birds. Nearly all the churches in Lima have a variety of caged birds next to the altar, and their singing often drowns the voice of the priest officiating at mass. Apart from the daily entertainment to be found inside the churches there are at least two processions a week in the city, and these are even cruder and more indecent than the ones which shocked me so much in Arequipa. Finally, to ensure that the edification and amusement of the pious population continue without interruption, there are also evening services which are conducted with much pomp, and where, one must suppose, the same regard for the proprieties is observed. Think how many schools could be set up with the money all these pointless ceremonies cost! And what a lot of useful things could be learned or done in the time thus wasted!

The two principal promenades are the *Almendral* and the *Paseo del Agua*: the latter is the more popular. It is beautiful, but badly situated; the river, which flows alongside, and the great trees on either side of the river, make it damp and harmful to the health in winter, and airless in summer. On Sundays and feast-days it is just like the Boulevard de Gand in Paris. The broad shady avenues are thronged with people, most of the women wearing the *saya*, and many of them sitting on benches in an attitude which exposes their legs right up to the knees. The road is full of light carriages, some moving at a foot pace, others stationary so that the ladies inside can parade their beauty and their fine clothes. People stay for four or five hours, which might well have seemed too long to me had I not been in the company of several ladies, in particular my aunt, whose wit is always at its most sparkling when she has something to criticise — and there was plenty of scope for her here.

The best time to be in Lima is the beginning of spring; the celebrations are really superb. They open on St John's day (June 24) with the procession known as *Amancaes*. I went with Dona Calista, one of my friends. The whole population was there: over a hundred carriages containing magnificently dressed ladies, countless cavalcades, and an immense crowd on foot. During the two winter months, May and June, the mountains are covered with yellow flowers called *amancaes* which give the festival its name. The road which leads to the mountains is very wide and at a certain height the view is enchanting. In several places tents are set up where refreshments are sold and very indecent dances are performed. Fashionable society flocks here for the two months the season lasts, and the tyranny of fashion, the desire to see and to be seen, is sufficient to override the many inconveniences. The road is very bad, the horses sink up to their hocks in the sand, the wind is cold, and if you are just a little late to leave in the evening, you risk being stopped by thieves. Nevertheless the city's inhabitants are passionately eager to go there; they make up dinner and supper parties and even spend the night in the mountains.

I did not confine myself to visiting the buildings and

the beauty spots of Lima: I also sought introduction to the principal residents so that I would discover how people lived. I had been recommended to several families, in addition to two of my cousins from Arequipa, Senora Balthazar de Benavidez and Senora Inez de Izcué. I was very well received in these two houses and sumptuous dinners were given in my honour. Nothing in the world is more tedious than these dinners: there is a great display of the best china, glass and everything else, but the chief extravagance is in the quality and variety of the food. Lima is remarkable for the advances it has made in the art of cookery: for the past ten years everything has been done in the French style. The country around provides very good meat and vegetables as well as a variety of fish and an abundance of exquisite fruit, so it is easy to enjoy a rich and varied diet at little expense. But as I am accustomed to dine in ten minutes, I found these banquets unimaginably tedious. Two courses are served, sometimes three, and one has to partake of everything in order not to offend against the rules of etiquette. I had to explain over and over again that I did not eat soup or meat, and that my diet was usually confined to vegetables, fruit and milk. People stay at table a good two hours, during which conversation alternates between praise of the food and fulsome compliments addressed to the master of the house. Here as in Arequipa they are in the habit of passing titbits around on the end of a fork, but this custom is dying out. The amount I have seen eaten on these occasions is truly prodigious. As a consequence, by the end of the meal nearly all the guests are unwell and in such a state of stupor that they are incapable of uttering a word. No doubt about it, these banquets are as bad for the mind as they are for the health, and my readers will not need to be told what a penance they were for me.

XVII

A seaside resort: a sugar-refinery

In my opinion the people of Lima have chosen as their seaside resort the most arid and disagreeable spot on the coast: it is called Chorrillos. The Izcué family, who had rented a house there for the season, invited me to come and stay as long as I liked.

Senor Izcué called for me at seven in the morning and we got straight into the carriage. We had ten miles to go, over sand, but the going was not too bad for the horses, as the sand is firm and they do not sink into it as they would in the sand of the pampas. The countryside is very varied: the vegetation is succeeded by a black and arid terrain with just the odd tree every now and then. Half-way there we went through the village of Miraflor, which has an abundance of trees, some charming houses and two towers which give a view of the whole countryside including Lima and the sea, which is less than a mile away. This was certainly the prettiest village I saw in South America, and after we had left it behind we came across one or two fields of potatoes or lucerne, but never any corn. When we arrived at two fine-looking houses belonging to M Lavalle, a former intendant of Arequipa, I noticed what magnificent gardens each of them had with groves of oranges, papayas, palm trees, sapotillas and every kind of fruit tree. Ten minutes more and we passed through El Baranco, a tiny hamlet situated amid lush vegetation, huge trees and an abundance of water. From this oasis to Chorrillos there is nothing but arid sand. There had been a thick damp mist all the way and I had become very cold, so I was ill by the time we arrived and after a cup of very hot coffee I went straight to bed.

I did not get up until dinner-time; then, as he saw I was better, Senor Izcué suggested a ride through the neighbouring countryside, where the land is fertile, to visit the sugar plantations. I was given a horse and we set out.

Up to then I had only seen sugar cane in the Botanical Gardens in Paris; but these vast forests of giant reeds eight to nine feet high, so dense that even a dog could hardly have penetrated them, surmounted by thousands of shoots bearing tiny flower-spikes, grew with a vigour and profusion seldom seen in our corn or potato fields; and I felt that in these favoured climes nature encouraged men to work because she was more bountiful. This plantation aroused my keen interest, and next day we went to visit one of the really big Peruvian estates.

Senor Lavalle's sugar refinery, five miles from Chorrillos, is a magnificent establishment with four hundred negroes, three hundred negresses and two hundred children. The proprietor courteously offered to take us on a tour of inspection and was happy to give us an explanation of everything we saw. I was very interested in the four mills used to crush the canes; they are powered by a waterfall. The aqueduct which brings water to the refinery is very fine and cost a great deal to build because of the difficulties of the terrain. I went over the huge shed where the vats for boiling the sugar are housed, then we proceeded to the adjoining refinery where the sugar is separated from the molasses. Senor Lavalle told me of his plans for improvements. 'But what drives me to despair, mademoiselle,' he added, 'is the impossibility of obtaining fresh negroes; it will be the ruin of all our refineries. We lose so many slaves, and three-quarters of the children die before the age of twelve. Once I had fifteen hundred negroes, now I have only nine hundred left, including the sickly children you see here.'

'Such a death rate is frightening and must give you cause for concern about your business. But how is it there is no balance between the births and the deaths? This is a healthy climate and I would have thought that the negroes would do just as well here as they do in Africa.'

'You are right about the climate but you do not know the negroes. Many of the women miscarry and the rest let their children die out of sheer laziness. You can get nothing out of them unless you use the whip.'

'Do you think that if they were free their needs would be enough to make them work?'

'In this climate their needs are so few that they would not have to work very hard. But then, it is my belief that no man, whatever his needs, can ever be persuaded to work regularly unless he is forced to do so; most of our Indians still do next to nothing and live in idleness and poverty; our missionaries have to beat them to make them cultivate the land. It is the same with the negroes: you French have already tried the experiment in Santo Domingo. Now that you have freed your slaves they will no longer work.'

'I agree with you that whether a man is white, black or red, he will not take easily to work when he has not been brought up to it; but slavery corrupts man because it makes him loathe work, so that it is impossible to prepare him for civilisation. I grant that Spanish laws regarding slaves are far more humane than those of any other nation, but the root of the evil is the same everywhere: slavery is a permanent condition. The slave has to work such long hours that it is impossible for him to exercise his right to purchase his freedom. If the products of his labour were to lose their value I am certain that slavery would be changed very much for the better.'

'How so, mademoiselle?'

'If the price of sugar bore the same relation to the cost of the labour that produces it as prices bear to labour costs in Europe, the master, having no compensation for the loss of his slave, would not make him work so hard and would take better care of him.'

'Mademoiselle, you speak of negroes like someone who knows them only from the fine speeches of philanthropists in parliament, but unfortunately it is only too true that you cannot make them work without the whip.'

'If that is so, monsieur, I can only pray for the ruin of your refineries, and I believe my prayers will soon be answered. A few years more, and the sugar beet will replace your sugar cane.'

'Oh, mademoiselle, if you have nothing worse than that to bring against us! . . . your sugar beet is just a joke, only good for sweetening cows' milk in winter.'

'Laugh if you like, monsieur, but in France we can already do without you. The sugar we produce is as good as yours; what is more, it has the supreme merit, in my eyes, of bringing down the price of sugar from the colonies, and I am convinced that this alone can bring about an improvement in the lot of the negroes and the eventual abolition of slavery.'

'The abolition of slavery . . . so you are not discouraged by what happened in Santo Domingo?'

'Monsieur, a revolution inspired by the noblest sentiments was bound to be outraged by the existence of slavery. Our Convention decreed the emancipation of the negroes out of a burning conviction, without realising that they needed to be prepared to make proper use of their liberty.'

'And what is more, your Convention, unlike the English parliament at the present time, neglected to compensate the slave owners.'

'The English parliament, with our example before it, has proceeded towards this great measure in a more rational manner than the Convention, it is true; but in its eagerness to achieve its ends it has acted so precipitately that it will be a long time before we see any good results. When you consider the formidable obstacles involved in freeing all the slaves at the same time, you are amazed that a nation as enlightened as the English should have risked such a step before ensuring that the slaves had acquired industrious habits and had been trained to use the freedom which is part of our social system. I am convinced that only a process of gradual emancipation offers a means of transforming the negroes into useful members of society. Liberty could have been granted as a reward for labour. The English parliament would have made faster progress if it had limited itself to freeing a certain number of slaves under the age of twenty each year, and placing them in rural schools where they could learn farming and various trades before being permitted to enjoy their freedom. In every European colony there are still enormous tracts of virgin soil where liberated slaves could have been settled, and there would also be plenty of work for those who had learned a trade. Had the English proceeded in this way, it would have taken thirty years to achieve full emancipation, but in every one of those years the liberated slaves would have gone to increase the working population and thereby increase the prosperity of the colonies; whereas under the present system the future holds nothing but poverty and disaster.'

'Mademoiselle, your views on slavery prove nothing except that you have a good heart and far too much imagination. All these beautiful dreams are superb in poetry, but I am only an old planter, and I am sorry to say that not one of your fine ideas would ever work.'

And talking to an old planter, I thought, was as much use as talking to the deaf, so I said no more. But slavery has always aroused my indignation, and I was overjoyed when I learned that a band of English ladies had vowed to stop eating sugar from the colonies and buy only sugar from India, even though the duties imposed on it make it more expensive, until the Bill of Emancipation had been passed by parliament. Their determination to accomplish so generous a resolution caused American sugar prices to fall and triumphed over the forces opposed to the Bill. May this noble example be followed on the continent!

M Lavalle had had an extremely elegant mansion built for himself, tastefully furnished with carpets from England, furniture, clocks and candelabra from France, and paintings and curios from China. He had also had a chapel built, big enough to hold a thousand people, where all his slaves attended mass on Sundays and festivals. He was good enough to get two of his slaves to dress up for my benefit: the man in blue and white striped jacket and trousers with a red neckerchief, and the woman in a skirt of the same striped material, with a length of red cotton cloth wound around her head and the upper part of her body. She also had black leather slippers tied with white ribbons. The children wore only a little apron about a foot square. On weekdays their dress was much simpler: the children wore nothing at all, while the women wore just a skirt and the men a pair of trousers or a loin-cloth. Their master was famous for the smart appearance of his slaves.

The hot countries are rich in fruit and M Lavalle's orchards contain them all. The soil suits them and they grow into magnificent specimens: you would think from its height that the sapodilla was determined to keep its large green apple, with its delicious juicy flesh, forever out of reach: while the mango is as tall as an oak and bears oval fibrous fruits which smell of turpentine. I never ceased to admire the beautiful big orange trees, their green branches weighed down with thousands of golden balls whose colour gladdened the eye and whose fragrance scented the whole atmosphere. I thought I had been transported to another Eden! Arbours of passionfruit and barbadines dropped their cool fruit into my waiting hand, while here and there banana trees, bent beneath the weight of their clustering fruit, trailed their long broken leaves upon the ground. A collection of various European flowers enhanced this tropical orchard with memories of home, and in one particularly fresh and fragrant spot there was a summerhouse with a magnificent view: on one side the sea dashing against the rocks, on the other the vast fields of sugar cane, so lovely when they are in flower, with an occasional clump of trees to vary the scene.

It was late when we left: as we were passing a sort of shed where the negroes were still at work, the bell for angelus sounded, and they all fell upon their knees, pressing their faces against the earth. They all looked sullen and miserable, even the children. I tried to talk to one or two, but all I could get out of them was *yes* or *no*, uttered in a flat toneless voice.

I went inside a cell where two negresses were imprisoned. They had let their children die by neglecting to give them milk; both of them were crouching completely naked in a corner. One was eating raw maize; the other, who was young and very beautiful, turned her large eyes upon me in a look which seemed to say: I let my child die because I knew he would never be free like you, and I would sooner have him dead than a slave. The sight of that woman upset me. Beneath a black skin there may well be a proud and noble soul; the negroes passed with brutal suddenness from independence to slavery and among them there must be some indomitable spirits who suffer torments and die without ever submitting to the yoke.

The next day we went to watch men casting the net. This method of fishing is terrifying and looked as laborious as it was dangerous. The fishermen go right out to meet the advancing wave carrying an immense net fastened around a huge ring. The rushing wave engulfs them completely, and when it recedes they drag the net back to the shore; there were twelve fishermen, and it was not until the fourth attempt that they caught nine fish. As I watched free men undergoing such arduous toil and taking such risks to earn their bread, I asked myself whether a country in which men were forced to practise such a trade in order to live had any need of slaves.

I have already said that I could not understand why the people of Lima were so fond of Chorrillos; the word means *sewers*, and the village owes its name to the little channels of water which trickle down from the top of the rocks surrounding the beach and form a pool of soft water at the bottom. It is near this little lake that people go to bathe, as the sea is calm here, and most bathers take advantage of the soft water to rinse the salt from their skin when they emerge from the sea. But apart from this the place is very inconvenient for bathing, though it would not cost so very much to make it as agreeable a resort as Dieppe. If Chorrillos retains its vogue, perhaps somebody will think about this some day.

El Baranco, the charming oasis I have already mentioned, would have been the ideal spot to establish a bathing resort; it is only a short distance from the sea, and it has fine trees, lush green vegetation, and water, the same water which gives Chorrillos its name; but Chorrillos itself, perched on top of a black and arid rock, has none of these advantages. Nothing could be more depressing and unattractive than this collection of huts: there is not one tree, not one blade of grass to gladden the eye, and the water is right at the foot of the rock. The houses are built of wood, and in some the floors are not even paved; there are also a few bamboo houses with no other opening save the door. They are all very uncomfortable and full of antiquated furniture.

Chorrillos produces absolutely nothing to eat and the market is very poorly supplied; what is more, everything is expensive and of poor quality. You cannot go out without sinking up to your knees in black sand; your shoes, stockings and the hem of your dress are ruined after such an outing. The wind and sea blow the sand into your eyes and you are blinded by the light reflected from the sun. In a word, this village is the most detestable place

I have ever encountered, yet it has grown so much in the past five years that it contained eight hundred houses at the time of my visit.

The life people lead when they gather here is an exact reflection of their behaviour when in Lima: idleness, pleasure and intrigue are all they live for. The women share the same tastes and habits as the men and are just as free to pursue them. They explore the region on horseback, bathe with the men, smoke from morn to night and gamble recklessly — my aunt Manuela lost ten thousand piastres in a single night. They openly conduct four or five intrigues at a time, amorous, political, and so on; go to banquets and the rustic balls which everybody gives; yet they still manage to spend a good part of the day reclining in a hammock and surrounded by five or six admirers. The pleasures of Chorrillos are ruining the wealthiest families in Lima; the sacrifices they make to spend a month or two there are incalculable. This sort of extravagance is more common in Lima than elsewhere; no doubt the climate has something to do with it, but the absence of the fine arts and the lack of any education or training which would occupy the brilliant imagination with which these people are endowed makes them commit every kind of folly, aided and abetted by their overflowing vitality.

After spending a week at Chorrillos I was heartily glad to return to Lima; my little apartment furnished in the French style and the good French fare were more welcome than ever, and the amusing conversation of Madame Denuelle seemed a thousand times more agreeable.

XVIII

The former First Lady of the Republic

— —

But despite the warm welcome my new friends had given me and the many distractions Lima had to offer, I was longing to depart. However lively its inhabitants, however beautiful its climate, this city was the last place on earth where I would have consented to live. There sensuality reigns supreme: the people have eyes, ears and a palate but no soul to respond to the stimulus of sight, sound and taste. I have never been more aware of the emptiness and aridity of my surroundings than during the two months I stayed in Lima.

In my impatience to return to Europe, which I loved and appreciated far more since I had left it, I considered going to Valparaiso, where I hoped to find a vessel ready to sail for Bordeaux; but I soon abandoned this plan as I was almost certain to come across Chabrié in Chile, so I resigned myself to the expense and tedium of staying in Lima.

Nevertheless it was some time before I could bring myself to book my passage, not that I particularly dreaded the bad food on board an English merchantman, but because I had a burning desire to return by way of North America. It was an exhausting voyage: M Briet had made it and it had nearly killed him, but I felt strong enough to make the attempt, and I would certainly have done so if I had had enough money to pay my way. I confess that this caused me great annoyance; I wrote to my uncle telling him how much I would like to see America, and hinting that only my straitened circumstances held me back. Ten times over I was on the point of asking him outright for the sum I needed, but my pride prevailed; my uncle's reaction to my plan made me fear a refusal, and I had no wish to expose myself to such a risk.

I booked my passage on the *William Rushton* from Liverpool, which was due to proceed straight to Falmouth. I had been gone from Arequipa for two months when this vessel arrived at Callao with Senora Pencha de Gamarra on board, accompanied by her secretary Escudero. Mr Smith brought me the news together with a packet of letters from Arequipa telling me what had been happening there during the latest upheaval.

To put it briefly: Senor Gamarra and his wife had entered Arequipa on Sunday 27 April. Under the threat of imprisonment and other military measures they raised enormous sums from the townsfolk, but lacked the authority or will to prevent their soldiers from committing every kind of depredation. The entire population was outraged; they were being held to ransom at every opportunity by the soldiers, who for their part could not venture abroad without the risk of being massacred by the peasants; one soldier was stabbed to death by a monk from whom he had demanded two *reals*. All the territory occupied by the Gamarrists was seething with discontent, and this rallied the people to the cause of Orbegoso; everywhere the cry was: Long live Nieto! The latter, entrenched in Tacna, was waiting for the opportunity to play an active part once more. The Gamarrists made yet another attempt to exploit his credulity, and despatched his brother-in-law to him with a letter from Bermudez announcing the collapse of Orbegoso; but this time Nieto did not swallow the bait, he rejected their advances and entered into negotiations with Santa-Cruz, the President of Bolivia, in order to obtain his help.

This is how matters stood when on Whitsunday, 18 May, two companies broke away from the Bermudez faction. Just when Senora Gamarra least expected it, Don Juan Lobaton, a major from the Ayacucho battalion, with two hundred men under him, seized the artillery and made the city square ring with cries of Long live Orbegoso! Long live Nieto! Up with the law! The people, who hated the military, thought this was a trick to capture any men rash enough to join them, and in their indignation they fell upon the insurgents. Between fifteen and twenty people were killed in the affray, including Lobaton, the leader of the revolt.

When the people saw the dead, the disorder reached its height; they rushed upon the house occupied by Senora Gamarra and sacked it. Senora Pencha had seen the approaching storm and taken refuge in a neighbouring house to escape the fury of the crowd, who were killing every officer and soldier in sight whether they had taken part in the uprising or not. The house San-Roman had occupied was plundered, and so was Colonel Quirroga's, but the colonel had fled.

In a very short time my uncle was appointed military commander by acclamation. The next day order was restored and the people submitted to the counsel of their chosen leaders. Their sufferings and their victory had raised their morale to such a pitch that the moment a rumour arose that the Gamarrists were coming, everybody, even the peasants, snatched up their weapons and went out to meet them.

The other leaders of this revolution, apart from Lobaton, were Arismendi, Landauri and Rivero, and it was they who assumed command and drove the Gamarrists out of Arequipa. The troops who had remained loyal to Bermudez lost heart and all in turn recognised Orbegoso as President. Nieto returned to Arequipa on 22 May, and, true to form, imposed an excessively high levy on the unfortunate proprietors. The bishop had to pay one hundred thousand piastres, and the others paid in proportion; but this time Don Pio, who was now a member of the supreme government, was exempt. Gamarra took refuge in Bolivia. His wife, who was the principal object of the people's hatred, was still in hiding, and only my uncle's influence enabled her to go into exile in Chile: even so she was obliged to leave by night in order to escape the vengeance of the people, who were determined to kill her.

Escudero, and Senora Gamarra as well, asked me to visit them on board the English vessel, as they were not allowed to go ashore, so I went to Callao immediately. As I stepped on board I was welcomed by Escudero, who shook me warmly by the hand. I returned this affectionate greeting and said to him in French: 'My dear colonel, how is it that after leaving you two months ago victor and master of Arequipa, I find you now a prisoner on this ship and driven out of the town?'

'Mademoiselle, this is the way chance tosses men about when they seek to play a part in countries prey to civil wars, where people have no understanding of politics and fight only for a *leader*. Ah! since you left I have thought about you very often; you were right, and I begin to think I could do better than to stay in America. Had it not been for recent events in Arequipa I might even have returned to Europe with you on board this vessel. I have thought about it more than once, but it is yet another of those plans that I am fated never to realise. You behold me shackled here for ever. Poor Senora Gamarra has been driven out everywhere, her cause is irretrievably lost. Her weak-minded cowardly husband has taken refuge with Santa-Cruz, and if any chances come his way he will be certain to bungle them. I cannot abandon this woman; your uncle's protection and my devotion have together succeeded in rescuing her from the vengeance of the people. As Santa-Cruz will not have her in his country, she is being deported to Chile; as for me, I am perfectly free. Nieto wants me to stay with him, and Santa-Cruz asks for me in all his letters; but you will understand, Florita, that in her misfortune Senora Gamarra has a right to my devotion, and as long as she is a prisoner, an exile, rejected by everybody, I must follow her to prison, into exile, and be everything to her.'

At that moment I thought Escudero was superb. I pressed his hand and said in tones which plainly let him know my thoughts, 'My poor friend, you deserved a better fate.'

I would have said more, but Senora Gamarra appeared on deck. 'Ah! Senorita Florita, how happy I am to see you! I am impatient to make your acquaintance. Do you know, you beautiful young lady, that you have made a conquest of our dear Escudero? He never stops talking to me about you and quotes your opinion on every subject. As for your uncle, everything he does is *inspired by you*. It was very naughty of you to leave Arequipa just two days before I arrived. To think that you were so curious to see San-Roman, the bogeyman of Arequipa, but not curious enough to see Dona Pencha, the terror of all Peru! I am sure I deserve a place in your journal as much as he does!'

So saying, she conducted me to the end of the poop-deck, made me sit beside her, and dismissed with a wave of her hand anybody importunate enough to wish to follow us. Though a prisoner, Dona Pencha was still the President's wife: her spontaneous gesture revealed a consciousness of her superiority. Not a single person remained on the poop, though as the awning had been put up, it was the only place sheltered from the burning sun; everybody stayed below. She examined me intently, and I looked at her with no less interest; everything about her revealed a being as exceptional for her will-power as for her intelligence. She was between thirty-four and thirty-six, of medium height and wiry frame, though she was very thin. Her face was assuredly not beautiful by accepted standards, but to judge from the effect it produced, it possessed something more than conventional beauty. She had a long, slightly turned-up nose and a large but very expressive mouth; her whole face was long, with prominent cheekbones and muscles, while her skin was very brown but full of vitality. She had an enormous head adorned with a mass of thick long hair which hung over her brow; it was a dark chestnut colour, with a lustrous and silky texture. Her voice was heavy, harsh, imperious; she spoke in an abrupt and jerky manner. Her movements were graceful enough, but they could not hide the tenor of her thoughts. Her fresh, elegant and distinguished toilette formed a strange contrast with the harshness of her voice, the austere dignity of her look and the gravity of her person. She was wearing a gown of heavy Indian silk the colour of bird-of-paradise, embroidered in white silk, with the finest pink silk stockings and white satin slippers. A brilliant red crêpe-de-Chine shawl embroidered in white, the most beautiful I ever saw in Lima, was thrown carelessly over her shoulders. She had rings on every finger, diamond ear-rings, and a superb necklace of fine pearls, beneath which hung a worn and dirty scapular. Seeing my surprise as I contemplated her, she said in her brusque manner: 'You must find me very ridiculous in this grotesque costume, my dear Florita, you dress so simply yourself; but now you have passed judgment on me, you probably realise that these clothes are not mine. It was my poor sister who persuaded me to wear them, to please her and my mother and all the rest of them; these good people imagine that my luck will change if I consent to wear European clothes. So I yielded to their entreaties and put on this gown which hampers my movements, these stockings which feel cold to my legs, this big shawl which I am afraid of burning with the ash from my cigar. I like clothes which are comfortable for riding, clothes which will stand up to the strains of campaigning, visiting camps and barracks, and going aboard Peruvian ships: those are the only clothes that suit me. For years I have been travelling all over the country in breeches of the coarse cloth they make in my native Cuzco, a greatcoat of the same material embroidered in gold, and boots with gold spurs. I love gold, it is the precious metal which gives the country its reputation, the finest ornament a Peruvian can have. I have a long cloak as well, a little heavy, but very warm; it was my father's and it has been very useful in the snow of our mountains. You are admiring my hair,' continued this alarming woman with the eagle eye, 'well, my dear Florita, in a career where my strength has often fallen short of my courage, my position has been threatened more than once, and to compensate for the weakness of our sex I have had to retain its attractions and exploit them as need arose in order to enlist the support of men.'

'So,' I could not stop myself crying out, 'this strong soul, this superior intelligence, has had to yield to brute force in order to gain domination.'

'Child,' retorted the ex-President's wife, crushing my hand in an iron grip and giving me a look I shall never forget, 'child, let me tell you that it is precisely because I have never been able to submit my invincible pride to brute force that you see me a prisoner here, driven into exile by the very men I commanded for three years. . . .'

In that moment I penetrated her mind; my soul took possession of hers. I felt stronger than she was and dominated her with the power of my gaze. She perceived this and grew pale; the colour drained from her lips, and with a sudden movement she flung her cigar into the sea and ground her teeth. Her expression would have made the boldest tremble, but she was under my spell and I read distinctly all that was passing inside her. In my turn, taking her hand which was cold and bathed in sweat, I said to her in a grave tone:

'Dona Pencha, the Jesuits said: Who desires the ends desires the means; and the Jesuits ruled the mighty of the earth . . .'

She looked at me for a long time without speaking: she too sought to penetrate my soul . . . She broke the silence in tones of irony and despair.

'Ah! Florita, your pride is leading you astray; you think you are stronger than I am; you are mad! You know nothing of the never-ending struggle I have had for the past eight years, the humiliations I have had to endure! I have begged, flattered, lied: I have tried everything and stopped at nothing ... and yet it was not enough. I thought that at last I had reached the point where I could reap the harvest of eight years of pain and sacrifice, but then the infernal blow struck and I saw myself driven out, lost, lost, Florita! ... I shall never return to Peru. Ah! glory, how dearly you are bought! What folly to sacrifice the joy of living, the whole of life, to obtain you! Glory is nothing but a flash of light, a puff of smoke, a cloud, an illusion; and yet, Florita, the day I lose all hope of living enveloped in that cloud, there will be no more sun to light me, no more air for me to breathe, and I shall die.'

These last words were uttered in a prophetic tone which matched the sombre expression of Dona Pencha's face; she gazed at the serene blue sky above our heads in rapt contemplation of her celestial vision and seemed no longer to belong to this world. I bowed before this superior being who had suffered all the torments reserved for natures such as hers in their passage on earth. I was about to continue the conversation, but she rose abruptly, and darting to the other end of the deck, she called her sister and two other ladies, saying, 'Come quickly, I feel ill.'

Escudero came up to me and said: 'I am sorry, mademoiselle, I am afraid that Dona Pencha is having one of her epileptic attacks, and at such times I am the only one who can look after her.'

'Colonel, I am leaving; I shall come back tomorrow. Go quickly to that poor woman, she needs your help and your affection so much.'

'Have no fear, Florita, I shall stay with her to the end.'

I asked my future captain to have me rowed across to

the frigate *Samarang* where Mr Smith, Madame Denuelle and several other people were awaiting me. I knew the commander of the *Samarang* very well, as he was another of Madame Denuelle's lodgers and I saw him every day at table. He was unlike the commander of the *Challenger* in every way: as ugly as the other was handsome, as gay as the other was sad, as careless in his attire as the other was neat and simple. There was the same contrast between the officers of the two vessels: servants copy their masters. The officers of the *Samarang* divided their day into three parts: in the mornings they rode about the countryside dressed up as rich Mexican bandits, then they paraded the town in the company of fallen women, after which they sat down to table and spent the rest of their time drinking grog and sleeping it off. Apart from this behaviour, which did no harm save to their health and their pockets, they were mild, likeable and easy-going men. The commander was conspicuous for his impeccable manners, which he had kept in the course of a life of dissipation. I had promised him I would visit his frigate on the day I went to see my ship. I confess I expected to find the same carelessness on board as I had already observed in the commander and his officers; what then was my surprise as I set foot on deck to see order and cleanliness reign supreme down to the smallest details! I have never come across anything like it: the between-decks, the sleeping-quarters, the appearance of the soldiers and the naval officers, all were admirable for their conformity. As I was looking about me with an air of astonishment the commander said with a smile: 'Ah, mademoiselle, I am sure you thought you would find the same confusion here that you see in my chamber when you pass my door.'

'Not exactly, commander, but I confess I did not expect to find everything in such perfect order on board your ship.'

'Permit me to tell you, mademoiselle, that I am surprised in my turn that a person who always shows so much good sense should hasten to pass judgement on something she knows nothing about. On land I am off duty, I am free to do as I like, and while my conduct may offend some people who are not as open as I am, I do not think it does society any harm. On board I am the commander of my frigate, and I understand the extent and the importance of the obligations attached to my command; in the fifteen years that I have had the honour of serving my country, I may say that I have never once failed in my duty, and not one of the officers you see treating me with such familiarity at table would be spared should he forget the least of his.'

This man, whose behaviour on land showed such superb disdain for public opinion, was on board ship one of the best officers in the English navy and one of the strictest disciplinarians. His was a proud and original course to follow, but it also demanded considerable self-control. He and all the officers were extremely sober and hard-working on board and allowed themselves no diversions; the only visible reminders of their life ashore were the women's portraits they kept in their cabins: I counted six in the commander's alone. Their grave manner was quite different from what I had seen at Madame Denuelle's; the commander had received me with cool politeness, and etiquette was strictly observed the whole time we were on board. We were so astonished at the change that we talked of nothing else all the way back to Lima.

My conversation with Senora Gamarra had upset me so much that I was unable to sleep. I shuddered when I thought that once I had planned to usurp her position; what torments would have been in store for me had I succeeded! Now my poverty and obscurity seemed infinitely preferable, nobler, even, for I still had my freedom. I felt ashamed to have believed even for a moment that ambition could bring happiness, and that anything could compensate for the loss of independence.

I returned to Callao next day to find that Senora

Gamarra had left the *William Rushton* for another English vessel, the *Young Henrietta*, which was leaving that very day for Valparaiso. When I arrived I found Escudero pale and depressed.

'What is the matter, my poor friend, you look so ill?'

'Yes, indeed, I have had a very bad night. Dona Pencha has suffered three severe attacks. I do not know what passed between you, but ever since you left she has been in a state of constant agitation.'

'It was the first time I had seen Dona Pencha, and perhaps what I said to her may have increased her bitterness instead of calming her distress. If that were so, I should be very sorry.'

'It is possible, as you say, that without your knowledge you may have wounded her pride, which is extremely susceptible.'

I had hardly been speaking with Escudero for a quarter of an hour when he was called away, leaving me to review in my mind all I had said to Dona Pencha the previous day in an attempt to discover what could have upset her so much, but only those who have once enjoyed all the trappings of power can fully understand the anguish of losing it, and my search was vain. I regretted having been so outspoken and not having been more reserved in the presence of a pain which transcended common afflictions.

I was interrupted in my reflections by Escudero; he tapped me gently on the shoulder and said in a voice it pained me to hear: 'Florita, poor Pencha has just had her worst attack; I was afraid she was going to die in my arms. She is conscious now and wants to see you. I beg you to be careful what you say to her; a single jarring word would be enough to bring on a fresh attack.'

My heart was beating violently as I descended. I went into the captain's cabin which was large and very handsome, and there I found Dona Pencha, half-dressed, lying on a mattress upon the floor. She gave me her hand and I sat beside her.

'No doubt you know that I suffer from a terrible disease, and . . .'

'I know,' I interrupted her, 'but is there no medicine which will cure it, or have you no confidence in the relief it offers?'

'I have consulted all the doctors and done exactly as they prescribed; but their remedies have been unsuccessful; the older I get, the worse the disease becomes. It has done me great harm in everything I have undertaken; any strong emotion brings on an immediate attack, so you can judge what an obstacle it has been to my career. Our soldiers are so badly trained and our officers so cowardly that in every serious engagement I had to take command myself. For the past ten years, long before I had any hope of getting my husband nominated president, I have taken part in every battle to accustom myself to fire. Often when the fight was fiercest I would grow so angry at the apathy and cowardice of the troops under my command that I would foam with rage, and then I would have one of my attacks. I had only enough time to throw myself to the ground; several times I was trampled by the horses and carried off for dead by my servants. Well, Florita, would you believe it, my enemies used my cruel illness to discredit me with the army; they gave out that *fear*, the noise of the cannon and the smell of gunpowder were attacking my nerves and making me faint away like some little lady of fashion! I confess it is slanders like these that have made me hard. I wanted to make them see that I was not afraid of blood or of death. Each reversal makes me more cruel, and if . . .'

She stopped, and raising her eyes to heaven, she seemed to be communicating with some being that she alone could see; then she said: 'Yes, I am leaving my country never to return, and before two months are up, I shall be with you . . .' Only some presence not of this world could have given her features the expression they wore as she spoke these words. I looked at her then: how changed I found her since the day before, with her wasted cheeks, livid complexion, pale lips, cold hands, and glittering sunken eyes! Life seemed about to abandon her. I dared not speak to her for fear of making her worse. I was leaning over her; one of my tears fell upon her arm and this had the effect of an electric spark upon the unfortunate woman. She came out of her trance, turned abruptly towards me, fixed me with her burning gaze and said in sepulchral tones: 'Why do you weep? Is it out of pity at my fate? Do you think I am banished for ever, lost, as good as dead?' I could find no words to reply; she had thrust me away, so I was now on my knees before her. I clasped my hands together in a mechanical gesture and continued to weep as I gazed at her. There was a long silence; she seemed to grow calmer and said in a voice that wrung my heart: 'So, you weep, do you? Ah! God be praised! You are young, there is still life in you; weep for me, I am finished, I am dead . . .'

As she finished speaking, she fell back upon her pillow, clasped her hands to her head, and uttered three faint cries. Her sister ran in, followed by Escudero; everybody lavished the most tender care upon her, while I stood watching by the door. She made no movement, she was no longer breathing, her glittering eyes were still wide open.

The captain drew me away from this sad sight by announcing that it was time for visitors to leave, as they were about to weigh anchor. Mr Smith came to collect me, I pencilled a few words of farewell to Escudero, and departed.

As we were getting into the carriage we saw the *Young Henrietta* drawing away. I noticed on the deck a woman with dishevelled hair, wrapped in a brown cloak and waving a white handkerchief. It was the former First Lady of Peru addressing her last farewells to her sister and the friends she was never to see again.

By the time I reached my apartment, I was ill. That

woman was still before my eyes: her heroic endurance in the face of suffering made her appear larger than life to me, and it wrung my heart to see one of God's élite, herself a victim of the very qualities which set her apart from her fellow creatures, forced by the fears of a cowardly people to flee her country, abandon her family and friends, and go, stricken with the most frightful infirmity, to end her painful existence in exile.

A lady who was born in Cuzco and had known Dona Pencha since childhood told me various particulars about this extraordinary woman which I think cannot fail to interest the reader.

Dona Pencha was the daughter of a Spanish officer who had married an extremely wealthy young lady from Cuzco. During her childhood she stood out among her companions by reason of her proud, bold, melancholy disposition. She was very devout: from the age of twelve it was her desire to enter a convent and become a nun, but her poor health did not permit her to realise her intention. When she was seventeen her parents made her return home so that she could receive the care and attention she needed. Her father's house was frequented by many officers, several of whom sought her hand, but she declared that she did not wish to marry, being resolved to return to her convent at the earliest opportunity. Her father arranged for her to travel, in the hope of restoring her to health; he took her to Lima, brought her out in society, and provided her with every distraction, but she remained melancholy and seemed insensitive to the pleasures normally associated with youth. She spent two years in travel, and soon after her return to Cuzco, she gave up all idea of becoming a nun and chose as her husband an ugly, stupid little officer, the least distinguished of all her suitors. She married Senor Gamarra, a simple captain. Although she was still in poor health and nearly always pregnant, she followed her husband wherever the war took him, and the constant exertion so strengthened her constitution that she was soon capable of covering enormous distances on horseback. For a long time she managed to conceal the cruel infirmity which afflicted her, and which was steadily growing worse. It was only when, as wife of the president, her life came under investigation, that the public got to know about it through her enemies. Her solicitation and intriguing had raised her husband to the presidency, and once he was installed she took Escudero as her confidant and skilfully exploited everybody she thought capable of furthering her interests. When she succeeded General de la Mar to power, the republic was in the most deplorable state; the country was rent asunder by civil war, there was not a single piastre in the treasury, soldiers sold their services to the highest bidder — in short, it was anarchy with all its horrors. Yet this woman, raised in a convent, without education, but gifted with a strong moral sense and an uncommonly powerful will, governed a people even Bolivar had found ungovernable with such success that in less than a year order was restored, rival factions were tamed, trade flourished, the army regained confidence in its leaders; and even if parts of Peru were still unsettled, most of the country enjoyed peace.

With such a character, Dona Pencha seemed destined to continue the work of Bolivar for many years to come, and she would certainly have done so had not her all too feminine exterior stood in her way. She was beautiful, she could be very gracious when she chose, and she had the power to inspire great passion. Her enemies spread the vilest slanders about her and, finding it easier to attack her morals than her political actions, attributed various vices to her to console themselves for her superiority.

Dona Pencha was too ambitious to take love seriously. Several officers in her retinue fell in love with her and others feigned love in order to advance their fortunes, but she repulsed them all, not with the indulgence a woman feels towards a love she cannot share, but with the anger and contempt of outraged pride. However she did not stop there: she conceived a violent hatred for them, ceased to trust them, and missed no opportunity of insulting them, even in public. Once when she was inspecting the troops she caught sight of a colonel who, it was said, had boasted of having once been her lover. She pounced upon him, tore off his epaulettes, struck him three or four times across the face with her riding-whip, and pushed him so roughly that he fell off his horse. Then she cried in ringing tones: 'This is the way I shall punish anyone who dares to slander the President's wife.'

On another occasion she invited four officers to dinner, was perfectly agreeable throughout the meal, then turned to one of them during dessert and said: 'Is it true, captain, that you told these three gentlemen you were tired of being my lover?' The unfortunate man turned pale and looked in terror at his comrades, who remained silent. 'What!' she continued, 'Have you lost your tongue? Answer me! If it is true I will have you whipped by your comrades; if they have maligned you, the two of us will make them pay for their cowardice.' It was only too apparent that the rash young man was indeed guilty of the remark in question, so she summoned four enormous negroes, had the doors locked, and made the three other officers thrash their comrade with birch-rods.

Such conduct was not in accordance with the morals of the country she governed and was bound to antagonise public opinion, because in a country where there is complete independence between the sexes, people do not think of virtue, in the conventional sense of the word, in connection with women, and the Peruvians considered themselves insulted by the arrogant behaviour of the president's wife. Not that Dona Pencha had any more concern for virtue than any other woman in Peru; in private life she would not have been in the least offended at the homage paid to her charms, and she would have been as indifferent to gossip about the number of lovers she had as any other lady in Lima. But she was intoxicated by her power and convinced that she belonged to a superior order of creation. Ministers had to submit every act of congress to her scrutiny; she struck out any passages which did not suit her and substituted her own, so that in the end she became an absolute ruler within a constitutional republic.

Senora Gamarra had all the virtues necessary for the exercise of power at this stage of Peru's development, yet she had great difficulty in serving her full three-year term of office. Her despotism had been so harsh, her yoke so heavy, she had wounded so many people's self-esteem, that a strong opposition rose against her. When she saw that she would not be able to get her husband re-elected, she resorted to a trick. Senor Gamarra declared in the Senate that his health did not permit him to continue in public life; Senora Gamarra wished to have one of her creatures nominated as president, a slave obedient to her will. So she and her husband transferred their support, and that of their friends, to Bermudez; but Orbegoso won the day, as we have seen.

To conclude the story of Dona Pencha: when she reached Valparaiso she rented a splendid furnished house where she installed herself with Escudero and her numerous retainers; but not one lady in the town went to call on her. All the foreigners she had offended joined in the outcry against her, and barely a handful of her former comrades-in-arms had the courtesy to go and see her. This proud and haughty woman must have suffered cruelly from the abandonment and isolation in which hatred kept her confined. To be condemned to inactivity was like being buried alive for one of her restless spirit. As I have not heard from Escudero since my departure from Lima, I cannot describe her sufferings in any detail; but seven weeks after she left Callao, she died.

The day after my visit to Senora Gamarra I felt really ill; it was the first time since I had been in Lima. I stayed in bed all day feeling miserable. Madame Denuelle came to spend the evening with me.

'Well, mademoiselle, how are you feeling?'

'No better, I am sad and I want someone to make me cry.'

'And I have come, on the contrary, to make you laugh. I am sure that it's your visits to Callao that have made you ill. That Dona Pencha with her epileptic fits must have got on your nerves; they say that yesterday she was falling down every few minutes. Thank God we are rid of her, the wicked woman!'

'How can you judge her like that?'

'Good Lord, it's not difficult: a virago as bold as a trooper, who used to box her officers' ears, the same as I do to my little black boy.'

'Then why were these officers so contemptible as to put up with it?'

'Because she was the mistress, she distributed promotion, jobs, favours.'

'Madame Denuelle, a soldier who will put up with such treatment deserves to receive it. Dona Pencha knew the sort of men she had under her command, and if she had done nothing worse than punish government officials who were failing to do their duty, you would still have her as your president's wife.'

Madame Denuelle was clever enough to change the course of my thoughts, and by the time she left I was almost cheerful.

At last the moment of departure arrived. I awaited the day with the keenest impatience; my curiosity was satisfied, and the materialistic life of Lima wearied me to excess.

In the last week I did not have an hour to myself; I had to bid farewell to all my acquaintances, receive their visits in return, write innumerable letters to Arequipa, and sell all the trifles I wished to dispose of. I accomplished everything, and on 15 July 1834 I left Lima at nine o'clock in the morning for Callao, accompanied by one of my cousins, M de Rivero. We dined with Mr Smith's correspondent, and after dinner I had my effects put on board the *William Rushton* and installed myself in the cabin which Senora Gamarra had occupied. The following day I had several visits from Lima; these were the final farewells. Towards five o'clock the ship weighed anchor and everybody left. I remained alone, completely alone, between two immensities, the sea and the sky.

Afterword

Tristan's story ends abruptly here, leaving the reader, too, at sea. The two further volumes of memoirs announced for publication in November 1838 never appeared. Tristan referred to the voyage home only once, and that was in her journal *Le Tour de France*, as part of the entry for 25 August 1844:

'Ten years ago at this time I was alone, lost in the middle of the ocean. Ill, in danger at any moment of dying a frightful death, terrified by the presence of that accursed madman Antonio, exposed to the insults of those rough sailors, I was placed in the most dreadful position in which a woman could find herself.'

What are we to make of this? Are we to imagine Flora adrift, to be picked up later by a passing vessel? And how could such a situation have come about? Was there a storm? A mutiny? It is unlikely that we shall ever know what happened. After a longer than average voyage of 113 days the *William Rushton* arrived at Falmouth on Thursday 6 November, according to the *Falmouth Packet* of Saturday 8 November 1834. There is no mention of any untoward incident at sea, just the routine report that on 3 November the ship was in communication with the *Mary Walker*, bound for London from Valparaiso. On 9 November the *William Rushton* sailed for London. It is not known whether Tristan was on board, or whether it was at this point that she made the journey from Falmouth to London by stage coach which she described in her *Lettres à un architecte anglais*, published in 1837. Nor is it known whether she spent any time in London, or whether she returned immediately to France. According to Stéphane Michaud, who has worked extensively on Tristan's correspondence, she was back in Paris in January 1835, though it is difficult to account for her movements for much of that year, as she was trying to avoid her husband and was leading a very quiet life.

I sometimes wonder whether it could have been Chabrié who sent the anonymous letter to André Chazal on 11 October 1835 informing him of his wife's address. Flora hinted at some treachery on Chabrié's part in the *Peregrinations*, when she was desperately seeking some way of destroying his love: 'I could not confess it (my marriage) to him; his indignation against me for having made him believe that I was not married would have passed all bounds, *as indeed I was later to have proof.*' She corresponded with him for some months after their parting, but eventually his letters ceased, and she was forced to conclude that he had been lost at sea. Her hopes of seeing him again revived briefly during her visit to England in 1839: while looking over Bethlem Hospital she was informed that one of the inmates was a Frenchman named Chabrier, but she soon discovered that this was not the captain of the *Mexicain*.

After her book was published Tristan had no further contact with her uncle Don Pio. He is said to have been so incensed by her description of him that he seized all the copies he could lay hands on and had them burnt in the public square. He certainly stopped her allowance.

Don Pio lived long enough to meet Flora's daughter Aline, who married Clovis Gauguin and was a widow by the time she reached Arequipa with her son Paul, as her husband had died on the voyage to Peru. The old man grew very fond of Aline because she reminded him of Flora; he would have liked to leave her part of his fortune, but his last wishes were not respected by the rest of the family.

Flora's impressions of her uncle and Althaus are

confirmed by the brief mention both men receive in John Miller's *Memoirs of General Miller in the Service of the Republic of Peru* (1828). General William Miller describes Althaus as 'not only a very intelligent and enterprising officer, but a jovial companion, possessed of an inexhaustible fund of humour'. He recounts how Althaus, when in a tight corner, captured a milk-white mule previously used to carry the Host in processions, and made his escape disguised as a chaplain. As for Don Pio, who was of course fighting for the royalist side, he was defeated early in the struggle for independence by General Belgrano, 'who marred his prospects by his confiding magnanimity in General Tristan, and generously permitted him to return to Peru, together with his officers and men, upon their engaging, with the usual solemnities, not to bear arms against the republic. Forgetful of his honour, Tristan violated his parole.' He was granted absolution for this sin by the Archbishop of Charcas and thereafter fought in every battle until the royalists were finally defeated at Ayacucho in 1824.

The civil war ten years later, which Tristan described so graphically, ended in victory for Orbegoso, who served for three years as president. In 1836 Peru and Bolivia formed a Confederation, whereupon the Peruvian exiles, with Gamarra at their head, obtained the intervention of Chile to break up the Confederation, and Gamarra became president again in 1839. He was killed in 1841 while invading Bolivia. Just over twenty years later, his former subordinate, Flora's dashing admirer San-Roman — by now a Marshal — took over the presidency, but he died in 1863 after only a year in office.

I was mildly curious to discover the identity of the captain of the frigate *Challenger*, that romantic figure whose tragic dilemma — years of separation from his adored wife and children in the pursuit of a distinguished naval career — moved Flora to one of her typical bursts of indignation. By coincidence I came across his name in *The*

Times in 1982, at the height of the Falklands campaign: he was Captain Michael Seymour, and a few months before his encounter of April 1834 with Flora Tristan, he had been responsible for landing the first British Governor on the Falkland Islands.

Select Bibliography

ON FLORA TRISTAN:

Baelen, Jean, *La Vie de Flora Tristan: socialisme et féminisme au XIXe siècle* (Paris 1972)

Gattey, C.N., *Gauguin's Astonishing Grandmother* (London 1969)

Michaud, Stéphane, *Lettres de Flora Tristan* (Paris 1980)

Puech, J.-L., *La Vie et l'Oeuvre de Flora Tristan* (Paris 1925)

Thibert, Marguérite, *Le féminisme dans le socialisme français 1830–1850* (Paris 1926)

ON PERU:

Dobyns and Doughty, *Peru: a Cultural History* (New York 1976)

Marett, Sir Robert, *Peru* (London 1969)

Miller, John, *Memoirs of General Miller in the Service of the Republic of Peru* (2 vols: London 1828)

Read, Jan, *The New Conquistadors*, (London 1980)

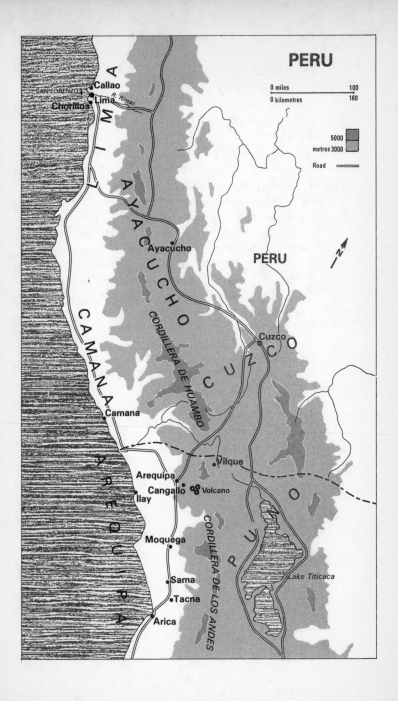

PERU

| 0 miles | 100 |
| 0 kilometres | 160 |

5000
metres 3000

Road

Callao
SAN LORENZO
Lima
Chorillos
R. Rimac

L I M A

A Y A C U C H O

Ayacucho

PERU

N

CAMANA

CORDILLERA DE HUAMBO

Cuzco

C U Z C O

Camana

Vilque

Arequipa
Cangallo
Ilay

Volcano

A R E Q U I P A

P U N O

Moquega

CORDILLERA DE LOS ANDES

Lake Titicaca

Sama

Tacna

Arica

Also of Interest

THE LONDON JOURNAL OF FLORA TRISTAN
Translated and edited by Jean Hawkes

In 1826 Flora Tristan visited England, and she came again in 1831, 1835 and 1839. She visited prisons, brothels, asylums, factories, gin palaces, infant schools, the Irish and Jewish ghettos, Chartist meetings, Ascot races and the Houses of Parliament (to which she gained entry by dressing as a Turk). She was an acute observer, and her wonderful journal brings to life in a remarkable way conditions of life in 'the monster city'. Vice – 80,000 prostitutes, many of them children, the wretched life of the poor, the dehumanising effects of the Industrial Revolution, the climate, the food, the architecture, the countryside, the daily lives of ordinary men and women, all come in for Gallic comment, sometimes enraged, always colourful, compassionate and full of life.

ROUGHING IT IN THE BUSH
Susanna Moodie

Susanna Moodie and her husband left Britain for Canada in 1832. By 1839 they had established a farm and home, put behind them the false starts and hardships of the early years, but Susanna Moodie was not one to revel in the triumph of ingenuity over adversity. A woman of refinement, she had a taste for things literary and was obliged to conceal her 'blue stockings' in deference to her 'less discerning' neighbours. She was not, in short, the heartiest of pioneers and applied herself instead to 'cultivating every branch of domestic usefulness' and to writing an account of Canadian life for the use of future immigrants. With a keen eye for the dramatic and the peculiar, she brilliantly brought to life situations and personalities: Tom Wilson who kept a pet bear, sported a false nose and stuck life in Canada for a mere four months; Brian the hunter who slit his throat but survived; the hazards of fire and whirlwind; neighbours with incessant borrowing habits and a penchant for gossip. 'Roughing it' may not have appealed to Susanna, but she wrote about it superbly. Her absorbing book, reissued in its full version and with an introduction by Margaret Atwood, has been out of print in Britain since 1852.

UNTRODDEN PEAKS AND UNFREQUENTED VALLEYS
Amelia Edwards

Unusual among Victorian women travellers, Amelia Edwards (1831-92) was a writer first, a traveller second. By the 1860s she had published novels, poetry, stories and history, and it was not until her journey to the little-explored mountains of the South-Eastern Tyrol in 1872 that travel began to dominate her life and work. Her 'ramble' with a woman companion in the Dolomites – impassable except by foot or mule and so relatively uncharted as to make the provision of food and shelter a triumph of ingenuity and good humour – was to prove a vital test of the resources demonstrated a year later on her famous trip up the Nile. Amelia Edwards was as observant of people and customs as she was thrilled by scenic grandeur, and she relished the novelty of her unorthodox undertaking. 'You are the first travellers who have come up this way,' remarks a road worker en route, astonished at the spectacle of two upright ladies making their way side-saddle along a mountain road which is about to give out. 'You must be Inglese!' Out of print since 1873, this a wonderfully lively evocation of the spirit of one of the nineteenth century's most celebrated women travellers.